AF412570

GHOST DANCING

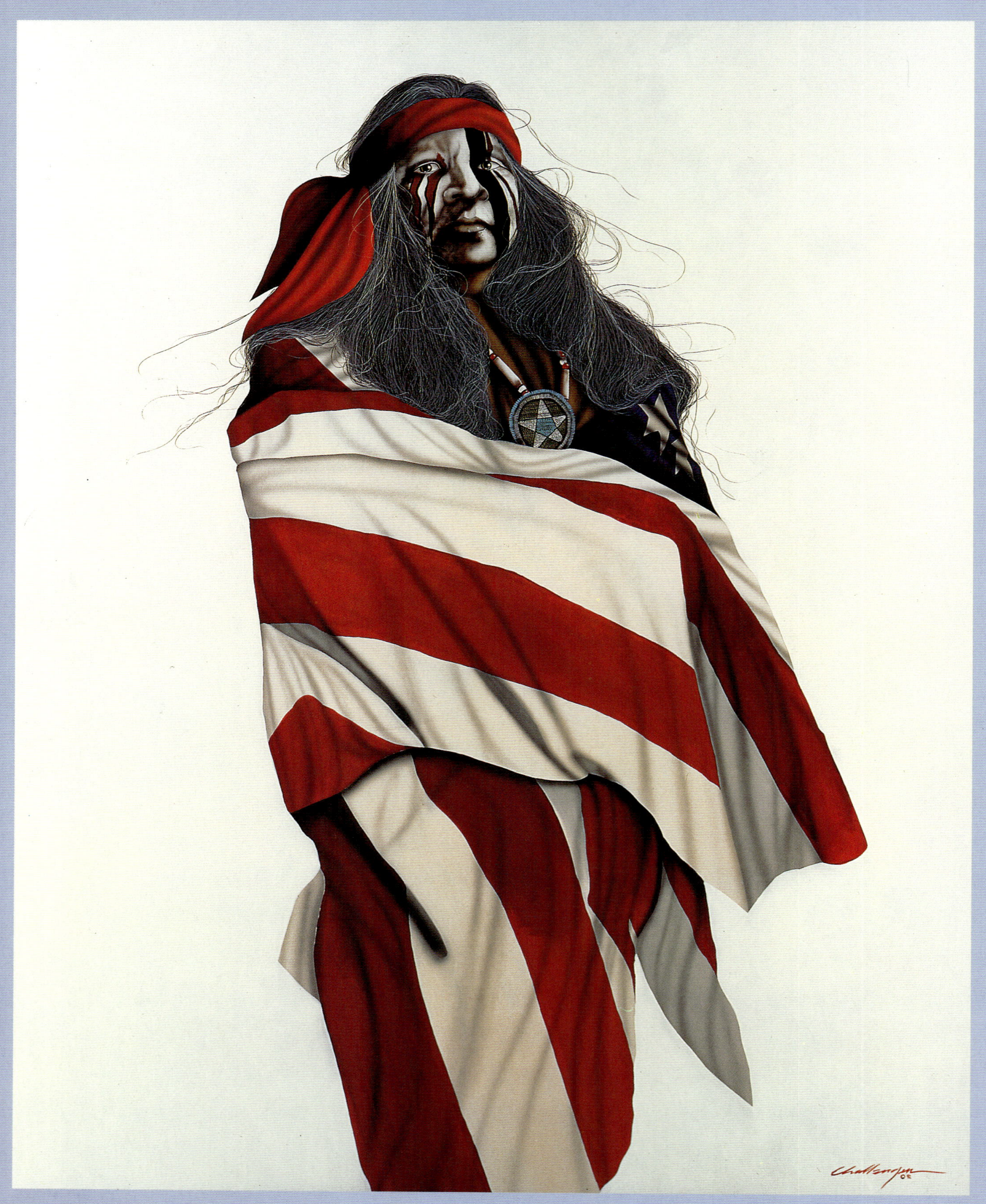

GHOST DANCING

Sacred Medicine and the Art of JD Challenger

Text by Edwin Daniels

Paintings and Drawings by JD Challenger

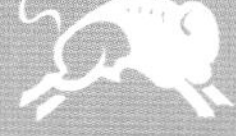

STEWART, TABORI & CHANG · NEW YORK

I would like to dedicate this book to

DENISE

my loving wife and my angel with green eyes.

JD CHALLENGER, 1997

Text copyright © 1998 Edwin Daniels
Illustrations copyright © 1998 JD Challenger

Somerset House Publishing, Inc. is the exclusive publisher of JD Challenger's limited edition
prints. For more information write to 10688 Haddington, Houston, Texas 77043
or call (800) 444-2540.

All Rights Reserved. No part of this publication may be reproduced, stored in a retrieval system,
or transmitted in any form or by any means, electronic, mechanical, photocopying, recording or
otherwise without written permission from the publisher. This includes but is not limited to
matting or framing any pages from this book with the intent to create other products for sale or
resale or profit in any manner whatsoever.

Publisher: Lena Tabori
Art Director: Nai Y. Chang
Editorial Director: Linda Sunshine
Editor: Alexandra Childs
Production: Deirdre Duggan

Published in 1998 and distributed in the U.S. by
Stewart, Tabori & Chang,
a division of U.S. Media Holdings, Inc.
115 West 18TH Street, New York, NY 10011

Distributed in Canada by General Publishing Company Ltd.
30 Lesmill Road, Don Mills, Ontario, Canada M3B 2T6
Distributed in Australia by Peribo Pty Ltd.
58 Beaumont Road, Mount Kuring-gai, NSW 2080, Australia
Distributed in all other territories by Grantham Book Services Ltd.
Isaac Newton Way, Alma Park Industrial Estate
Grantham, Lincolnshire, NG31 9SD, England

Library of Congress Cataloging-in-Publication Data

Daniels, Edwin.
Ghost dancing : sacred medicine and the art of JD Challenger
by Edwin Daniels ; paintings and drawings by JD Challenger.
p. cm.
Includes bibliographical references.
ISBN 1-55670-824-6
1. Ghost dance. 2. Dakota Indians—Rites and ceremonies. 3. Dakota Indians—Religion.
4. Dakota Indians—Portraits. I. Challenger, J. D. II. Title.
E99.DID35   1998
299'.74–DC21   97-53241
                                             CIP

PRINTED IN SINGAPORE
10 9 8 7 6 5 4 3 2 1

PREFACE

Pausing in the morning twilight, among the spines and thorns and blades and tar-black slicks of rock in this far west Texas canyon, I listen to a whirlwind circling up the draw. I can't see the telltale snake of dust rising above the gravel floor, but I can hear it approaching. I recognize the clatter a whirlwind makes through the brush, shaking the dry yucca pods, flush with seed and scattering the detritus of seasons passed in its wake. It sounds like a mystery.

I watch for movement in the hummocks of bear grass in the canyon's bed, then startle as the whirlwind suddenly alights, whipping the grass mounds and tossing sotol blooms into the air. I stand spellbound, willing the whirlwind to me, wanting to be engulfed in its frenzy and fearful that I will be absorbed by it. But its ferocity dissipates as the wind draws nearer, stirring the grasses tenderly, only bending the blades, never breaking them.

The whirlwind passes by, just on the edge of my path, pushing the air across my ear like a secret revealed in a whisper. It starts the lechuguilla stalks swaying and arouses the perfume of the blooming acacia, then retreats, vanishing as suddenly as it appeared, into a world far above the sky.

EDWIN DANIELS, 1997

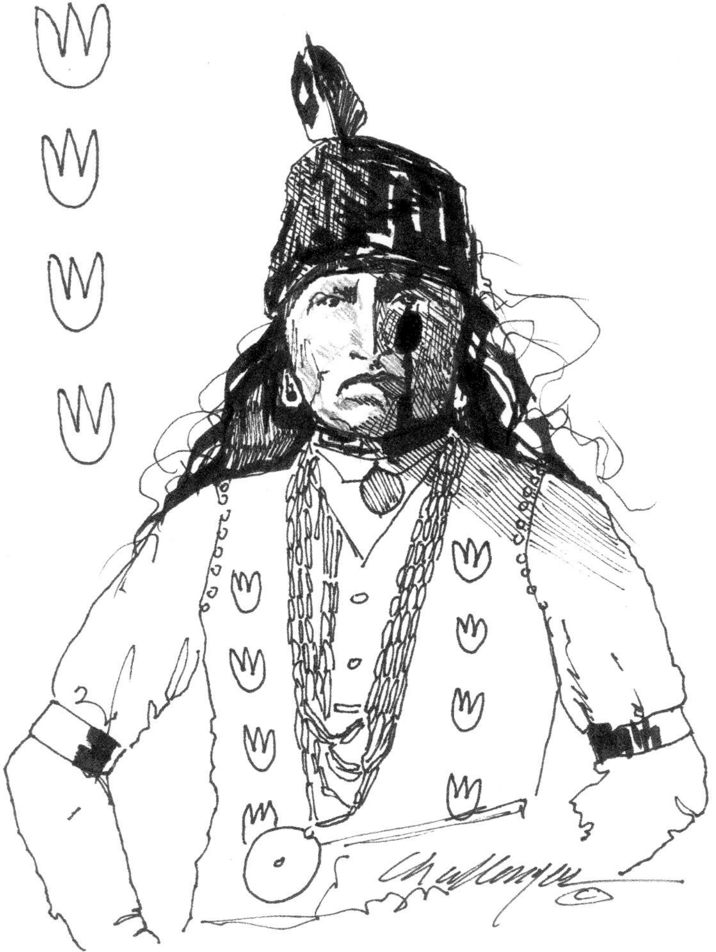

FOREWORD

"Beautiful . . . I've got to have one for my collection . . . Very stoic . . . What a way for an Indian to think . . . Stunning . . . Only an Indian would have thought of it . . . Magnificent . . . " These are just some of the comments I have overheard during an exhibition of paintings by JD Challenger. JD's work has made such an impact on the southwest art scene that in many ways it has taken Native American art to another level. His work often depicts important symbols of American history including the Bill of Rights, the Constitution of the United States of America, and the American flag while keeping the original people of this continent in the forefront of the viewer's mind. It is a controversial statement for an artist to make, and at times it comes as a shock to some people when they learn that JD is not an American Indian.

I consider JD Challenger to be my very great friend and embrace him as a brother. Often, when he and I talk about our successes and complain about not having enough hours in a day or days in the week to finish all the work we would like to complete, we remember the times when we were broke and struggling, when feasts were few and far between and famine was the rule. I think all artists, whether painters like JD or actors like myself, struggle through a period of difficulty. But the artists who really persevere and stick to it come out on top. JD is a great example of this, of someone who struggled and worked hard to achieve his dream, sometimes having to invent new ways to cook Spam, someone who just kept at it until he succeeded. He has proven that good things really do come to those who persevere.

I don't believe that artistic talent can be bought. It is a gift from the Great Creator. Which is how JD defines his talent—a gift that has been refined and has matured through life's experiences that stretch all the way back to his childhood.

JD's work is constantly undergoing change. He is always creating new challenges, riding on the cutting edge, and always taking American Indian art to a higher and deeper level. Yet he never takes his talent for granted. Instead, he is humble and appreciative whenever his exhibitions sell out or one of his paintings impacts the world in some larger way.

What you see on the following pages is the result of an artist dedicated to new ideas and to enlightening the world about American Indians and their constant struggle to remain free and proud. Take a close look at the paintings and drawings, at the fine detail of traditional clothing, and the intense facial expressions. Feel the passion that the artist has put into each painting. Behold the beauty of the warriors and dancers and heroes as they embrace their dignity and power. Understand the love this artist has for his work.

It is with great pleasure that I write about such an artist as JD Challenger—husband, son, brother, friend, mentor, but most of all, one of the nicest human beings you would ever want to be around.

JD, congratulations on reaching a wonderful milestone in this life. You are blessed by the Creator and I am proud to call you my brother and my friend.

A-ho Ka - Gay
We - bla - hūn,

RODNEY A. GRANT
Mon-Gay-Ska (White Breast)
Omaha Tribe of Nebraska

CONTENTS

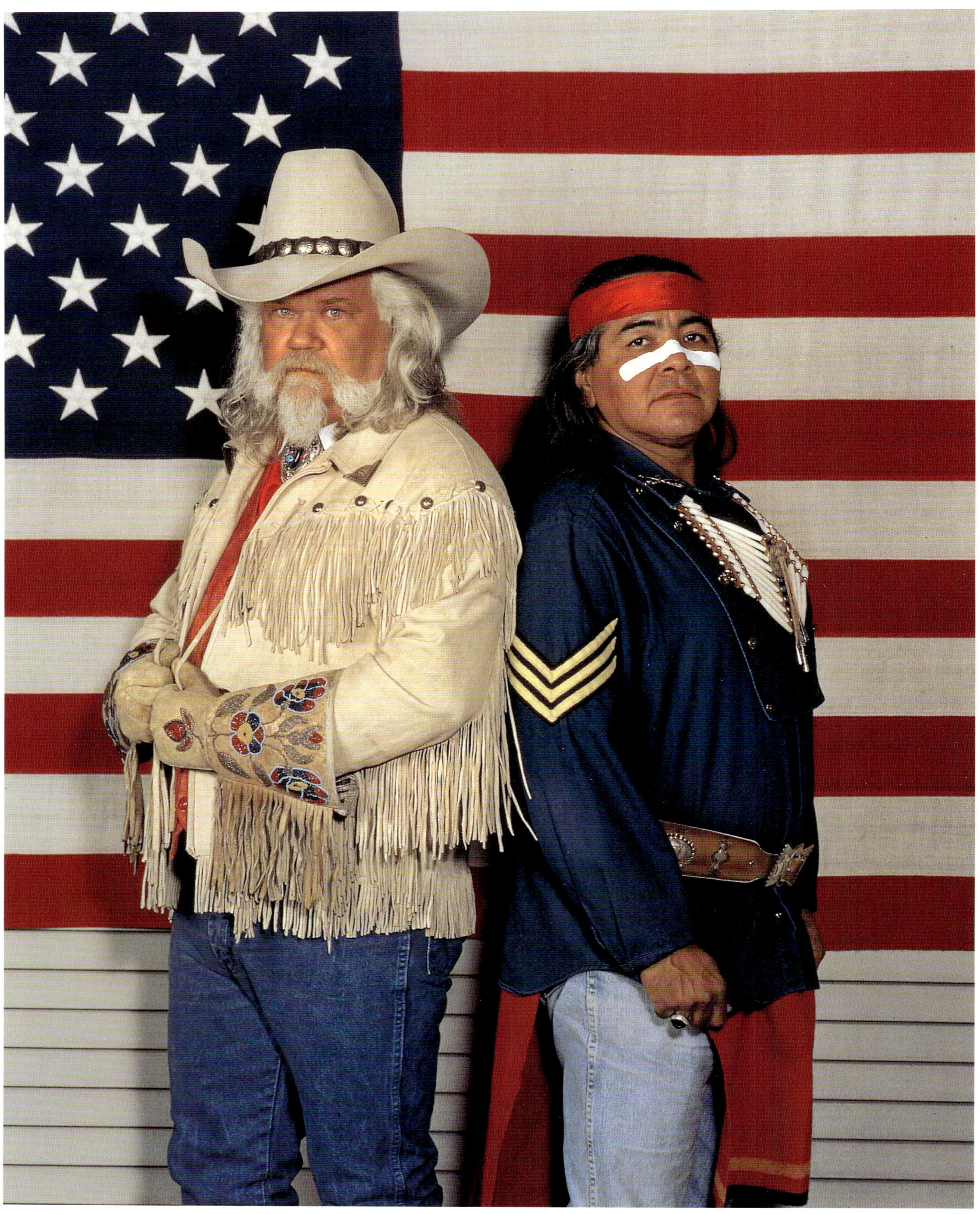

INTRODUCTION

When I first thought about JD Challenger, it was at least a year before I actually met him. I thought about him because I saw his paintings and, after seeing them, believed that he understood my feelings—my sadness when I think of the atrocities against Native people, my happiness when I think of our warriors' deeds of the past, and my concern when I think about our culture's salvation and the future for our children. The titles and themes that JD Challenger chooses and the statements he makes with his paintings made me think that he had to be Native. I thought this also because of the way he did not hold back and because of his bravery in portraying us the way that we want to be portrayed. His paintings remind us of who we are and to be proud of where we came from, and they will help us to remind our future generations of where they came from as well.

When Mr. Challenger paints, he doesn't paint guns and tomahawks and the aggressive nature of war. The paintings that Mr. Challenger creates puts the viewer in front of a human being with two arms, two legs, and a heart just like yours. And he's asking the world to look—to look at my people, to look at me. This is who I am, this is what I am. I am you. If you feel that war is wrong, I do too. If you feel that you don't want outside forces to come in and invade your country and dictate to you where you should live, I feel the same way. All the feelings that you have in protecting this country, if you look back and see, that is what I have felt too. If you see killing is wrong, I see it too. If you see that there is a need for a moral order in the universe, I see it too, and I live by it.

When John F. Kennedy was in the White House, he was very observant of many of the world's problems and, for the American Indian people in particular, he felt that something had to be done. In one of his speeches of 1961, he spoke of the responsibility of the American people to recognize their wrongful deeds during the so-called Indian wars. He said, "Before we can set out on the road to success, we have to know where we are going. And before we can know that, we must determine where we have been in the past . . . America has much to learn about the heritage of our American Indians. Only through this study can we, as a nation, do what must be done if our treatment of the American Indian is not to be marked down for all time as a national disgrace."

But for so many of the American Indians, since that speech, very little has been done. Thirty years later, Congress authorized and requested that President George Bush issue a proclamation designating 1992 as the Year of the American Indian. But no one, not one state did a thing to honor it. America has designated special days throughout the year for many of the cultures and leaders that have come to this country over the last several hundred years. But not one day has ever been set aside for the people or leaders or culture who were already Americans before any of these other cultures and leaders arrived.

Yet think of all the contributions American Indians have made to your life. Who in the world today would have seen a tomato, a potato, or sweet potato, or beans or corn? Those are the some of the basic foods for the world's societies today. They only existed here with the American Indian people. The American Indian people contributed to ballets, symphonies, rock, and the pop world. American Indians contributed to the pharmaceutical world, giving us one of the simplest forms of medication that exist today. Who would have known how to cure a headache had it not been for the American Indian sharing the wisdom of the willow, from which comes the aspirin? So much has been

OPPOSITE:
JD CHALLENGER
AND
AUGIE GRAYFOX

contributed, but not because you were asking questions. Because American Indians offered it. And that is something the world needs to come to terms with and understand and appreciate. You didn't come to me and ask for it; I gave it to you freely. Of my own choice, I gave it to you.

When I see Mr. Challenger's paintings, I see that he understands this. For all the world to say that the American Indian was a part of an army that the United States fought against, it must also understand that we did not choose the battle or the war. You came and invaded this country. You arrived hungry and suffering from your journey. We gave you medicine and we gave you food. We allowed you to live with us. We shared the wealth of this country with you. When you became strong after eating, your stomach full and your energy restored, you turned against us. Mr. JD Challenger sees this and expresses it. He also sees that I want to be happy and that I am willing to come out to you today and say that I am your friend and accept you as a friend and not as an enemy from the past. To prove my friendship, I have gone and lain in the mud, and the waters, and the sand and the forest and jungles and fought alongside your sons and brothers and fathers for this country. What more could you want from me? You've taken all that I have ever had. And I have given you far more than what you have asked for. Now accept me for who I am, respect my culture, accept the responsibilities of the past, and give me the rights that all American citizens are entitled to. Let me choose the way that I want to raise my children. Let me raise my children the way my ancestors would have loved to see them raised. Do not destroy my sacred places. Do not control my world. Do not let me suffer in poverty. Let me be free.

I have come to meet JD Challenger, the man behind the paintings, and I've come to see that this man's soul is as old as mine. He understands the same things I understand, the ideals and values that have been dictated to me through the clan leaders. For the pictures that he paints of the dances and the ceremonies show us that he understands the power behind the dances and ceremonies. The power behind the dances and the songs is God. If you look at his paintings and see the singers and dancers and they frighten you and you feel that there is more here than just a song or a dance, then you have to believe that there is more to this world, more to this universe than you are allowed to see. And that this singer and dancer, as they take part in this religion, can feel in their hearts the power beyond this world. And this faith, to believe in something that is felt but not seen, defines the very nature of all religion.

A man from the Crow Nation named Plenty Coups spoke of moral order and what he saw in his day and the atrocities his people endured. He talked about the people who tried to destroy the Native American culture, telling the world that ". . . they spoke very loudly when they said their laws were made for everybody. We soon learned that, although they expected us to keep them, they thought nothing of breaking them themselves. They said we might have their religion. But when we tried to understand it, we found that there were too many kinds of religions among whites for us to understand. We saw that the whites did not take their religion any more seriously than they did their laws and that they kept them both behind them, like helpers, to use when they might do them good in their dealings with strangers. These are not our ways. We keep the laws we made and live our religion."

For our people, when I think of all the prophecies and all the atrocities that our people have experienced and see that the prophecies have been borne out in events, I look around and wonder if the rest of the world knows where it is going. What is American Indian spiritualism? For us, it is to know that there is a way out. American Indian spiritualism tells me that this is the place, if I choose to make it so, where life will never have to end. If I choose to make it so, this is where all life will end. Spirituality tells me that if I practice my religion without wavering, I can make it a place where life never ends. So if you look around in this country and see the American Indian singing and dancing, know that we are not doing it just for ourselves. Through our spiritual beliefs, we are doing it to try and save this land for what we know will eventually come. We ask for another day in which we can sing and dance and in which we can be brothers with all life.

The paintings of JD Challenger remind us of the time when warriors were warriors. They were also preachers, ministers, doctors, healers, and fathers, and they raised families with respect for their children. And those warriors were also brothers, brothers to all life around them. When they saw water, they asked permission of the water to drink. They asked permission of the trees to use the wood. When they gathered anything from the earth, they asked permission from the spirit of that existence. They never took anything without asking permission first. When I look at the paintings of JD Challenger, I see that those are the warriors that I was told about. They were heroes but they were also human. They died. Yet the paintings show me that they are not dead. As long as a painting, shown to you, can evoke a feeling, then that painting is alive because it has awakened something in you that tells you to look and to see.

I want the world to know that I wish to be JD Challenger's friend. In our society, we don't have a word for friend. They tell us that there is no word for friendship. We don't have a word for hello or goodbye. We don't have a word for saying that I am going to die today. And we don't have a word for friend. The word we use for saying that I am your friend is a word that goes back thousands of years. It sounds like "Ama-cha-meh." It means that I will lay down my life for you. If a person is not willing to lay down his or her life for you, then that person is not your friend. If a person wants to be an acquaintance, to say hello and goodbye occasionally, then he or she is not your friend. When a person sees your life is at stake and says, "Take mine and leave him alone," then that person is your friend. It is a word we will rarely speak to another human being, the word that says "I will lay my life down for you." JD Challenger is my friend.

RONNIE JIMMIE
SEMINOLE

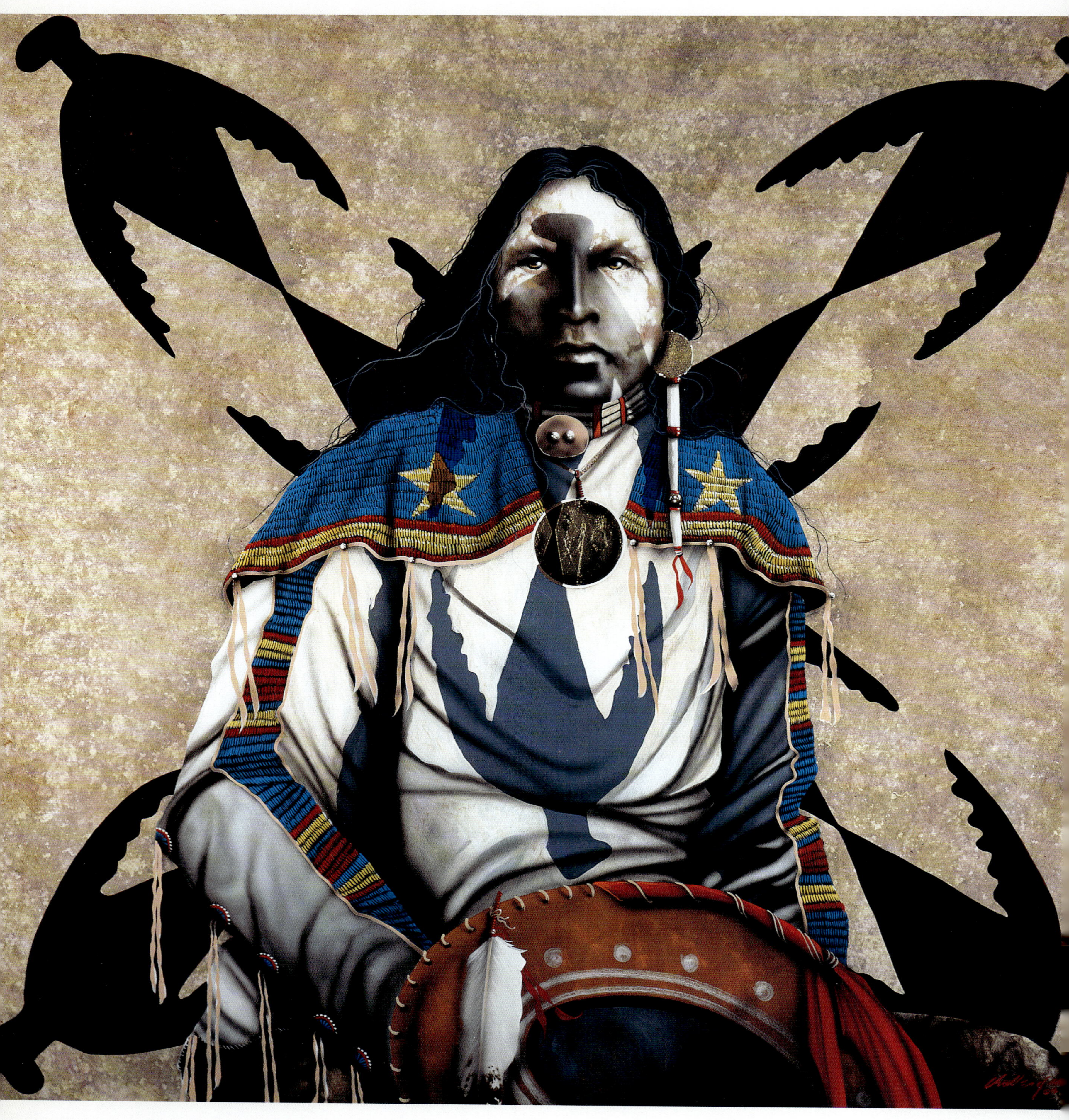

CHAPTER 1

ALL OVER THE SKY SACRED VOICES ARE CALLING

VISIONS AND VISIONARIES

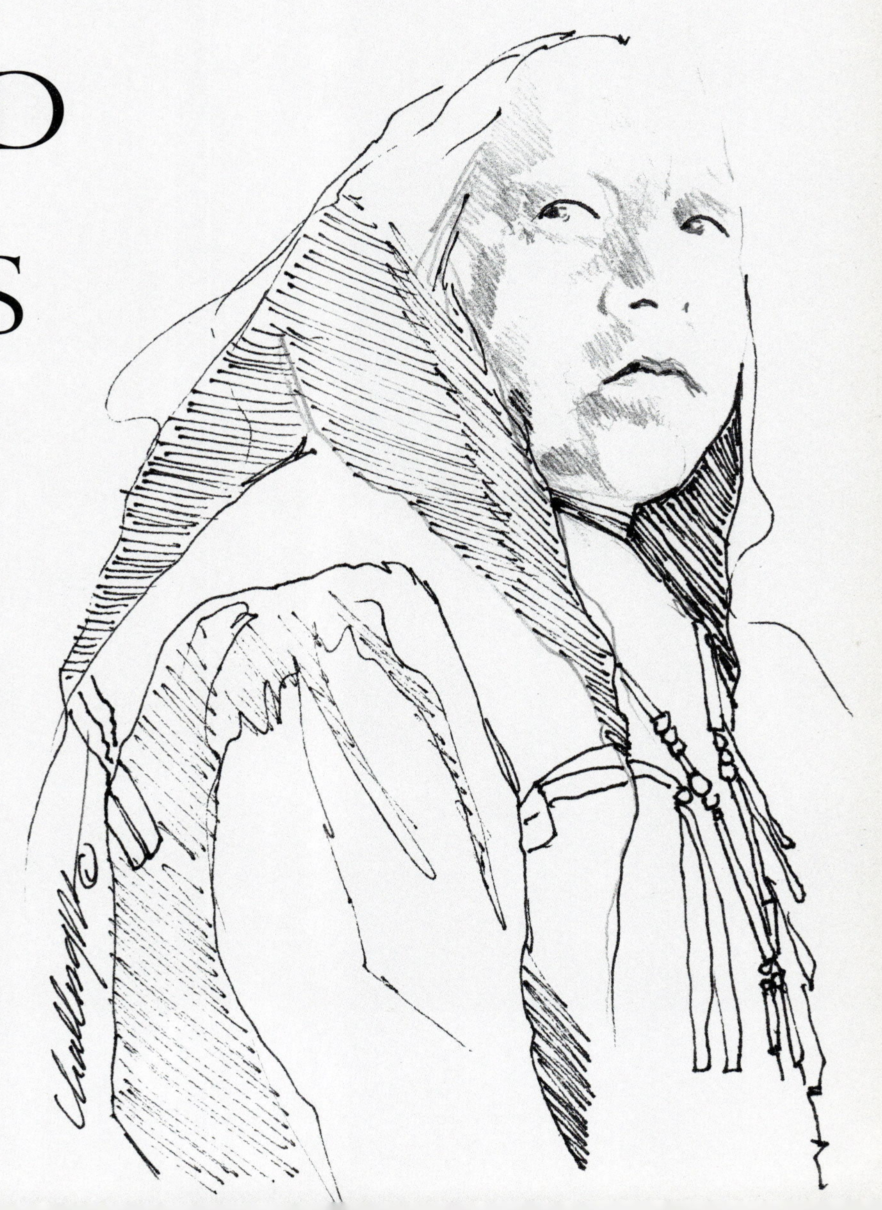

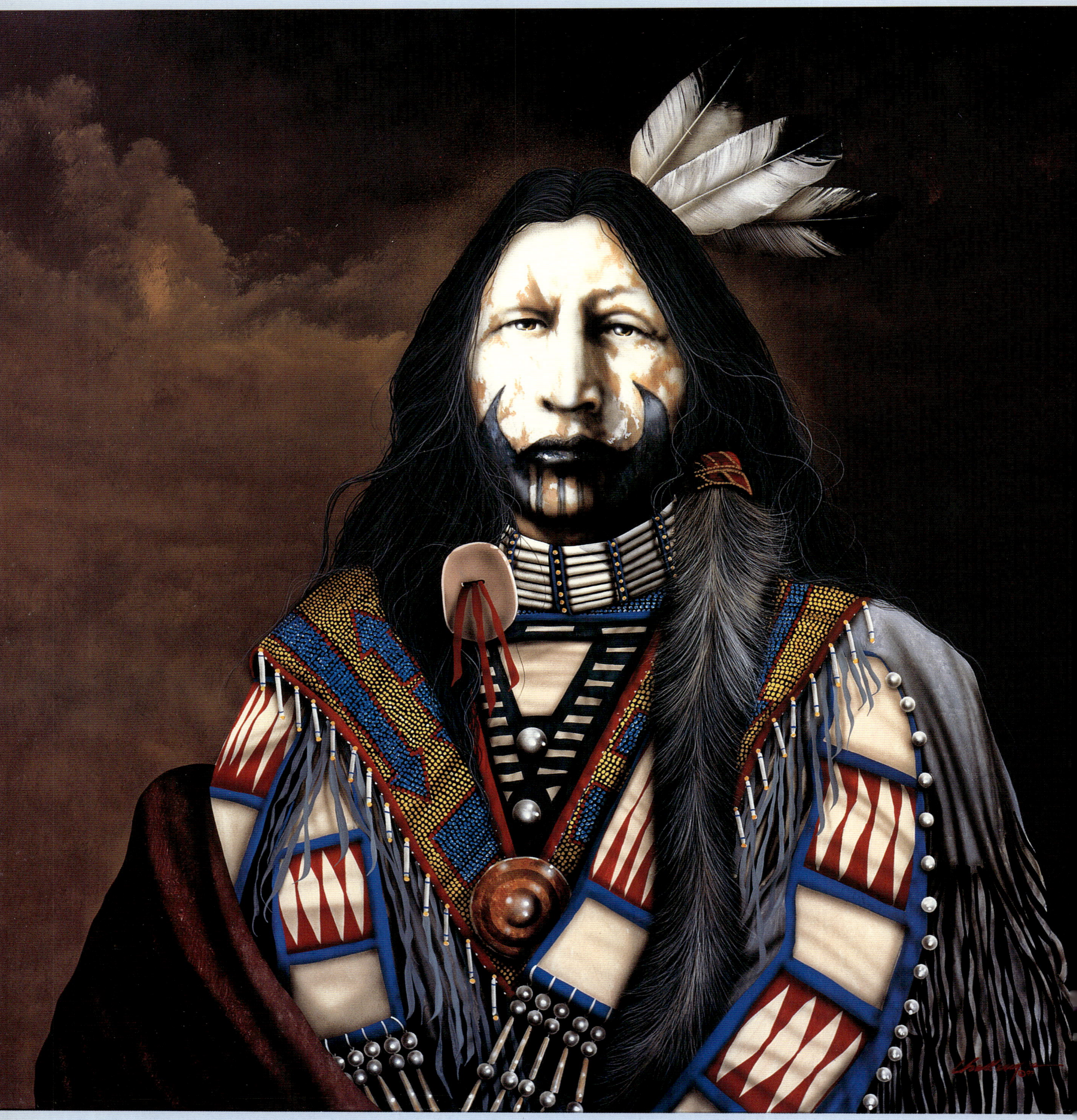

For a Paiute visionary named Wovoka and his people inhabiting the dry, desert wilderness of the American Northwest, the world began with water. The Paiute story, revealed in visions and dreams, tells of this ocean genesis, cool and pellucid as crystal, giving birth to all things known.

The mountain giant Kurangwa rose up from this flux, roiling the waters and spitting fire from its peak. Waves, blown by a great wind and cresting over the mountain, threatened to quell the flames. But the sacred sage hen appeared and settled upon the peak, keeping the waters at bay with her wings as her breast feathers blackened in the flames. The sacred bird's courage enabled the Paiute people to capture the first fire, drawn from the mountain's eruption, bringing warmth to cold nights and light to the darkness. As time passed, the ocean receded like a fan, slowly unveiling the full, beautiful face of earth.

The world's creation chronicles, religious traditions, inspired prophecies, and spiritual revolutions all seem to emanate from the realm of visions and dreams. It is here, in the bliss of twilight, that sacred knowledge wakes to consciousness. The vision or dreaming place, whether on a mountain top or in desert wilderness, is the sacred center, the medium between message and messenger and a sanctuary in which to seek reassurances and new understandings. Jerusalem, Mecca, Mount Sinai, and Lourdes are all sacred geographies—centers of inspiration defined by visions. Kurangwa, or Mount Grant, in the desert of Nevada, is also such a place.

This sacred mountain crowns the sierra cradle of Mason Valley, a thirty-mile expanse of sage prairie and the birthplace of Wovoka. It is here in the 1870s, beneath the shelter of Kurangwa, that the young Pauite man had a vision.

As a great shadow passed over the sky, shielding the sun and cloaking the earth in darkness, Wovoka rose up from the earth and entered the spirit world. Populated with plentiful game and buffalo, this world radiated serenity and peace, sheltering the contented ancestors of Wovoka's people—fathers, mothers, husbands, brothers, wives, and children no longer sick or starving or old. The Great Father appeared before Wovoka and showed him all this, then told Wovoka to return to earth and tell his people that they must love one another, not create war and not make trouble with the white men. The Father instructed Wovoka to lead his people in a dance that must last for five days. Once the dance was over, everyone must bathe in the river. Do not cry for the dead, said the Father,

OPPOSITE:
VOICES IN THE SKY

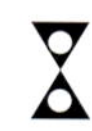

PAGE 12:
TOUCHED BY A VISION

15

as they will live again, and do not be afraid when the earth begins to shake. A new world is coming. Upon Wovoka's awakening, the Ghost dance religion began.

Wovoka followed the instructions given to him by the Father and taught his people the dance. One of the many Ghost dance practitioners, Porcupine, remembers Wovoka and the words the visionary spoke.

> "I have sent for you and am glad to see you. I am going to talk to you after a while about your relatives who are dead and gone. My children, I want you to listen to all I have to say to you. I will teach you, too, how to dance a dance, and I want you to dance it . . ." We danced until late in the night, when he told us we had danced enough.
>
> In the night when I first saw him I thought he was an Indian, but the next day when I could see better he looked different. He was not so dark as an Indian, nor so light as a white man. He had no beard or whiskers, but very heavy eyebrows. He was a good-looking man . . . He would talk to us all day.
>
> When we were assembled, he began to sing, and he commenced to tremble all over, violently for a while, and then sat down . . . He said he wanted to talk to us again and for us to listen. He said: "I am the man who made everything you see around you. I am not lying to you, my children. I made this earth and everything on it. I have been to heaven and seen your dead friends and have seen my own father and mother . . . My father told me the earth was getting old and worn out, and the people were getting bad, and that I was to renew everything as it used to be and make it better."
>
> He told us also that all our dead were to be resurrected; that they were all to come back to earth and that as the earth was too small for them and us, he would do away with heaven and make the earth itself large enough to contain us all; that we must tell all the people we meet about these things. He spoke to us about fighting, and said that was bad, and we must keep from it; that the earth was to be all good hereafter, and we must all be friends with one another . . . He told us not to quarrel, or fight, or strike each other, nor shoot one another; that the whites and Indians were to be all one people . . ."

Many of Wovoka's followers carried the dance beyond Mason Valley to other Native American camps and communities. The Ghost dance doctrine caught fire at once, spreading more quickly than perhaps any other documented religion in American history, affecting communities throughout the country with its spectral flame. The doctrine traveled by messengers, dancers, leaders, and educated Native Americans who would translate the message from the language of one tribe into another. The Ghost dance progressed south, from the Paiute of Nevada to the Cohonino, Walapai, Chemehuevi, and Mojave along the Colorado River and farther still to the Apache, Pima, and Maricopa of the southern deserts. The dance moved northward to the Shoshoni and Bannock of Idaho, the Flatheads, Nez Percé, Northern Arapaho, and Asiniboin of northern Montana. Eastward, many members of the Chippewa reservations, the Sioux reservations, Native Americans of the vast Oklahoma Indian Territory, and of the Cheyenne, Caddo, and Pawnee tribes embraced the ceremonies. Native Americans from the Mission reservation along the

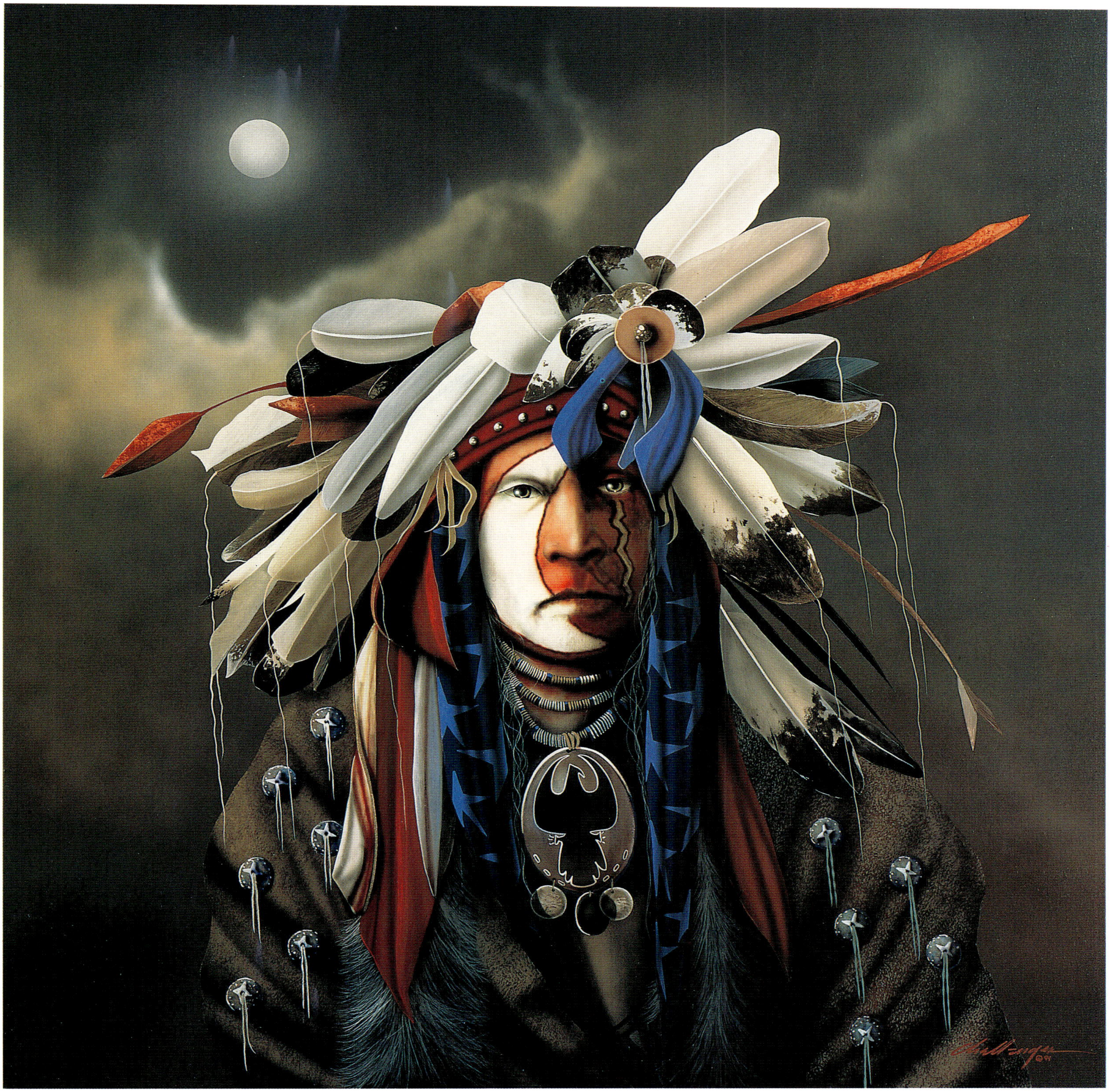

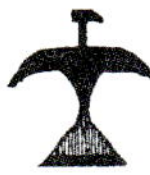

SEEKING THE VISION

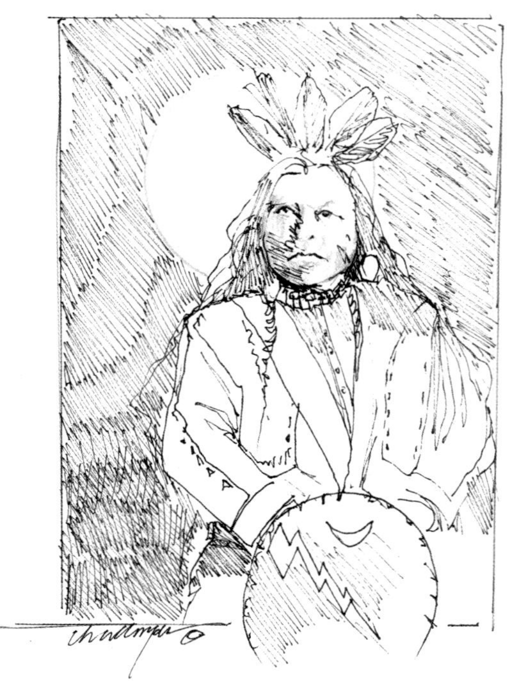

border of southern California to the Makah reservation at the northwest tip of the Olympic Peninsula welcomed the message. It was a remarkable advance spanning the continent from the Pacific Coast Klamath River reservation to the Cherokee's Qualla reservation in North Carolina. Estimates suggest that by 1890, members of over thirty-five tribes, approximately sixty thousand people, were practicing the Ghost dance religion. Native American men, women, and children from across the nation were gathering together to dance a dance that promised to bring the rebirth of the world.

The religion's celebration is movement. Visions, trances, hypnosis, dancers, and leaders are its media. Rebirth is its salvation. The Ghost dance is remarkable as much for the similarities it shares with many other religions of the world as for the inability of its detractors to recognize those kinships. Hebrews danced for atonement, Greeks and Romans danced to honor their gods, and Christians danced uncontrollably in tribute to Saint John in the 1300s. Shakers, Quakers, and Ranters saw visions and sought ecstasy in dance and ritual movements. The French prophets, the Welsh Jumpers, and the English Methodists all engaged in trance inducing dances. Adventists, Holy Rollers, Wilderness Worshipers, and Heavenly Recruits depended on the vision and the trance for inspiration. Fundamental Revivalists still travel the country roads of the late twentieth century, preaching holy inspiration and succumbing to divine physical intervention. Japan's Shinto cult danced the Bugaku prayer dance. Burma had its spirit dancers. The Kathakali danced in southern India. Islam set the Dervishes whirling.

The Paiute named their ceremony the "dance in a circle" because, unlike other Paiute dances, the circular movement was a primary feature of the Ghost dance. The Comanche named it the dance "with joined hands" and "the Father's dance." The Caddos gave it the names "my children dance" and "the prayer of all to the Father." The Shoshoni, referring to the way the feet moved and stirred up dust, called it "everybody dragging." "Dance with clasped hands" and "dance craziness" were the Kiowa names. The prairie tribes, such as the Arapaho and Sioux, gave the ceremony the name it came to be known by in history—the "spirit" or "Ghost" dance. But no matter what tribe or name, the Ghost dance promised the same to all who performed it—to bring back their ancestors from the spirit world, to return the buffalo and other natural game to the plains where they had been systematically slaughtered, and to terminate the European American stranglehold on the Native American world.

"By the late 1800s, the Native American needed nothing greater than for the white man to leave him, his family, his religion, and his land alone," Ghost-dance artist JD Challenger explains. "Whites had taken his land and forced him into a dependent relationship with the government. It was no wonder that the Ghost dance doctrine and the idea of a new world were embraced by so many Native Americans. Understanding Wovoka's vision of the earth's resurrection required the believer to imagine a world perfect for the Native American, a world that would not include other humans who forced them from their homes, defiled their sacred places, wastefully slaughtered the wildlife, and ridiculed their beliefs."

The strength and spreading influence of the Ghost dance were not lost on the European American population encroaching across Native lands. Throughout the past, Native American religions created communities of people who believed that sharing was one of the highest virtues, who had no need for locks on doors, no need for orphanages, and who taught that shame, not punishment, is disrespect's reward. Yet Native American religious practices, including the Ghost dance ceremonies, were considered heathen and

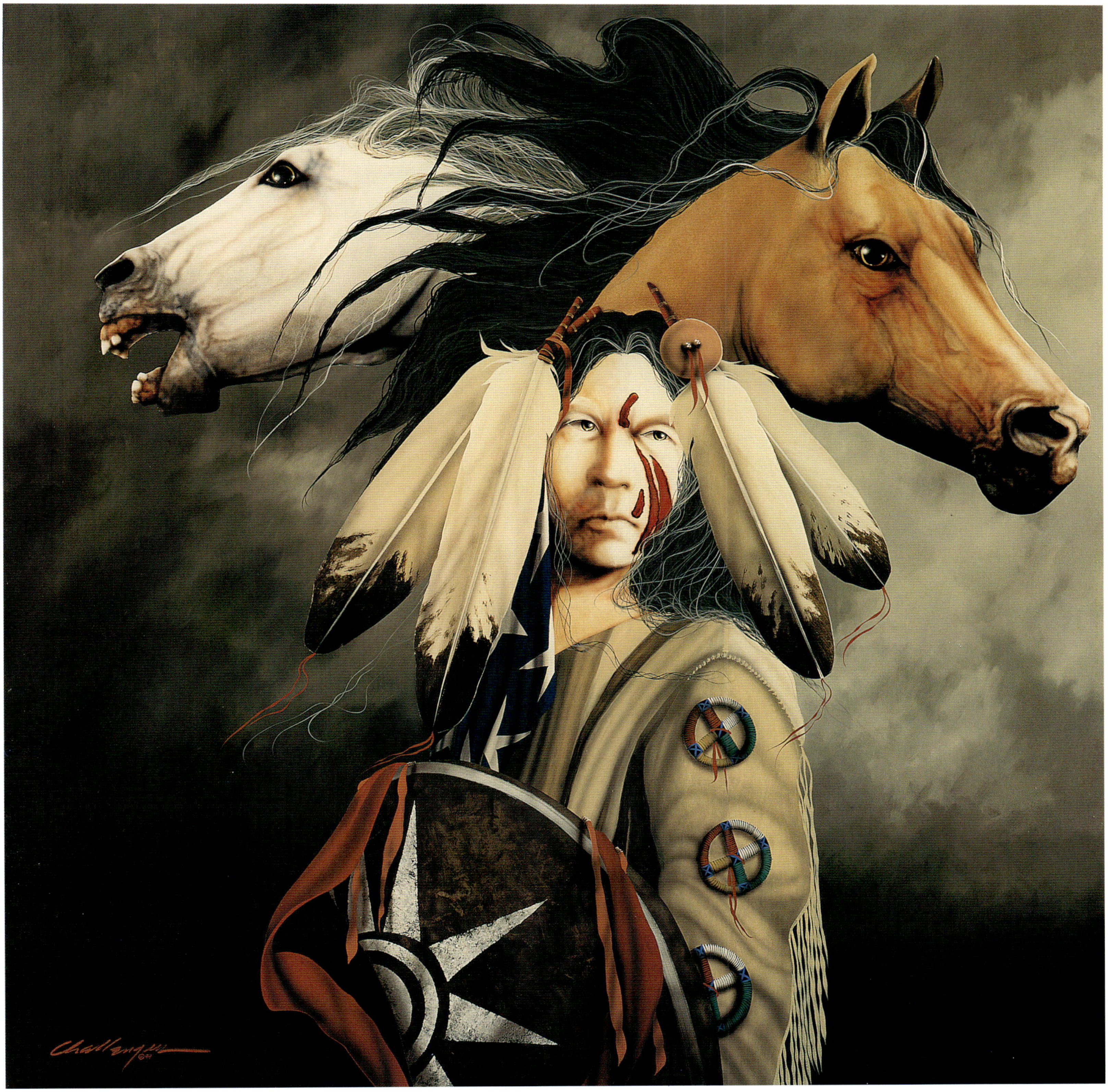

VOICES OF THE THUNDER BEINGS

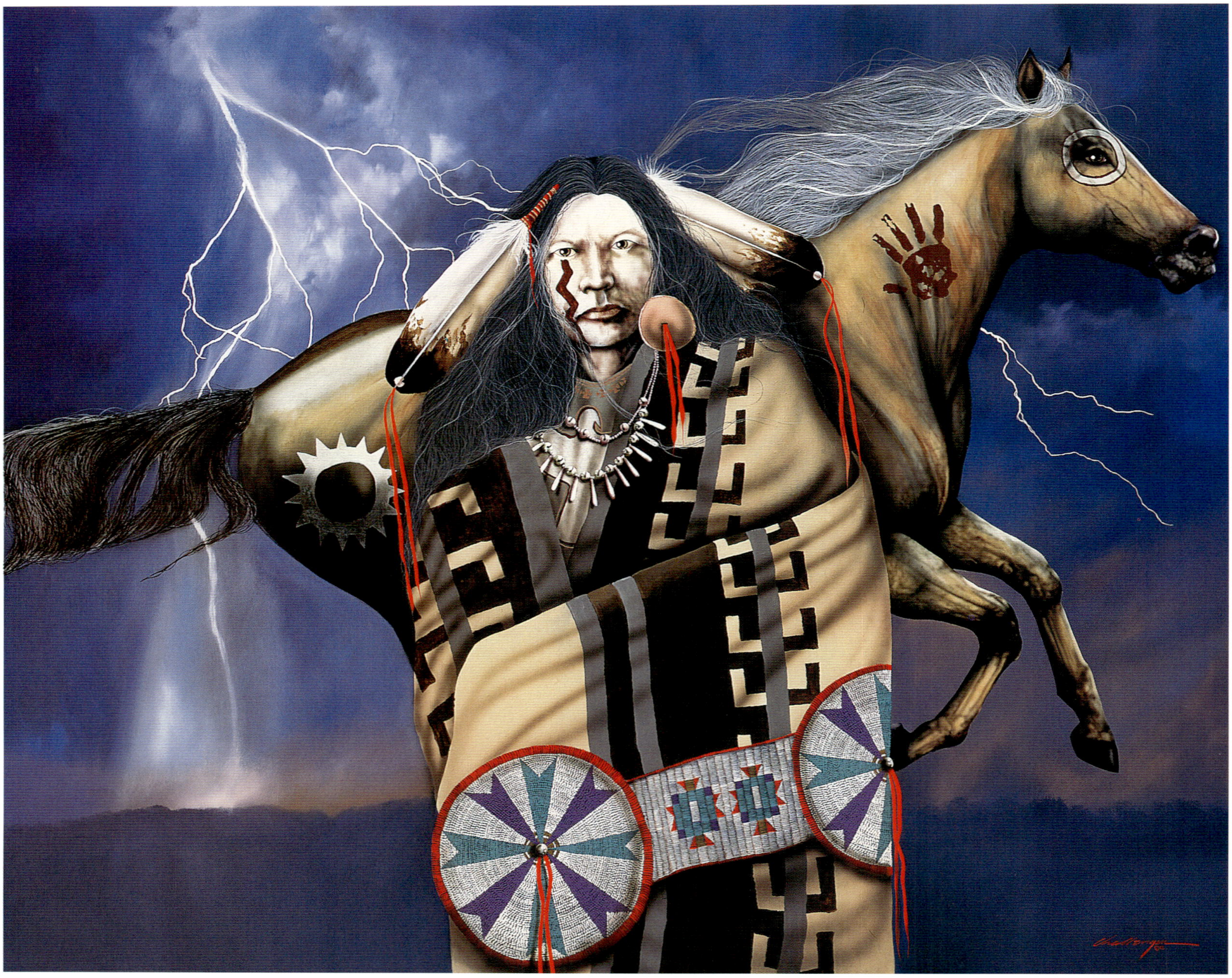

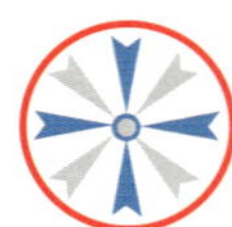

SPIRITS OF THE WILD WORLD

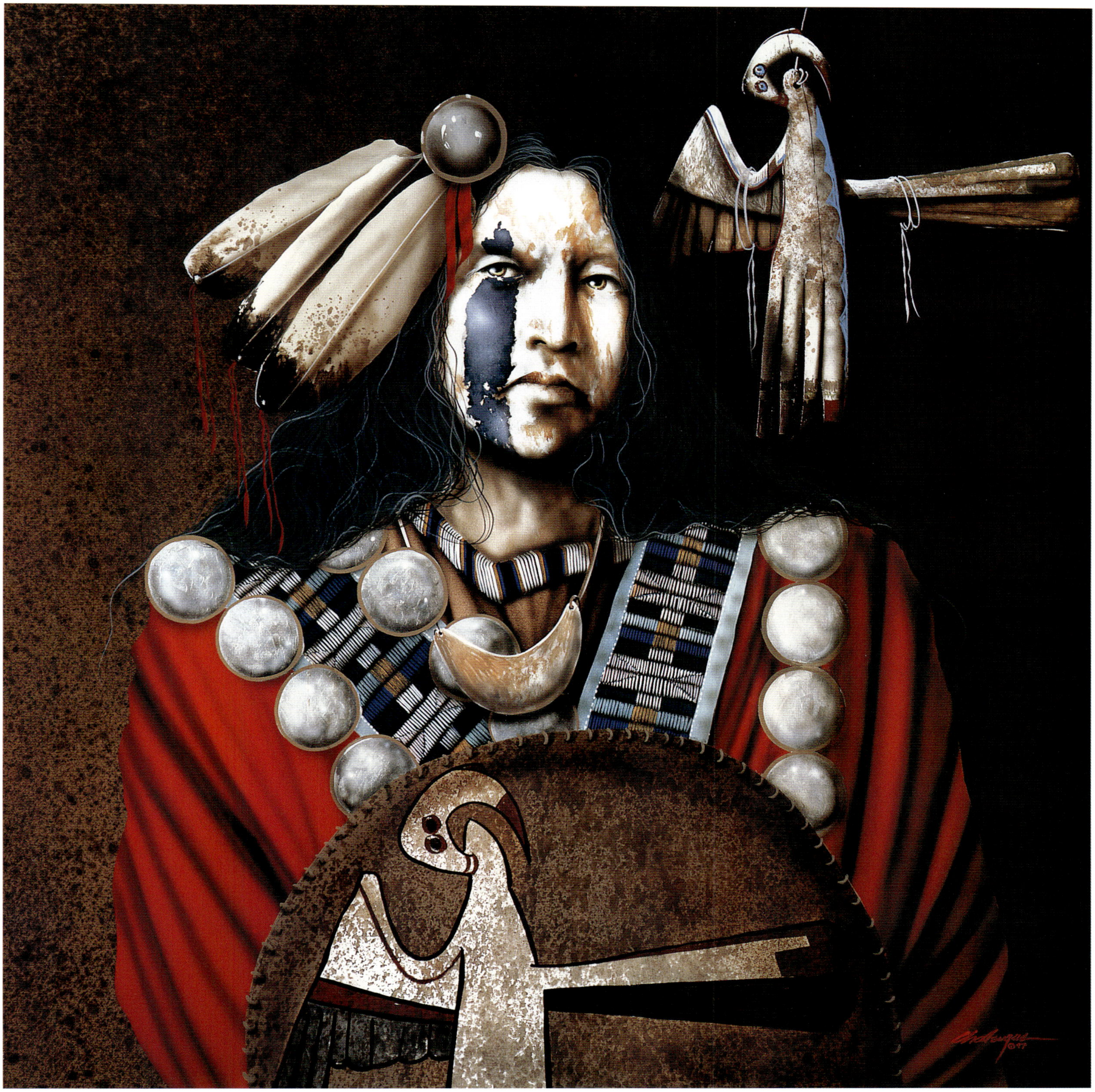

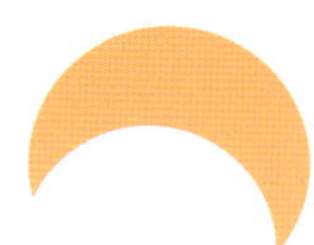

TALLBIRD'S VISION

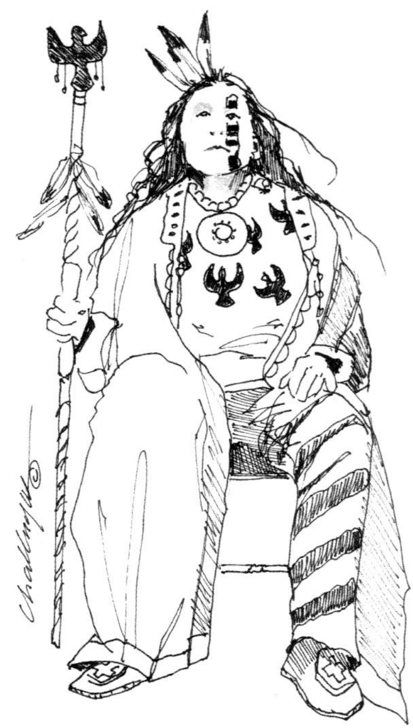

without merit by emigrating Europeans, American settlers, and the U.S. government, and every attempt was made to eliminate them.

Within this dramatically suppressive environment rose the genesis of hope—revealed in a dream and consecrated with a dance. Together with detailed narratives disclosed through the visions of practitioners, the Ghost dance religion combined the elements of the natural world including thunder, wind, and lightning with the dramatic events arcing through the lives of late nineteenth-century Native Americans.

Many religious doctrines derived from visions tend to evolve as they are passed from convert to convert. The changes made in them are often based on the needs and desires of their followers. As the Ghost dance doctrine's influence grew, the shaking of the earth in Wovoka's vision and the new world in his teachings became the Apocalypse. And in this vision of the future crafted by the Ghost dance magic, the European American ceased to exist.

> *The yellow-hide, the white-skin.*
> *I have now put him aside—*
> *I have now put him aside—*
> *I have no more sympathy with him.*

Many members of the Paiute believed that when the time came for the earth's rebirth, Native Americans would travel into the mountains and a great flood would come and drown all European Americans. Non-believing Native Americans would turn to wood and burn. Some believed the flood was a mix of mud and water and that skeptics would turn to stone. Some of the southern plains tribes believed that the world was worn out and both the Native Americans and European Americans would die and return to live in separate worlds. Several tribes made it known that they had no hostility toward European Americans, but when the apocalypse was upon the earth, nothing could be done to save them.

As the doctrine traveled east across the mountains, the renewal required that all believers succumb to a deep sleep and wake to a new world once the dramatic upheaval was complete. Many members of the Shoshoni of Wyoming stated that this sleep would last for five days, and upon awakening, all people would live together peacefully. Some Ghost dance practitioners of the Cheyenne, Arapaho, and Kiowa tribes believed that this new world would slip over the old world, covering everything as it approached from the west. Native Americans would be lifted above it by wings created from the sacred dance feathers adorning their hair.

The Sioux, suffering the loss of tribal members to starvation and tribal lands to broken treaties, embraced the most dramatic apocalypse. The earth would tremble and a great landslide would be followed by a flood, pouring into the mouths of European Americans and gagging them with mud. Storms and whirlwinds would devastate the earth as Native Americans rose above, riding on the sacred feather to a land of endless prairie and buffalo.

But perhaps the most succinct interpretation of the apocalypse came from the Arapaho Sitting Bull. He believed in a great wall of fire that would push all European Americans across the ocean and back to their own country.

Despite its catastrophic prophecy, much of the doctrine promoted kindness, love, and charity to others. It also provided comfort to a bereaved people who dealt with unwarranted loss on a daily basis. By the 1880s, game was scarce, the buffalo had been slaughtered to near extinction, and many of the tribes had been ushered onto reservations and forced to depend on meager government rations. Malnutrition and starvation were common. European Americans, in particular missionaries, habitually encroached on remote communities that had remained isolated from European viruses and disease. Within a short period of time, entire Native American families would often succumb to an unknown killer. The return of so many loved ones from the land of the dead was not an unreasonable desire.

Faith in dreams and love of family are two of the most powerful influences in the human psyche. They were also perhaps the primary forces driving the Ghost dance practitioners. James Mooney, ethnographer of the late 1800s, tells of the importance of the Ghost dance beliefs to the young Cheyenne Little Woman and her husband, the Arapaho Grant Left-hand:

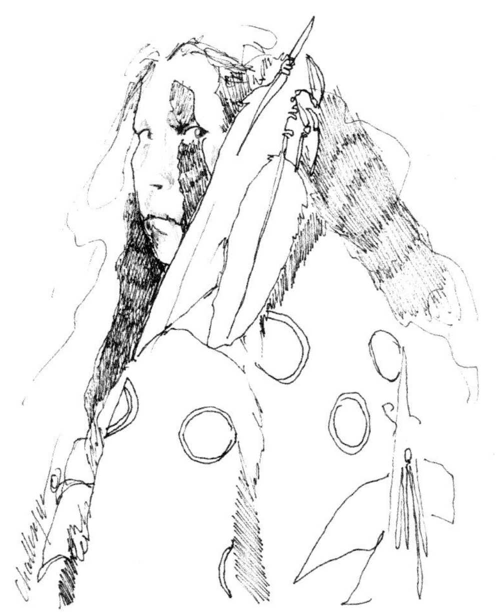

> Her first child died soon after birth, and the young mother was keenly affected by the bereavement. Afterward a boy was born to them, and became the idol of his parents, especially of the father. He grew up into a bright and active little fellow, but when about four years of age he was suddenly seized with a spasm in the night and died in a few minutes, almost before his father could reach his bed. This second loss brought deep sorrow to them both, and the mother brooded over it so that there was serious fear for her own life. Then came the Ghost dance and the new doctrine of a reunion with departed friends. The mother went to the dance, fell into a trance, met her children as in life, and played with her little boy. On awaking and returning home she told her husband. He could hardly believe it at first, but it required but little persuasion to induce him to attend the next Ghost dance with her, because, as he said, "I want to see my little boy." He himself fell into a trance, saw his children, and rode with his little boy on the horse behind him over the green prairies of the spirit land. From that time both became devoted adherents and leaders of the Ghost dance; their trances have been frequent, and every dance is welcomed as another opportunity of reunion with departed friends. The young man was deeply affected as he spoke of his love for his children, the sudden death of the little boy, and their second meeting in the other world, and as his wife sat by his side looking up into our faces and listening intently to every word, although she understood but little English, it could not be doubted that their faith in the reality of the vision was real and earnest. Every Indian parent who has lost a child, every child who has lost a parent, and every young man and woman who has lost a brother, sister, or friend affirms a similar reason for belief in the Ghost dance.

The crow woman—
To her home,
She is going.
She will see it,
She will see it.
Her children,
Her children.
She will see them,
She will see them.

Wovoka heads a long line of visionaries who brought hope to Native Americans in times of crisis and subjugation. Wovoka's own father, Tavibo, was also a visionary and passed along his revelations to the scattered bands of the Pauite tribe, the Shoshoni and Bannock, and other tribes of Oregon and Idaho.

Tavibo created a childhood of spiritual quest and devotion for his son and died when Wovoka was only fourteen. During his life, Tavibo exposed his son to the sacred ceremonies that were performed in their home. Wovoka had many opportunities to hear his father speak of sacred things and witness the respect bestowed upon him by the people who listened and believed. Wovoka attributes divine powers to his father, calling him a "dreamer." Tavibo's doctrine shared many of the same beliefs held by past visionaries, and some of them would show up again in Wovoka's Ghost dance revelations.

Wovoka was, by accounts, introspective in nature and sensitive to the voice of visions. Once in full command of his religious teachings, Wovoka inspired others to pursue their own vision quests. Kicking Bear, band chief of the Minneconjou Sioux, became a leader of the Ghost dance. He made several pilgrimages to see Wovoka and recounted his second visit before a council held on White Clay Creek at the Pine Ridge reservation in South Dakota. Kicking Bear revealed that he, along with his delegation and Wovoka, ascended a ladder made of clouds and passed through an opening in the sky. When they reached the Spirit Land, they were greeted by Wakantanka, the Great Spirit, and were shown the old camping grounds and lodges, friends and relatives long dead, endless prairies of uncultivated grass, and great herds of buffalo. Kicking Bear and his delegation watched this new world unfold for three days. Everywhere the village was active with ancestors. Buffalo meat was being prepared over cook fires. They ate from a boiling kettle. Then the Great Spirit ushered them into a large tepee filled with ghosts of the deceased.

Thick clouds descended on the village, and Kicking Bear's band could no longer see. When the fog eventually dissipated, everything had vanished. A wicked-looking man covered in short hair from head to foot approached them and spoke to the Great Spirit, demanding half the people of the world. The Great Spirit denied his request, but this evil man persisted until the Great Spirit relented, claiming all Native Americans as his chosen people and giving up all white men to this devil. The Great Spirit then informed the delegates of his intentions to cover the earth with new soil. The depth of this new earth would be five times the height of a man and would bury all white people. He would cover the surface with running water and grasses, buffalo and ponies, and make all oceans surrounding this new land impassable. Then the Great Spirit sent Kicking Bear and his delegation back to this world.

Visionaries can be found at the forefront of many Native American campaigns designed to end oppression. Drawn from the realm of dreams, visions are often the key to resolving struggles and understanding complexities plaguing the waking world. Charged by the power of trances, meditation, dances, and chanting, visionaries like Wovoka enter "the world where there is nothing but the spirits of all things. That is the real world that is behind this one, and everything we see here is something like a shadow from that world."

Two hundred years before the Ghost dance began, the Pueblo Indians of the late 1600s, in their struggle over land and religion with the invading Catholic Spaniards, turned to the Tewa medicine-man Pope'. Upon his return from a pilgrimage to the north,

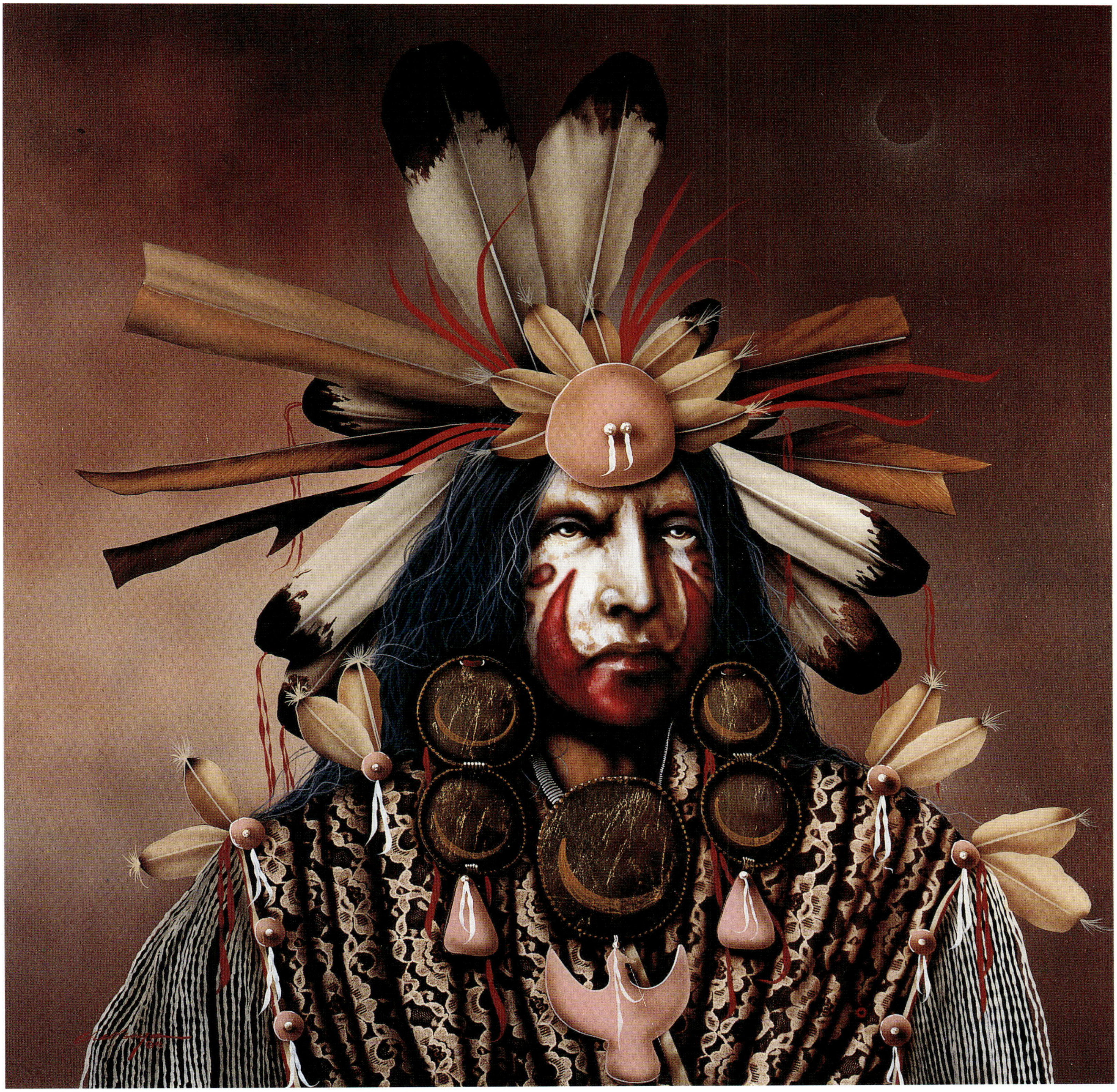

THE PROPHET

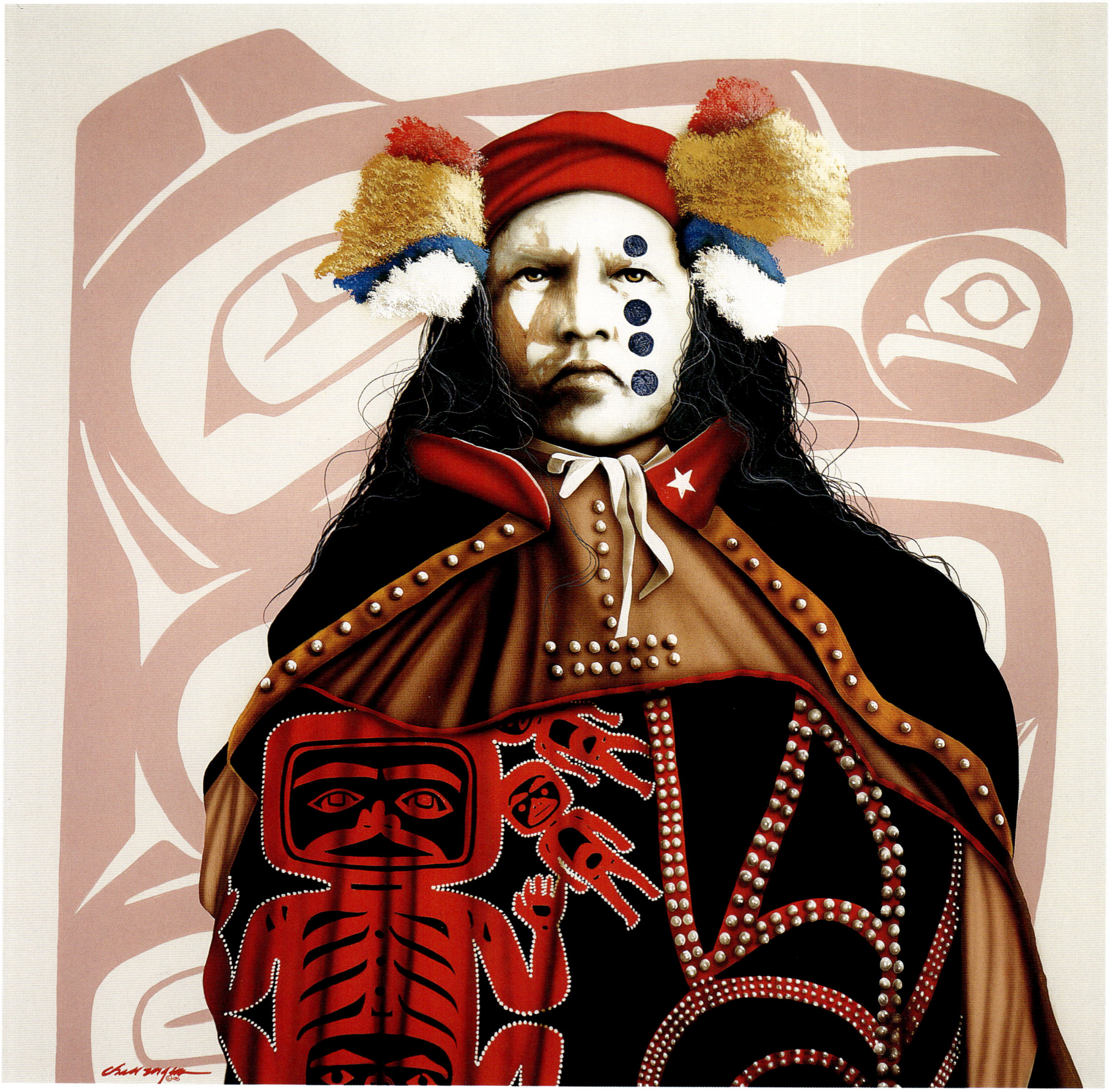

THE MYSTIC

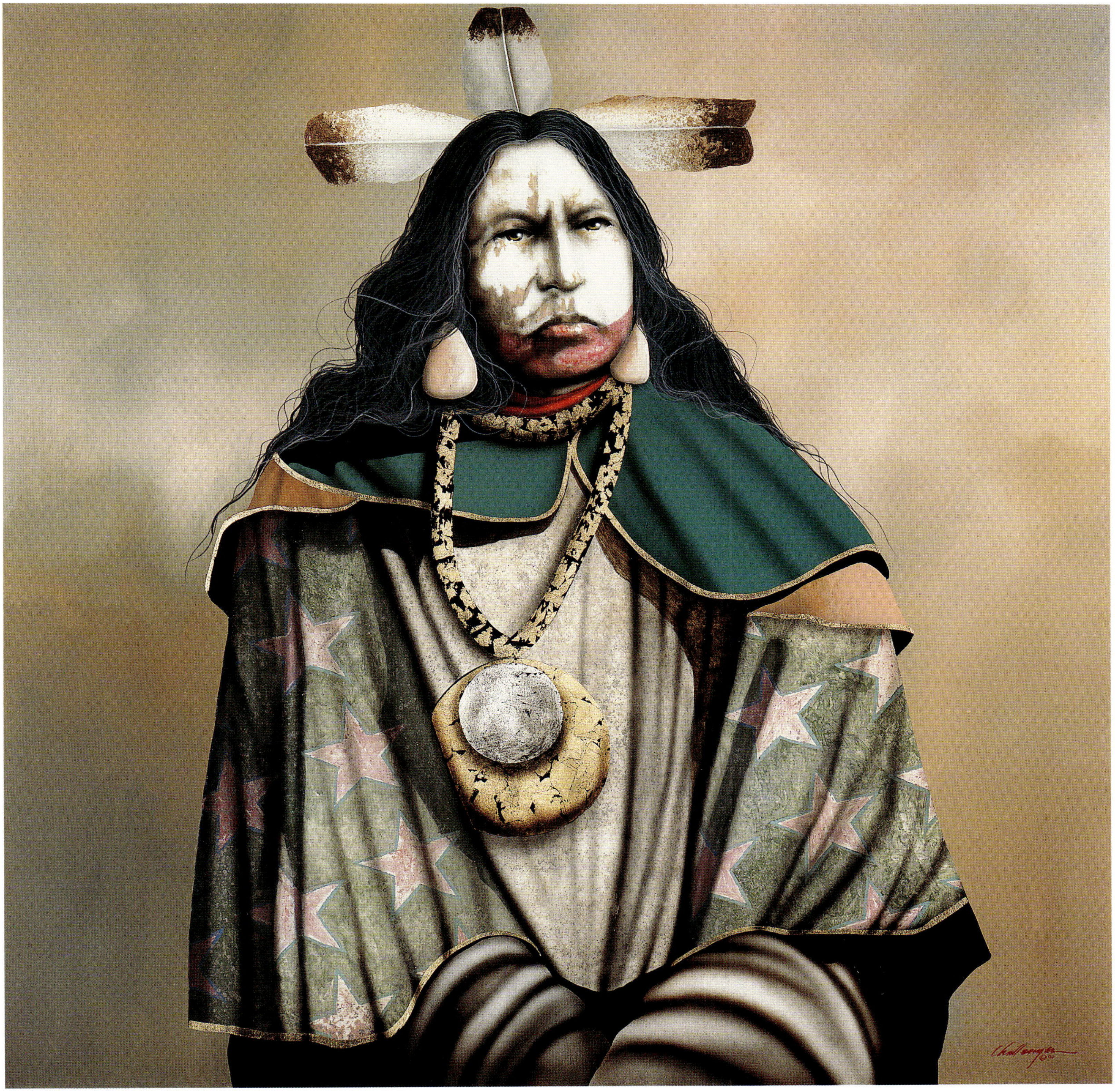

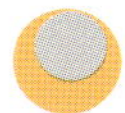

WISDOM OF THE SHAMAN

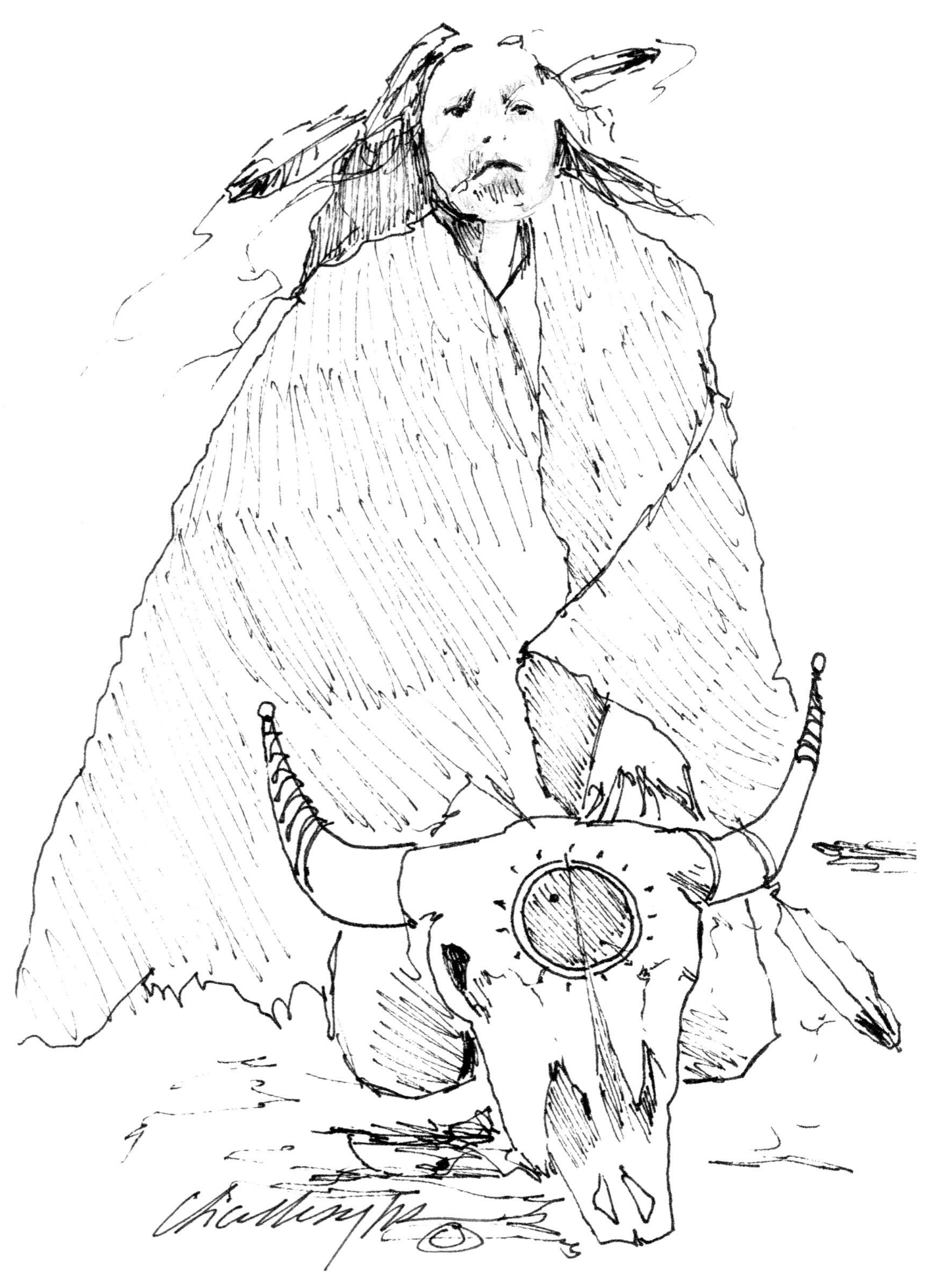

Pope' told of his visit to the lake of Shipapu, the sacred place where his people originated and home to their returning souls. The residing spirits entrusted Pope' with divine powers and told him to return to his people and help them rise up against their oppressors.

"Wonderful beings were these spirit messengers," reveals Mooney. "Swift as light and impalpable as thought, they passed under the earth from the magic lake to the secret subterranean chamber of the oracle and stood before him as shapes of fire and spoke, telling him to prepare the strings of yucca knots and send them with the message to all the Pueblos far and near, so that in every village the chiefs might untie one knot from the string each day and know when they came to the last knot that then was the time to strike."

The Apache of southern Arizona produced the prophet Nakai'-dokli'ni in the early 1880s and then lost him to a skirmish with U.S. troops. His prophecies, prayers, and ceremonies intimidated the stronghold at nearby Fort Apache and propelled the soldiers to action. The prophet's talk that whites would no longer occupy the country once the corn was ripe, his ability to commune with spirits, and the dance he created for his people were viewed as dangerous and he was shot dead in an attempt to arrest him. Nakai'-dokli'ni's dance took the shape of a spoked wheel with all the dancers facing the center. It was here the prophet stood, dusting them with the sacred pollen of the tule' rush.

In the 1870s Smohalla, the Dream prophet, moved through the tribes of Washington and Oregon along the Columbia River, gathering over two thousand followers. His doctrine, much like the Ghost dance doctrine twenty years later, told of a new world inhabited only by Native Americans, including the resurrected dead. Smohalla, like most visionaries, practiced meditative states of consciousness to receive messages from the Father above, or Sa'ghalee Tyee, as he is called by the Dream prophet.

Major J. W. MacMurray of the U.S. military witnesses one of Smohalla's trance states:

He falls into trances and lies rigid for considerable periods. Unbelievers have experimented by sticking needles through his flesh, cutting him with knives, and otherwise testing his sensibility to pain, without provoking any responsive action. It was asserted that he was surely dead, because blood did not flow from the wounds. These trances always excite great interest and often alarm, as he threatens to abandon his earthly body altogether because of the disobedience of his people, and on each occasion they are in a state of suspense as to whether the *Sa'ghalee Tyee* will send his soul back to earth to reoccupy his body, or will, on the contrary, abandon and leave them without his guidance. It is this going into long trances, out of which he comes as from a heavy sleep and almost immediately relates his experiences in the spirit land, that gave rise to the title of "Dreamers," or believers in dreams, commonly given to his followers by the neighboring whites.

Smohalla also brought back a dance from the world of dreams and taught it to his followers. General Howard of the U.S. military witnesses one of these dance ceremonies.

A long rank of men, followed by women and children, with faces painted, the red paint extending back into the partings of the hair—the men's hair braided and tied up with showy strings—ornamented in dress, in hats, in blankets with variegated colors, in leggings of buckskin and moccasins beaded and plain; women with bright shawls or blankets, and skirts to the ankle and top moccasins. All were mounted on Indian ponies as various in color as the dress of the riders. These picturesque people, after keeping us waiting long enough for effect, came in sight from up the valley from the direction of their temporary camp just above the company gardens. They drew near to the hollow square of the post and in front of the small company to be interviewed. Then they struck up their song. They were not armed except with a few tomahawk pipes that could be smoked with the peaceful tobacco or penetrate the skull bone of an enemy, at the will of the holder. Yet somehow this wild sound produced a

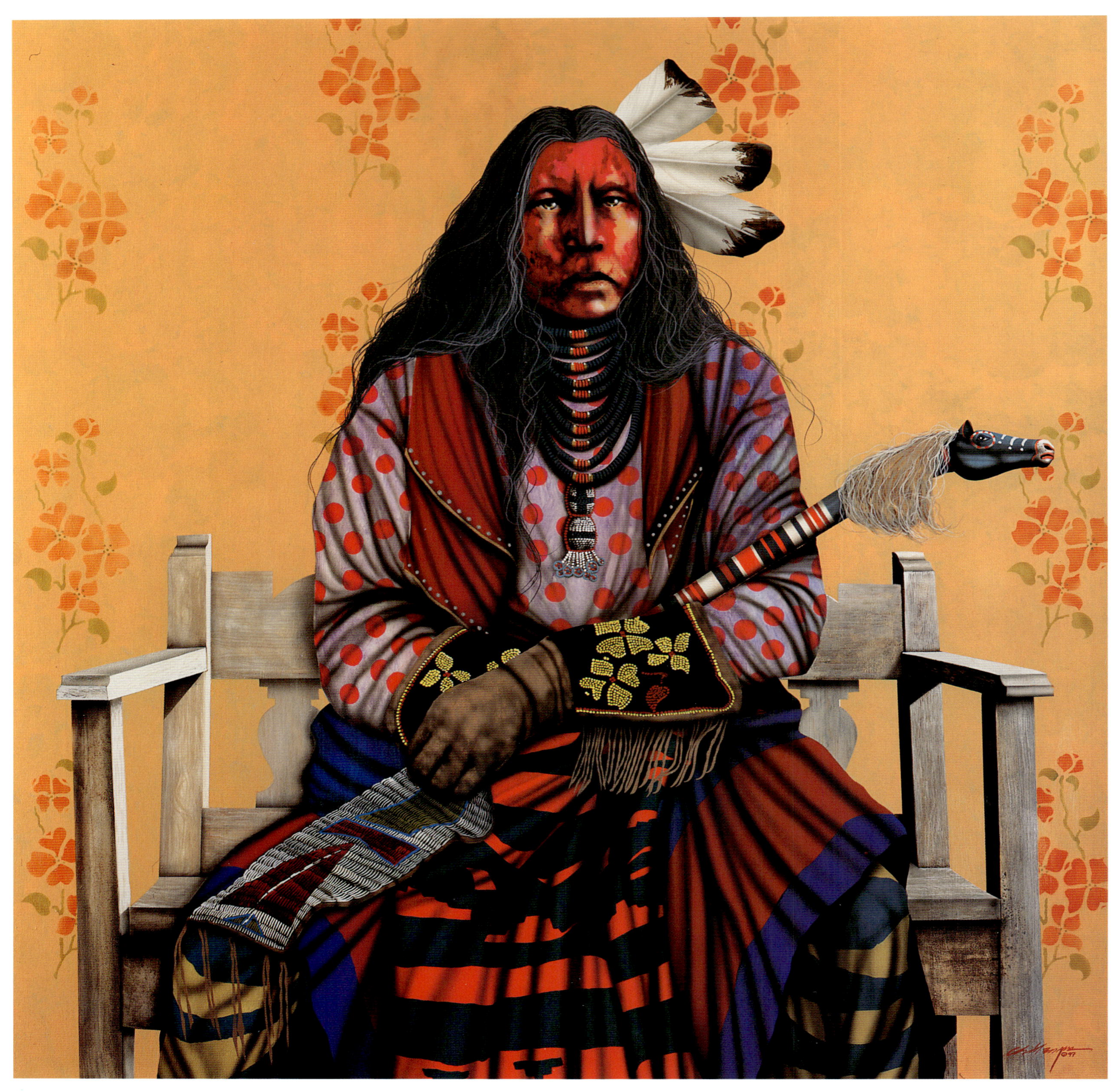

FLOWERS WITH NO SMELL

• • •

strange effect. It made one feel glad that there were but fifty of them, and not
five hundred. It was shrill and searching; sad, like a wail, and yet defiant in its
close. The Indians swept around outside the fence and made the entire circuit,
still keeping up the song as they rode. The buildings broke the refrain into
irregular bubblings of sound until the ceremony was completed.

Black Elk, an Ogalala Sioux and perhaps one of the most famous visionaries in American
history, also became one of the Ghost dance religion's most passionate converts. His first
view of the ceremony, on Wounded Knee Creek at Pine Ridge reservation, confirmed the
events he had seen in his childhood visions:

> I was surprised, and could hardly believe what I saw; because so much of
> my vision seemed to be in it. The dancers, both women and men, were holding
> hands in a big circle, and in the center of the circle they had a tree painted red
> with most of its branches cut off and some dead leaves on it. This was exactly
> like the part of my vision where the holy tree was dying, and the circle of the
> men and women holding hands was like the sacred hoop that should have
> power to make the tree to bloom again. I saw too that the sacred articles the
> people had offered were scarlet, as in my vision, and all their faces were painted
> red. Also, they used the pipe and the eagle feathers. I sat there looking on and
> feeling sad. It all seemed to be from my great vision somehow and I had done
> nothing yet to make the tree to bloom.
>
> Then all at once great happiness overcame me, and it all took hold of me
> right there. This was to remind me to get to work at once and help to bring my
> people back into the sacred hoop, that they might again walk the red road in a
> sacred manner pleasing to the Powers of the Universe that are One Power. I
> remembered how the spirits had taken me to the center of the earth and shown
> me the good things, and how my people should prosper. I remembered how the
> Six Grandfathers had told me that through their power I should make my people
> live and the holy tree should bloom. I believed my vision was coming true at last,
> and happiness overcame me.
>
> When I went to the dance, I went only to see and to learn what the people
> believed; but now I was going to stay and use the power that had been given me.
> The dance was over for that day, but they would dance again next day, and I
> would dance with them.

My children—
My children—
Here it is, I hand it to you.
The earth.

The Ghost dance vision and the doctrine it inspired are based on faith and hope, the
two underlying tenets common to all cultures, religious and secular alike. Revealed in a
remote desert valley of Nevada and traveling over vast stretches of land to the four corners of the country, this dream would ultimately galvanize a nation of people on the verge
of oblivion.

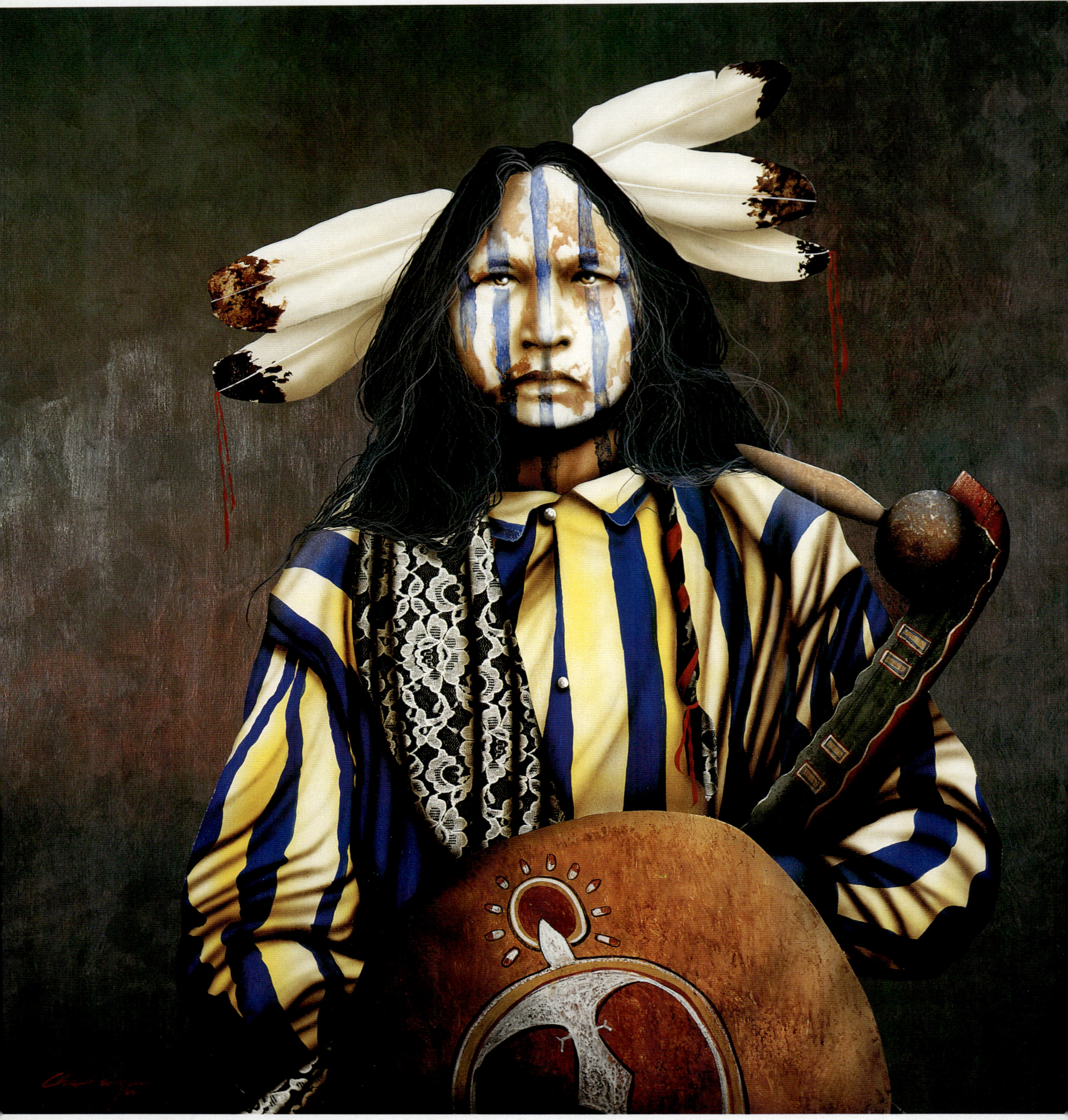

CHAPTER 2

DRAWING DOWN THE WHIRLWIND

THE GHOST DANCE CEREMONY

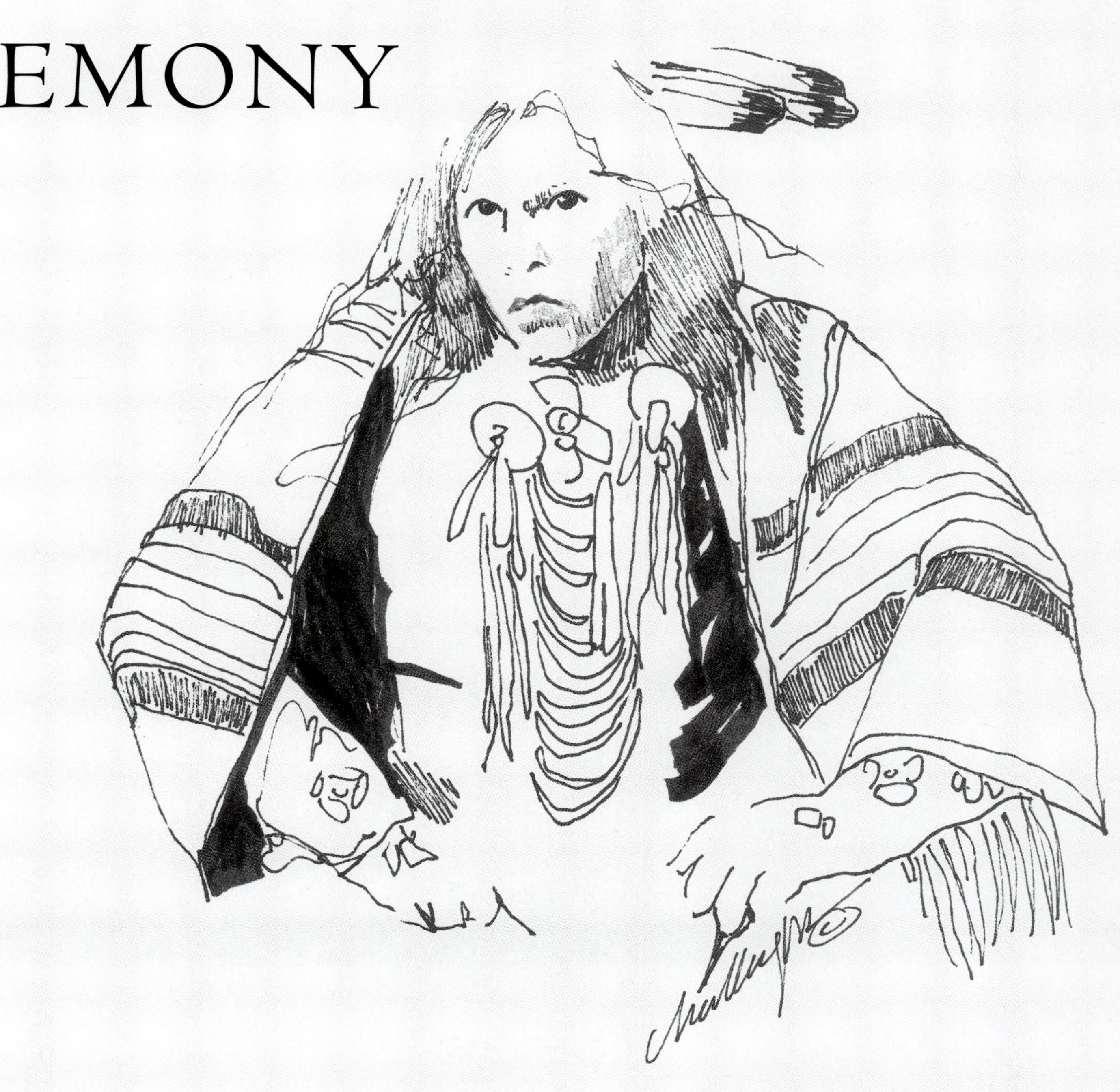

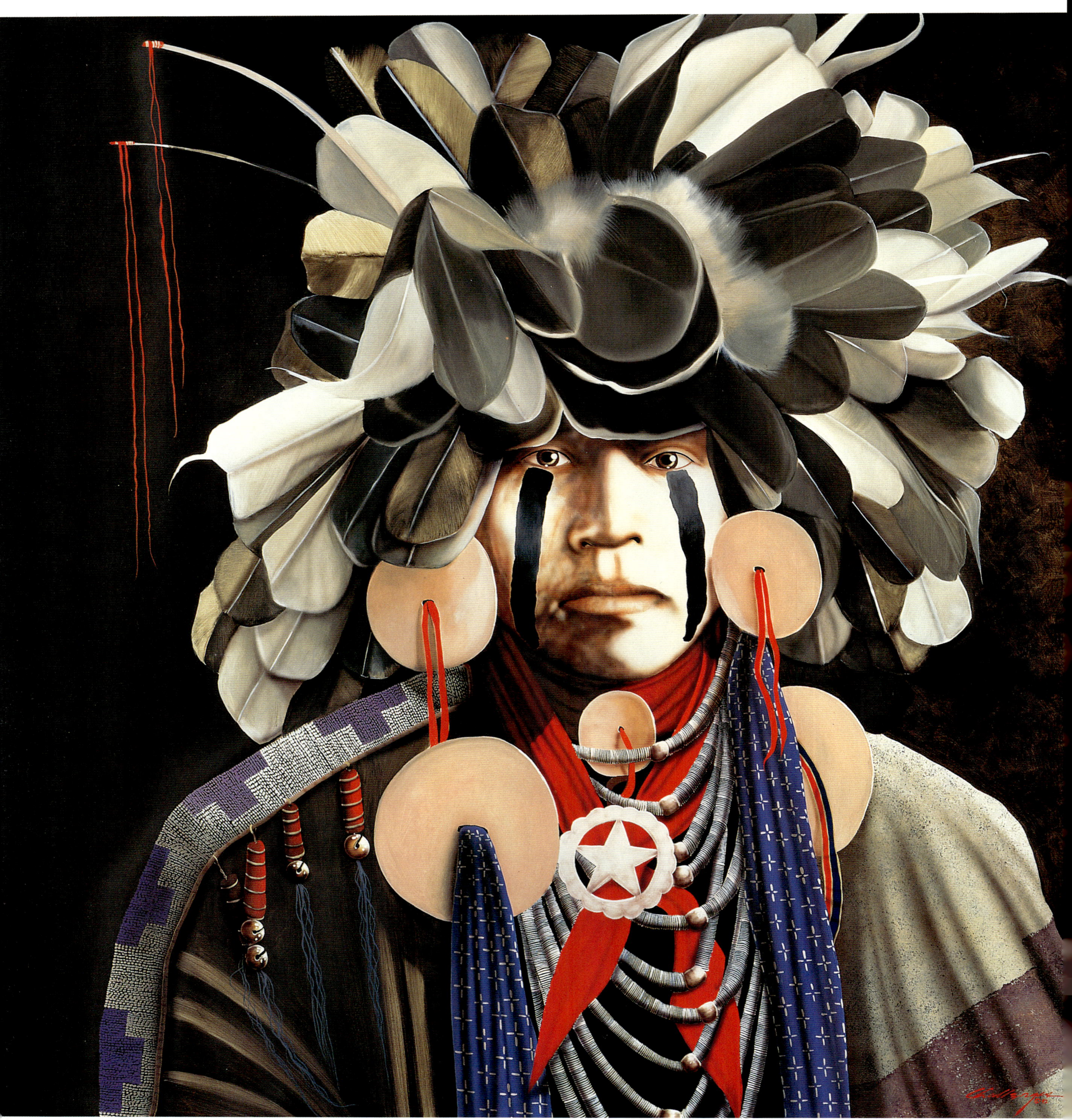

Shadowed by the indigo of high sierras, the dance circle eddies in a valley of dusty sagebrush, bending the amber shafts of buffalo grass to the earth. The circle encompasses a broad swath of leveled ground especially prepared for the many hundreds of dancers who will ultimately embrace its circumference. Shelters of willow wood dot the perimeter.

Sacred powder drifts across this swept land as the Ghost dance ceremony preparations begin. A cedar tree, chosen for its mystical evergreen limbs, graces the circle's center. Feathers and strips of red cloth hang from the branches and flutter in the evening breeze.

Prayers bless the dance ground as seven men and seven women gather in the dusk. They have been chosen to lead the dance. Each accepts a single eagle feather or two crow feathers bound to a whittled stick, which they bind into their hair. The crow, they sing, is the sacred bird of the Ghost dance.

Dancers begin to assemble, some wearing brilliant feathers embellished with ornaments and crowned with painted down, multicolored feathers inspired by visions, feathers adorning spoked hoops, fur streamers, cottonwood splints, gorgets of shell, and bonnets of feathers decorated in accordance with the world of spirits.

Elegant designs cross many of the dancers' cheeks and foreheads—painted stars, suns, birds, crosses, circles, streaks of lightning, and crescent moons in blue, yellow, red, white, and green paint. Some dancers select symbols seen in their visions as they appear on the faces of the loved and the dead.

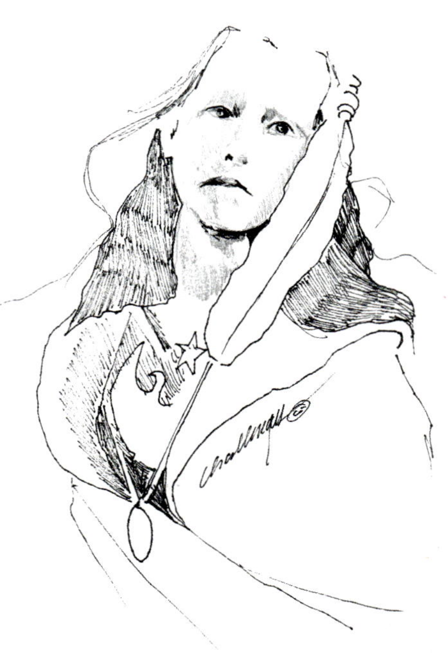

OPPOSITE:
CEREMONIAL SERIES

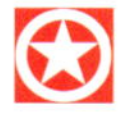

PAGE 32:
SUNRISE VISION

35

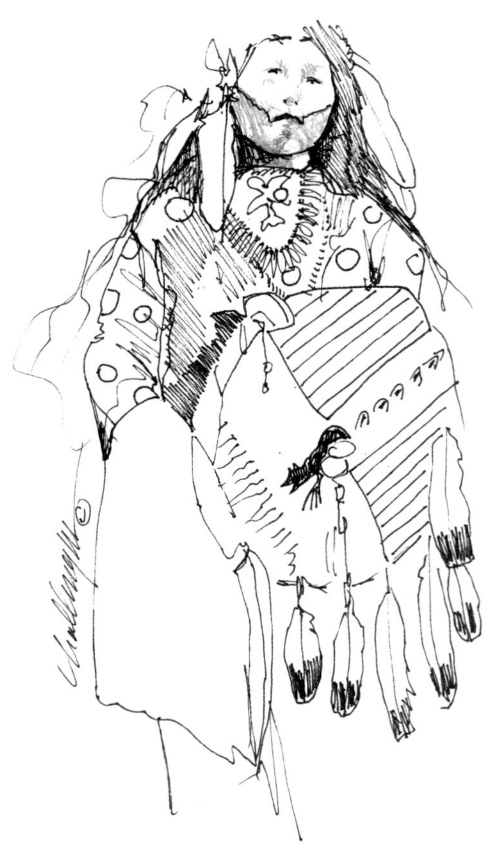

Others stand before the dance leader and, placing their hands upon the leader's head, request, "My father, I have come to be painted, so that I may see my friends; have pity on me and paint me." The paint is blessed, helping to focus the dancers' visions and bring them strength.

A blessing is bestowed upon each dancer by the spiritual leader of the dance. The leader performs a series of secret passes across the dancer's face, blowing away all evil with puffs of air, then bows the head in prayer, and finally releases the dancer with a light squeeze of the hand. Men, women, and children are all blessed in the same manner.

Once blessed and painted, the dancers slip into their Ghost dance vestments— fringed shirts and dresses of tanned hide or white cloth painted with figures of the crow, eagle, magpie, sage hen, turtle, buffalo, Thunderbird, sun, moon, and stars. Their bodies are rubbed with sweet-smelling grass, then the grass is set on fire.

"The sky is opening. I can smell the perfumes of the grasses used in the dance," cries an ancestor. Smoke veils the dying twilight. The incense filters through the air and rides the wind, signaling to those near and far that the Spirit is descending.

A young woman stands in the dance circle with four bone-tipped arrows dipped in steer's blood, a substitute for the buffalo that has vanished from the plains, and fires them in an arc to the four directions. The sacred arrows are gathered together and brought to the center, tied to the branches of the cedar tree along with the bow, small gaming wheels, and the ghost stick—a wooden staff exceeding five feet in length, embellished with red cloth and red-painted feathers and crowned with horns.

The Ghost dance begins in the open night air. Stars shine down on snow peaked mountains. The Milky Way, celestial road to the spirit world, scatters across the sky. The leaders move to the dance circle and, facing inward, join hands. They sing the opening song softly.

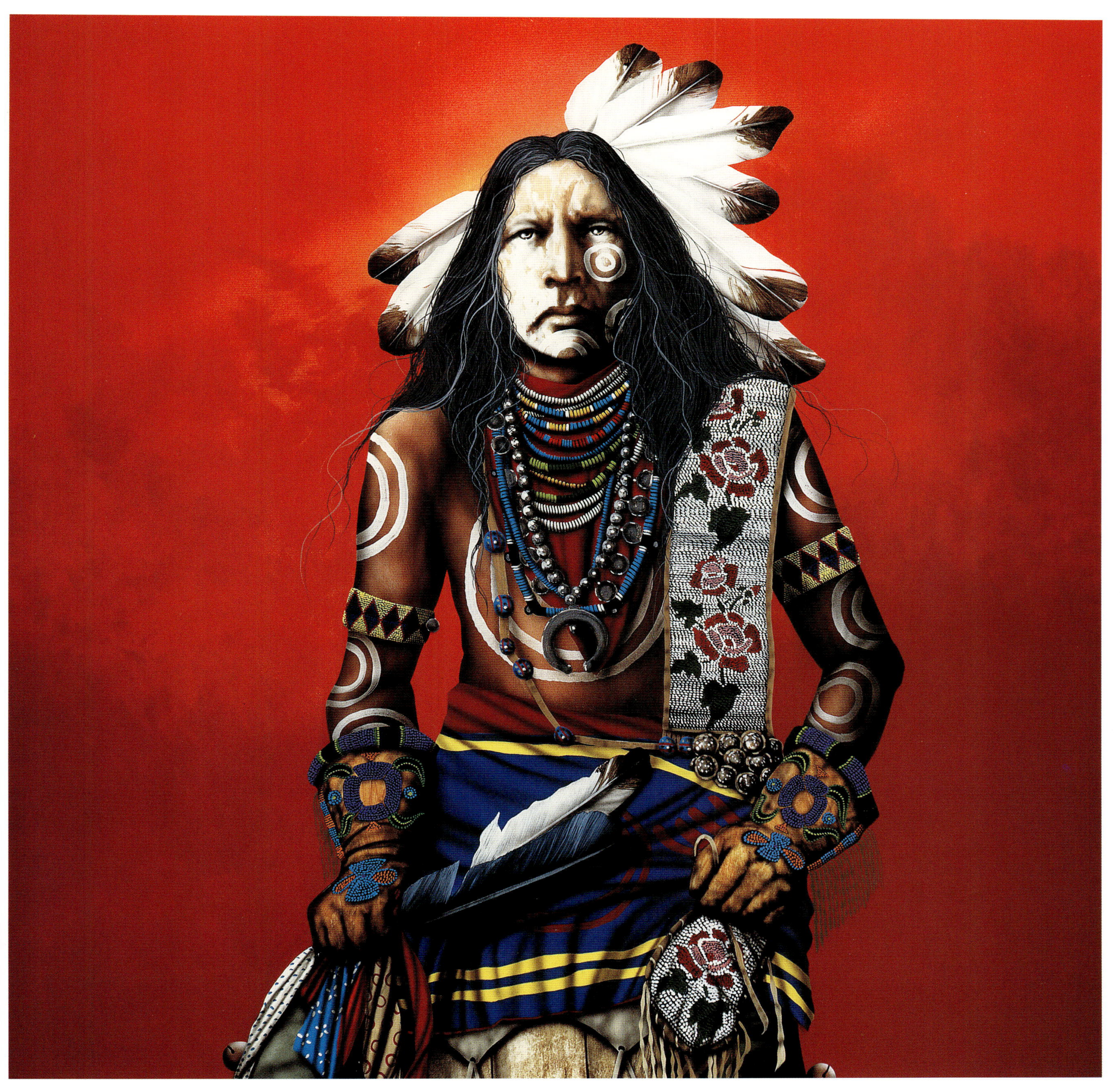

WORDS OF FIRE PRAYER AND HOPE

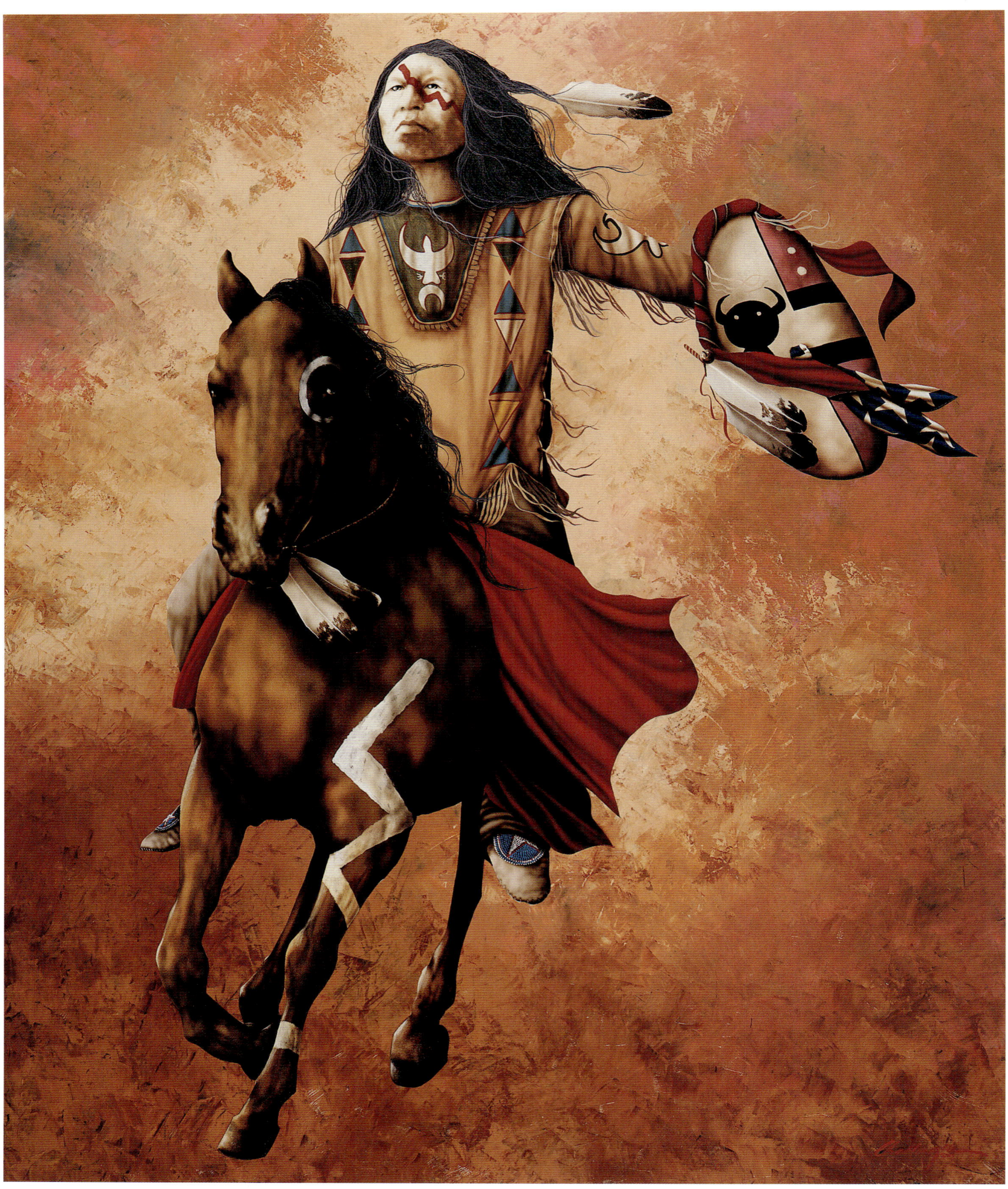

The song is sung again in full voice as the leaders begin to move slowly around in a circle, barely lifting their feet from the ground, moving right to left with the course of the sun. As the song swells, men, women, and children enter the dance. The circle grows larger and the movement steadily increases. The pace becomes lively, and the dancers seemed charged with an inner electricity. As the energy builds, the trances begin.

"Then we began dancing, and most of the people wailed and cried as they danced, holding hands in a circle; but some of them laughed with happiness," remembers the Ogalala Sioux visionary Black Elk. "After a while I began to feel very queer. First, my legs seemed to be full of ants. I was dancing with my eyes closed, as the others did. Suddenly it seemed that I was swinging off the ground and not touching it any longer. The queer feeling came up from my legs and was in my heart now. It seemed I would glide forward like a swing, and then glide back again in longer and longer swoops. There was no fear with this, just a growing happiness."

Many dancers rely on the spiritual leaders to usher them into their visions. The leaders move within the dance ring, holding the consecrated eagle feather or a scarf before the dancers as they rotate around. As the dancers' enthusiasm for the songs and the movements increase, they begin to succumb to the excitement.

Ethnographer James Mooney remembers watching as a dancer entered her trance.

The first indication that she is becoming affected is a slight muscular tremor, distinctly felt by her two partners who hold her hands on either side. The medicine-man is on the watch, and as soon as he notices the woman's condition he comes over and stands immediately in front of her, looking intently into her face and whirling the feather or the handkerchief, or both, rapidly in front her eyes, moving slowly around with the dancers at the same time, but constantly facing the woman. All this time he keeps up a series of sharp exclamations, *Hu! Hu! Hu!* like the rapid breathing of an exhausted runner...For a while the woman continues to move around with the circle of dancers, singing the song with the others, but usually before the circuit is completed she loses control of herself entirely, and, breaking away from the partners who have hold of her hands on either side, she staggers into the ring, while the circle at once closes up again behind her. She is now standing before the medicine-man,

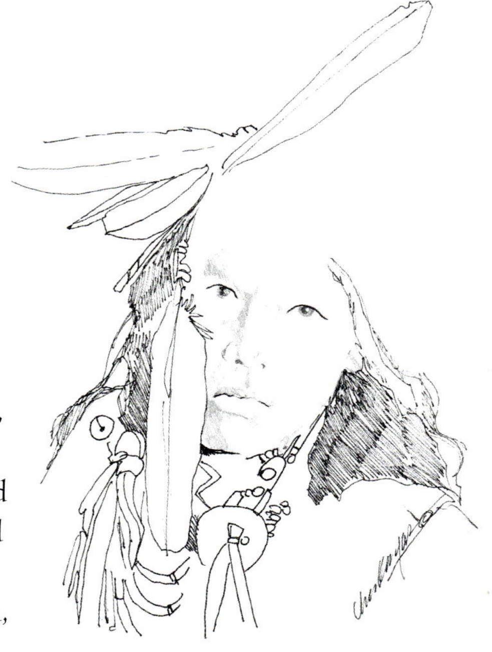

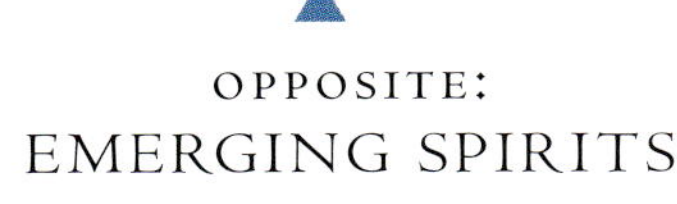

OPPOSITE:
EMERGING SPIRITS

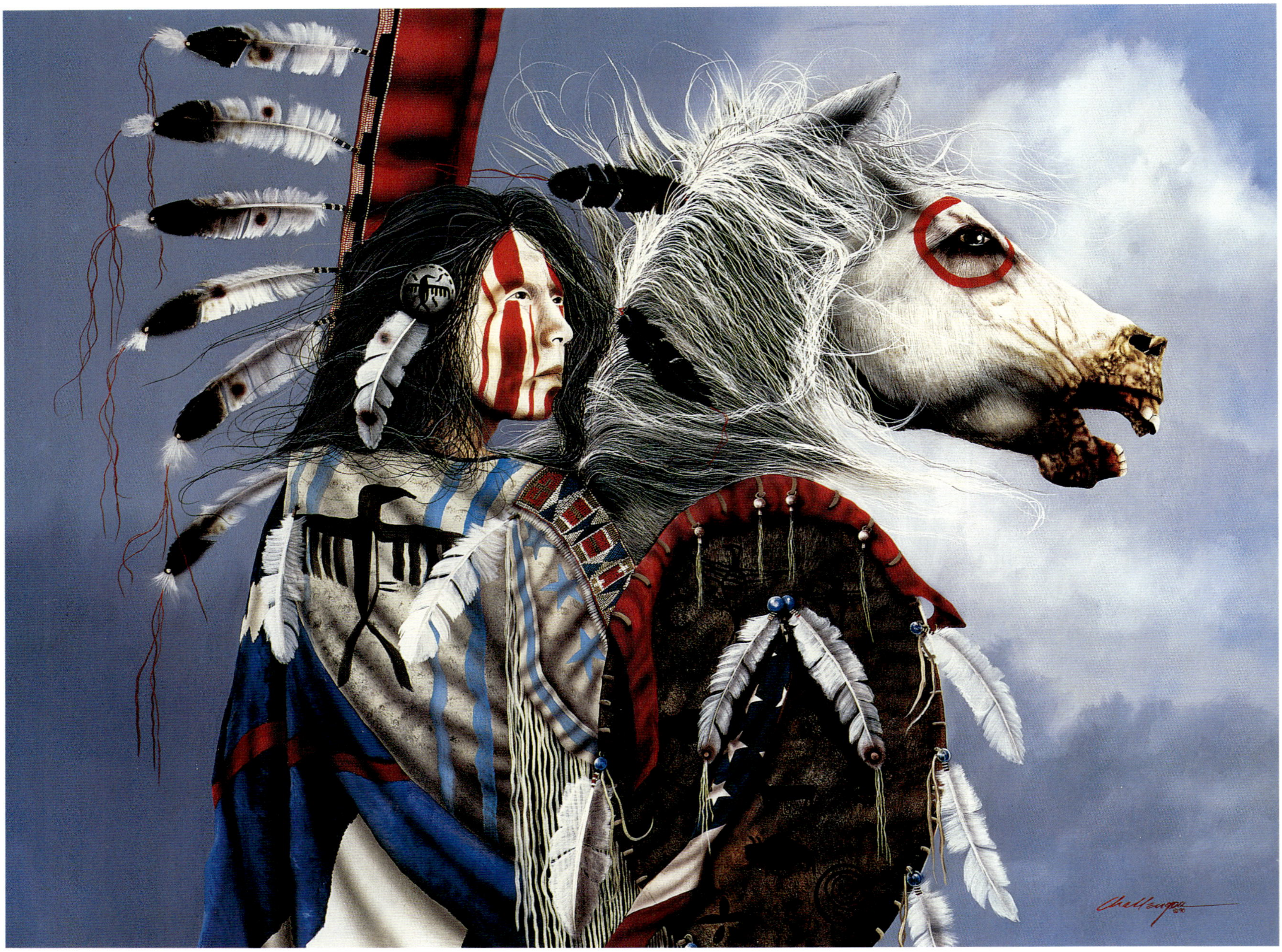

ABOVE:
SPIRIT RIDER

OPPOSITE:
RIDES THE CLOUDS

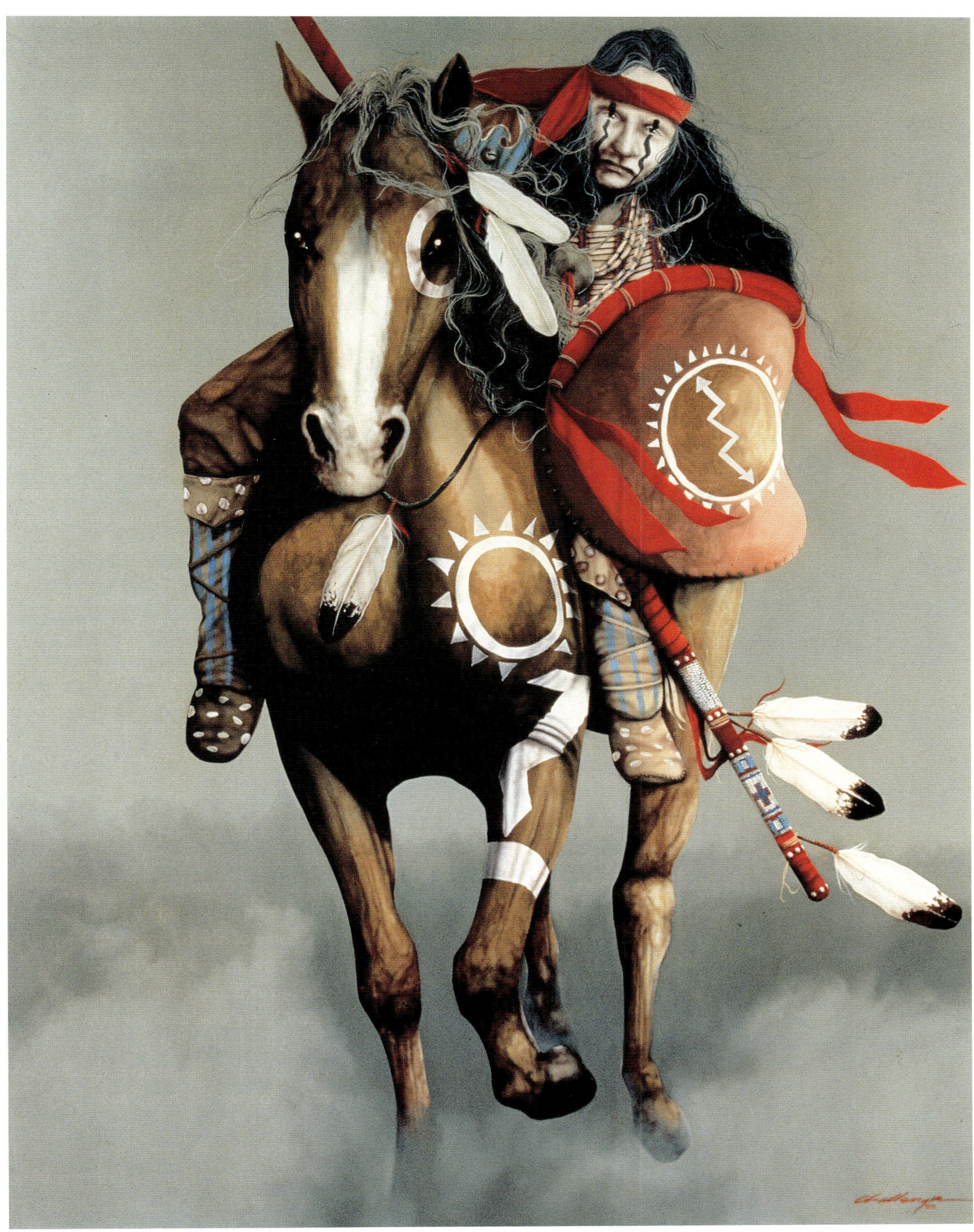

who gives his whole attention to her, whirling the feather swiftly in front of her eyes, waving his hands before her face as though fanning her, and drawing his hand slowly from the level of her eyes away to one side or upward into the air, while her gaze follows with a fixed stare. All the time he keeps up the *Hu! Hu! Hu!* while the song and the dance go on around them without a pause… Then the words become unintelligible sounds, and her movements violently spasmodic, until at last she becomes rigid, with her eyes shut or fixed and staring…for an indefinite time, but at last falls heavily to the ground, unconscious and motionless…but no one goes near to disturb her, as her soul is now communing with the spirit world.

My children, my children,
I am flying about the earth.
I am a bird, my children,
Says the father,
Says the father.

The dance continues into the night as hundreds of dancers raise a column of dust into the air that, if lit by sun or moon, can be seen for miles. All join in who wish to dance. The more enthusiastic dancers are careful to pace the dance for the young and old when they enter the circle. If a woman with a child on her back should join in, those around her watch over her, leading her from the crowd if she should begin to enter a trance. Dogs are kept out of the dance circle so as not to disturb dancers who are overcome. Once the dancers succumb to the power of the dance, nothing must disrupt their visions.

As George Sword, an Ogalala Sioux, observes, "They dance around in the circle in a continuous time until some of them become so tired and overtired that they become crazy and finally drop as though dead, with foam from the mouth and all wet by perspiration. The persons dropped in the dance all lie in the great dust the dancing makes."

"One woman fell a few feet from me," exclaims Mrs. Z. A. Parker, a teacher on the Pine Ridge reservation.

She came toward us, her hair flying over her face, which was purple, looking as if the blood would burst through; her hands and arms moving wildly; every breath a pant and a groan; and she fell on her back, and went down like a log. I stepped up to her as she lay there motionless, but with every muscle twitching and quivering. She seemed to be perfectly unconscious. Some of the the men and a few of the women would run, stepping high and pawing the air in a frightful manner. Some told me afterwards that they had a sensation as if the ground were rising toward them and would strike them in the face. Others would drop where they stood. One woman fell directly into the ring, and her husband stepped out and stood over her to prevent them from trampling upon her. No one ever disturbed those who fell or took any notice of them except to keep the crowd away.

They kept up dancing until fully one hundred persons were lying unconscious. Then they stopped and seated themselves in a circle, and as each one recovered from his trance he was brought to the center of the ring to relate his experience. Each told his story to the medicine-man and he shouted it to the crowd.

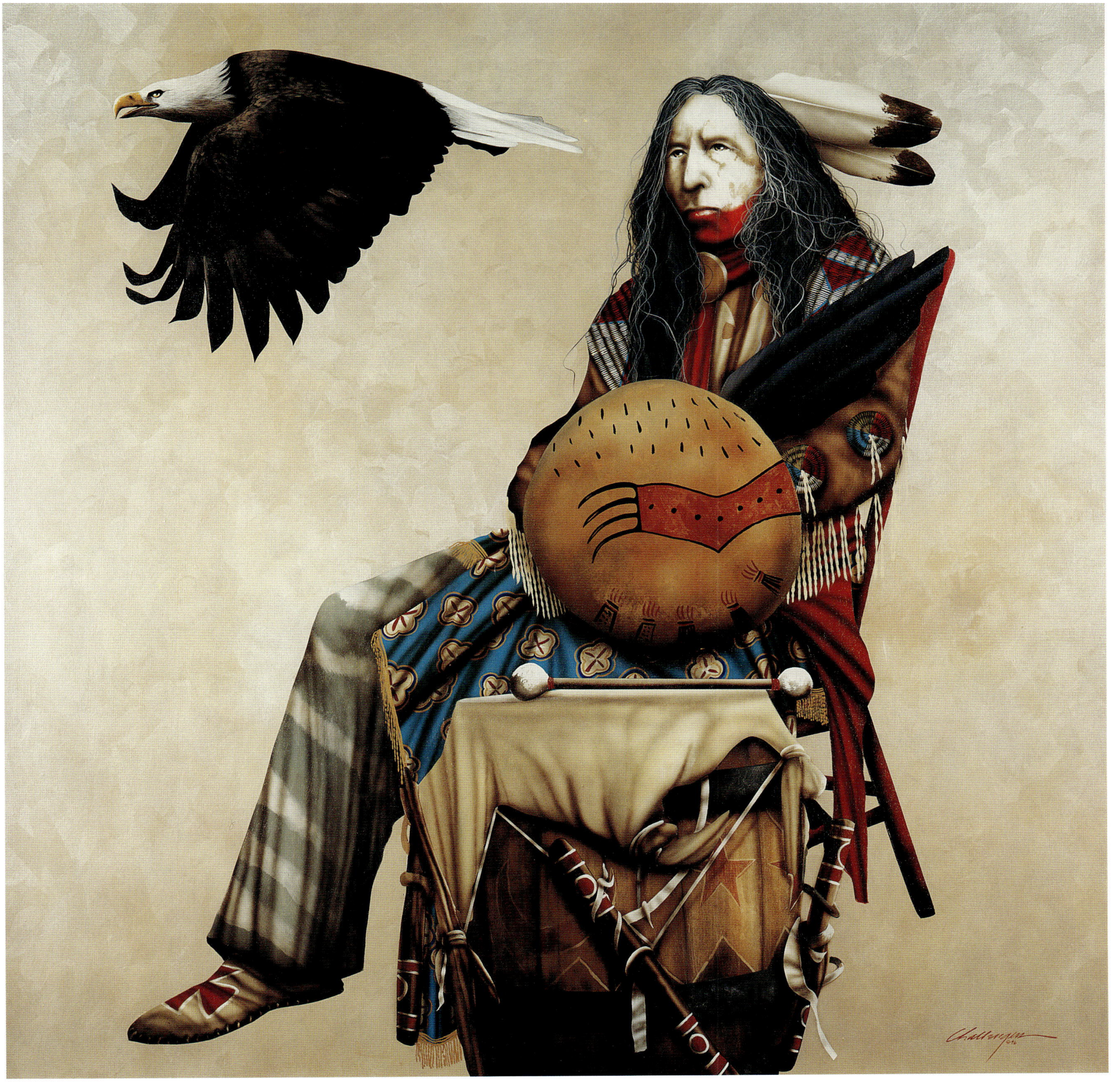

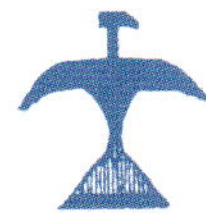

THE VOICE OF THE DRUM

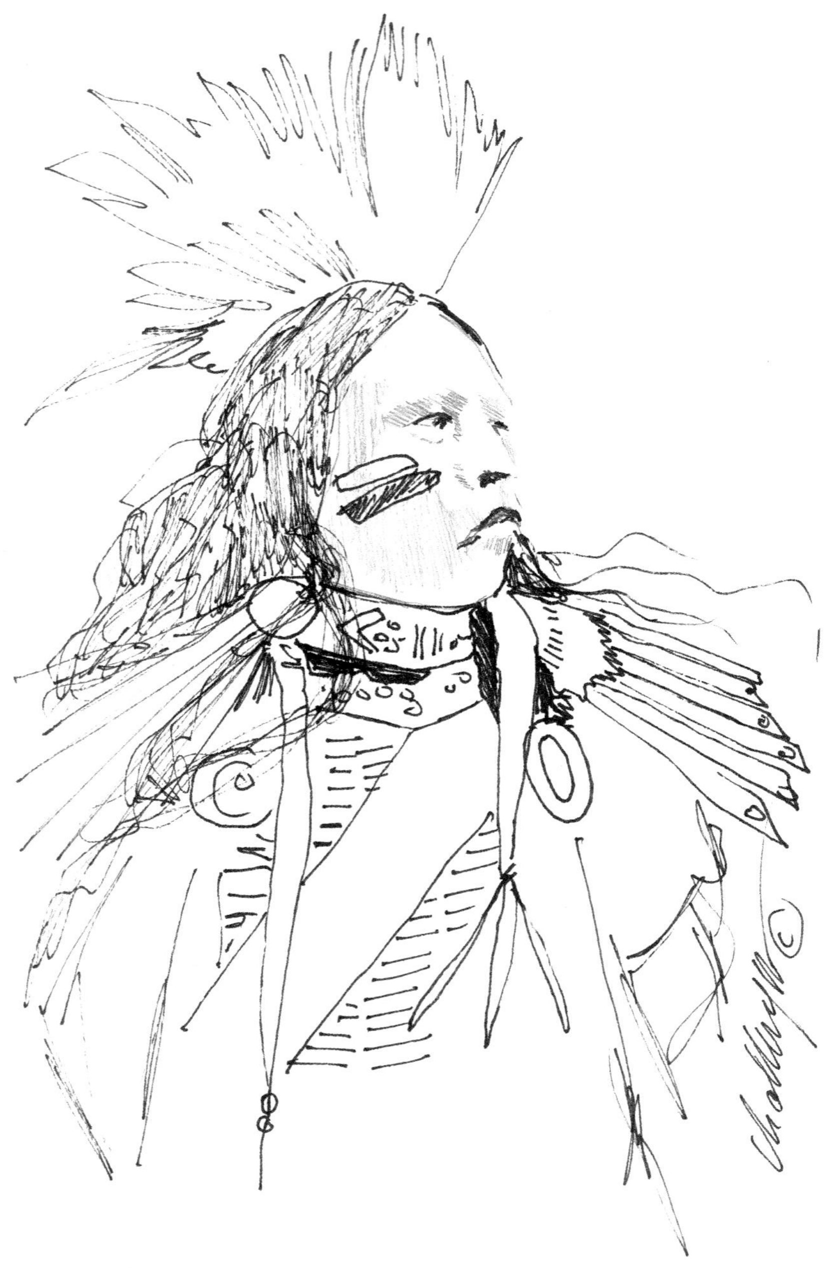

"I saw an eagle," explains a Ghost dancer, "coming towards me. It flew round and round, drawing nearer and nearer until I put out my hand to take it. Then it was gone."

Father, the Morning Star!
Look on us, we have danced until daylight.
Take pity on us—Hi'i'i'!
Take pity on us—Hi'i'i'!

The Ghost dance often lasts until the first light of dawn. A song is sung to the sacred morning star, and then the dancers take a moment to rest.

Thus says our father, the Crow,
Thus says our father, the Crow.
Go around five times more—
Go around five times more—
Says the father,
Says the father.

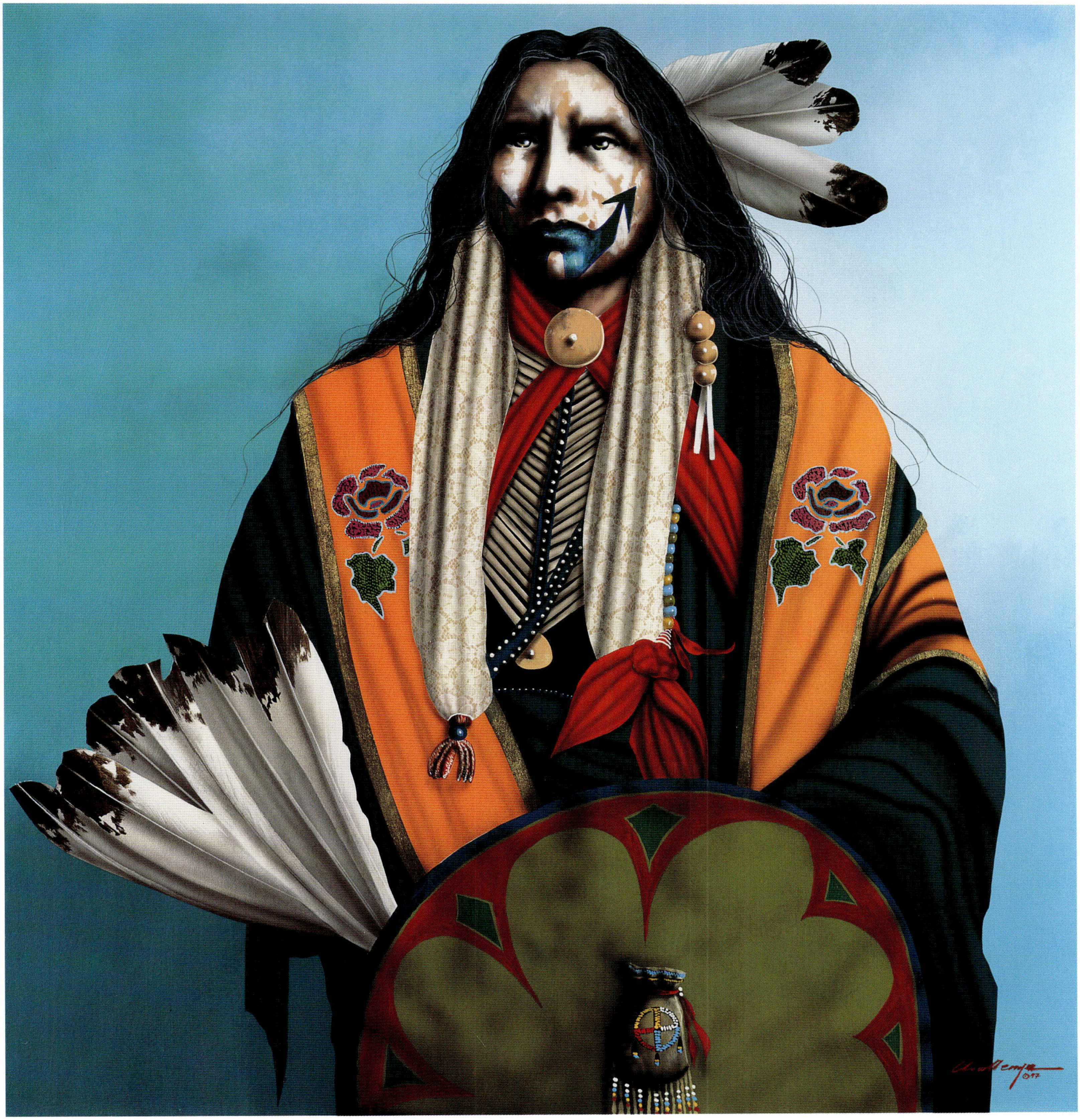

HIGH EAGLE SONG

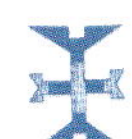

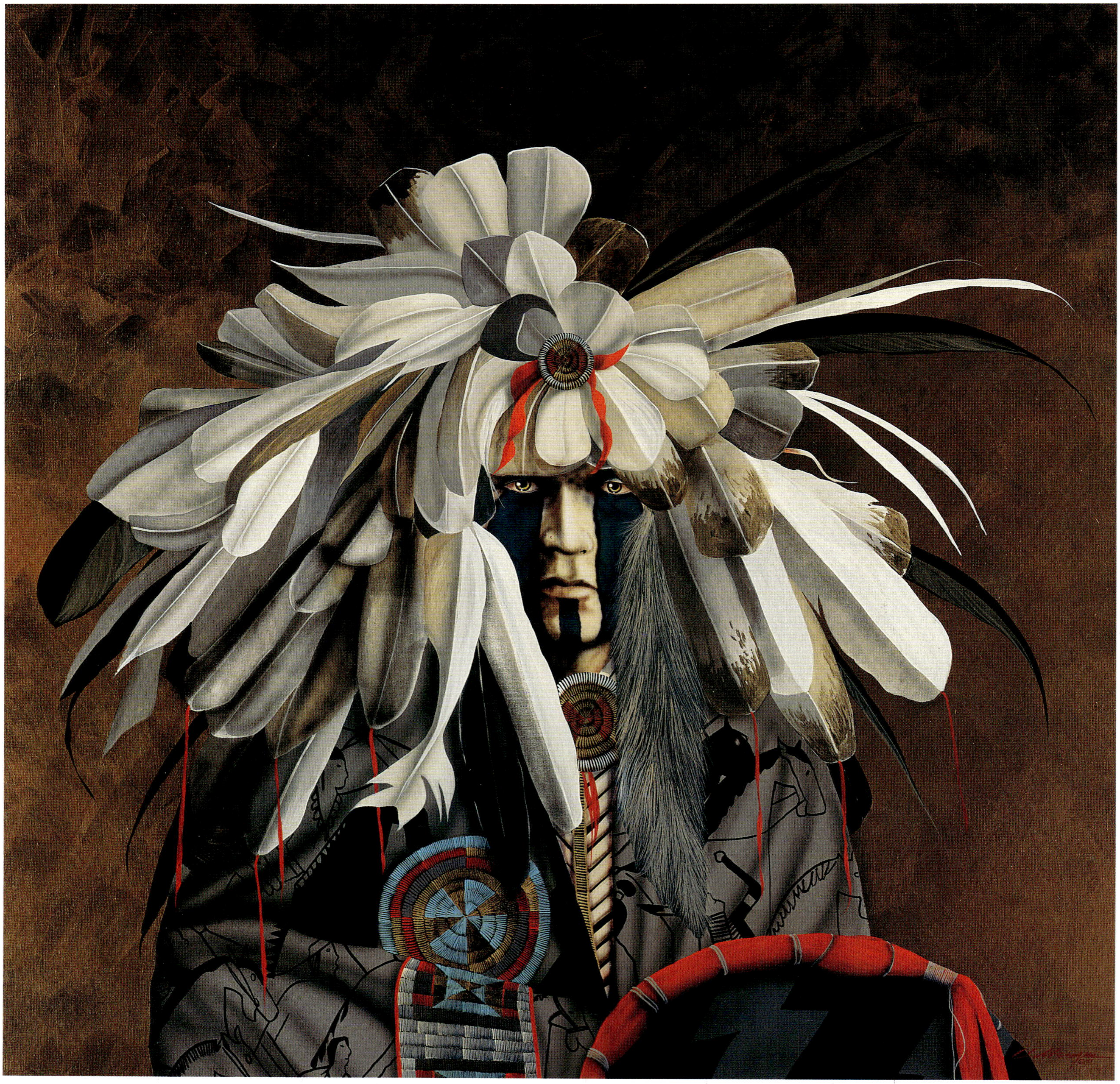

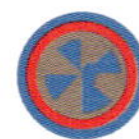

END OF THE DANCE

Five more times the dancers circle around to complete the ceremony before they release hands. After shaking their blankets skyward to scatter any evil forces, the dancers make their way to the river. Dividing into separate groups of men and women, the dancers bathe in the fresh water before retiring to their camps. The dance has ended for now.

Tomorrow the dance will begin again as the Father has instructed, continuing for four more days. In other dance circles across the country, tribes are accommodating their own dance histories by modifying the Ghost dance details. Some will transplant a living tree into the center of the dance circle while others will cut down a cedar near their camp. Some will build fires inside the dance circle. Others will construct four pilings around the perimeter, tall cones of log poles erected like tepees, and ignite them, allowing them to burn throughout the ceremony, signifying each of the cardinal points. Some will not allow fires at all.

Despite variations in the ceremony, the true meaning of the dance remains basically the same for all tribes embracing the Ghost dance doctrine. Dancing the dance will mean the return of traditions, the securing of necessities, and, above all, the freedom from oppression for the Native American people.

The whole world is coming,
A nation is coming, a nation is coming,
The Eagle has brought the message to the tribe.
The father says so, the father says so.
Over the whole earth they are coming.
The buffalo are coming, the buffalo are coming,
The Crow has brought the message to the tribe,
The father says so, the father says so.

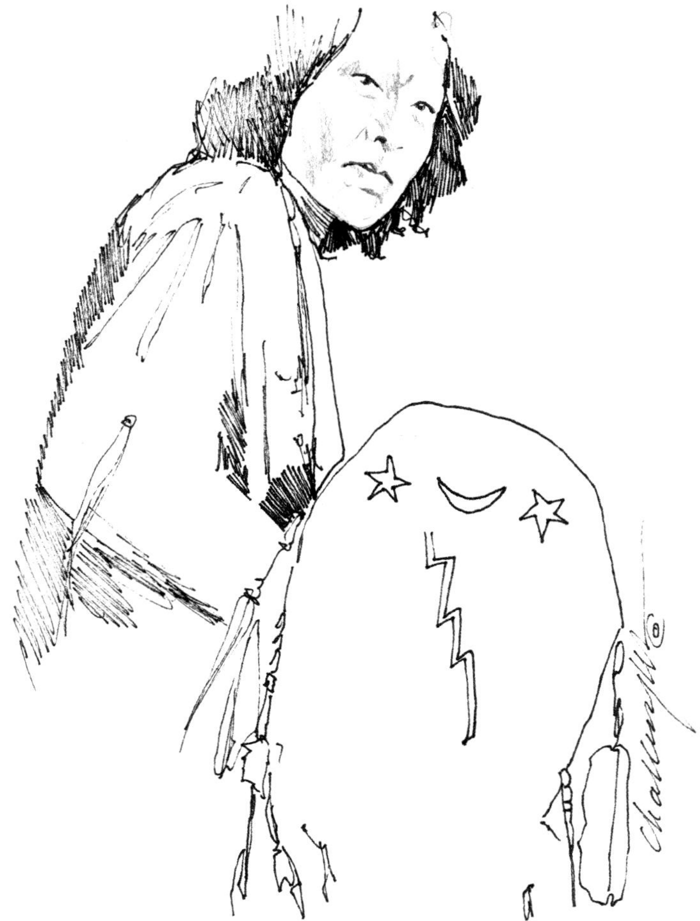

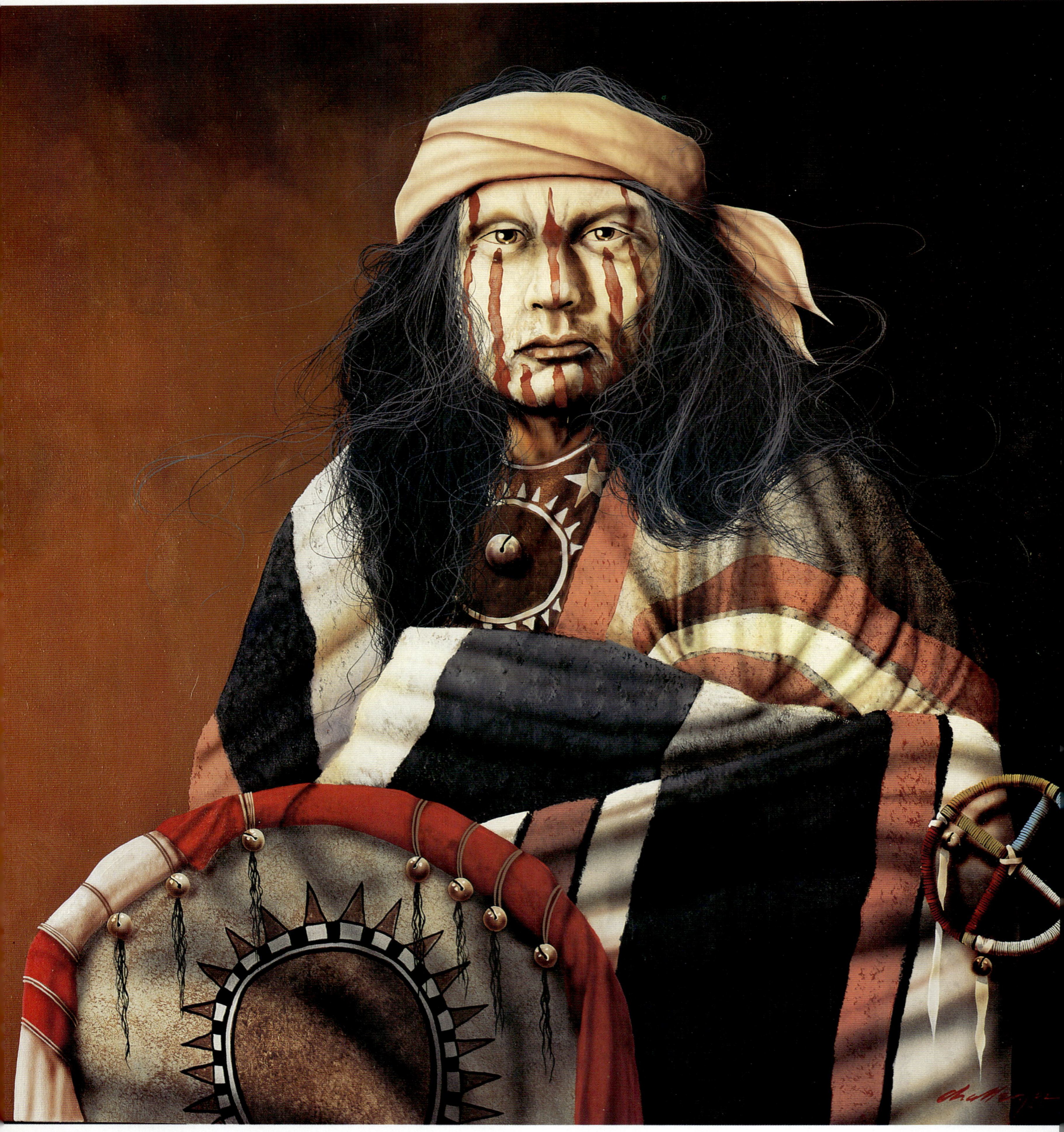

CHAPTER 3

IT IS I WHO WEAR THE MORNING STAR

SACRED MEDICINE, SIGNS, AND SYMBOLS

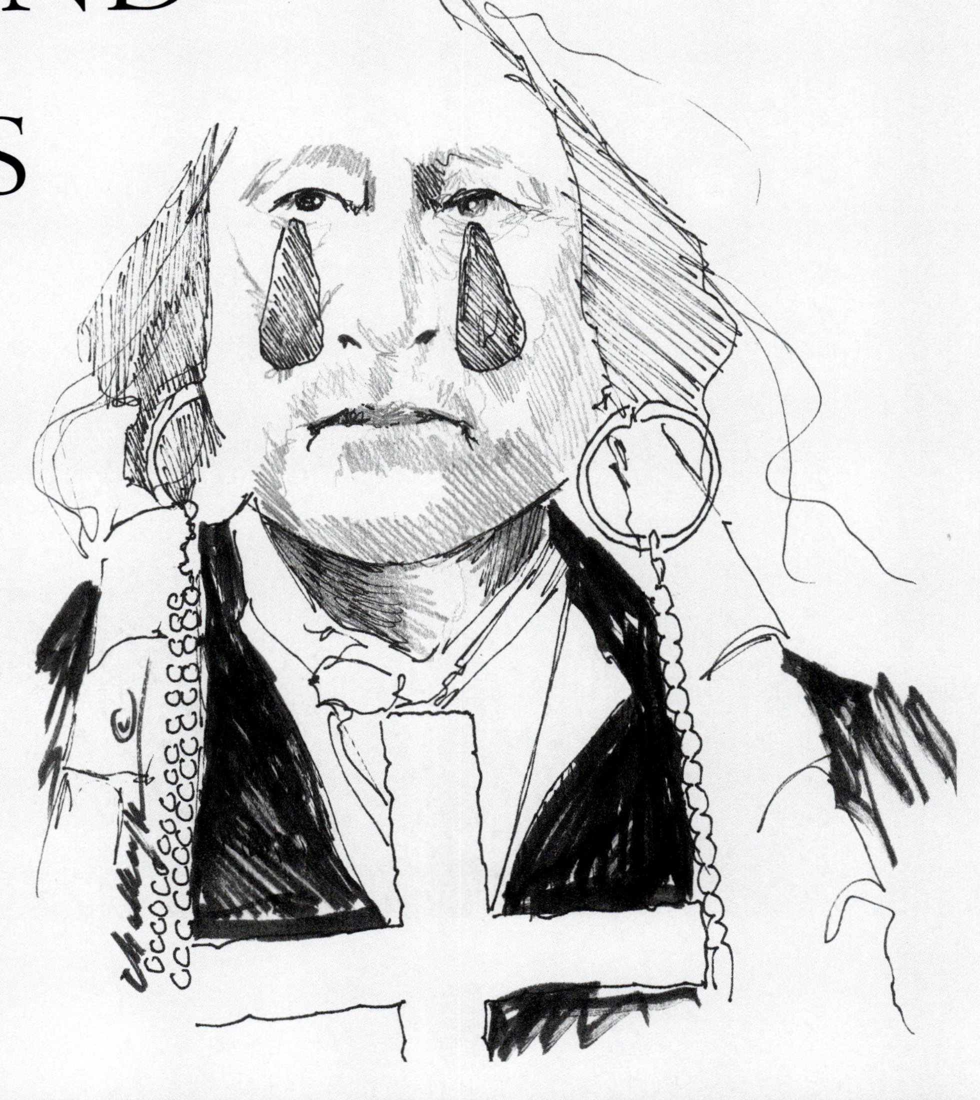

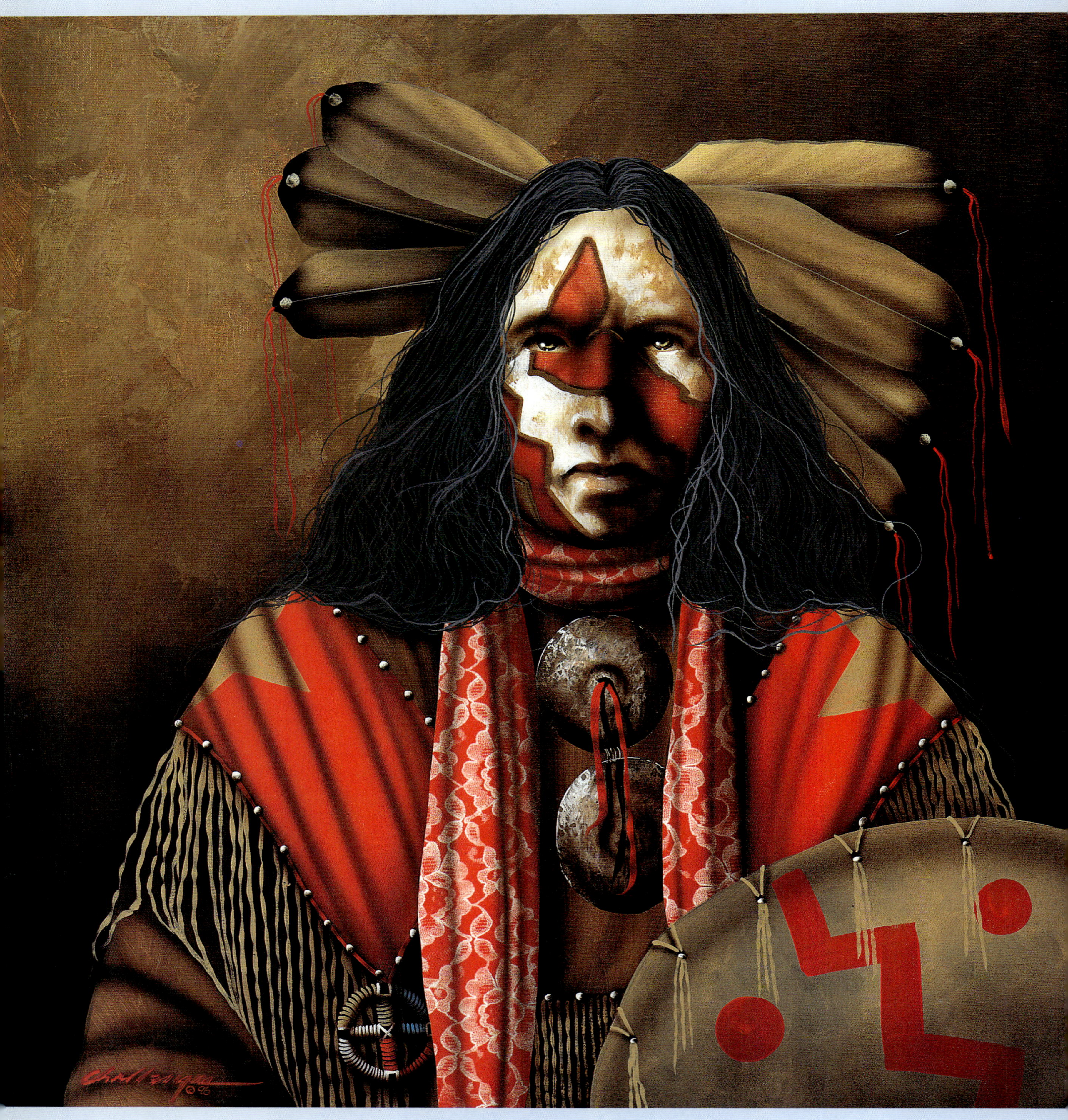

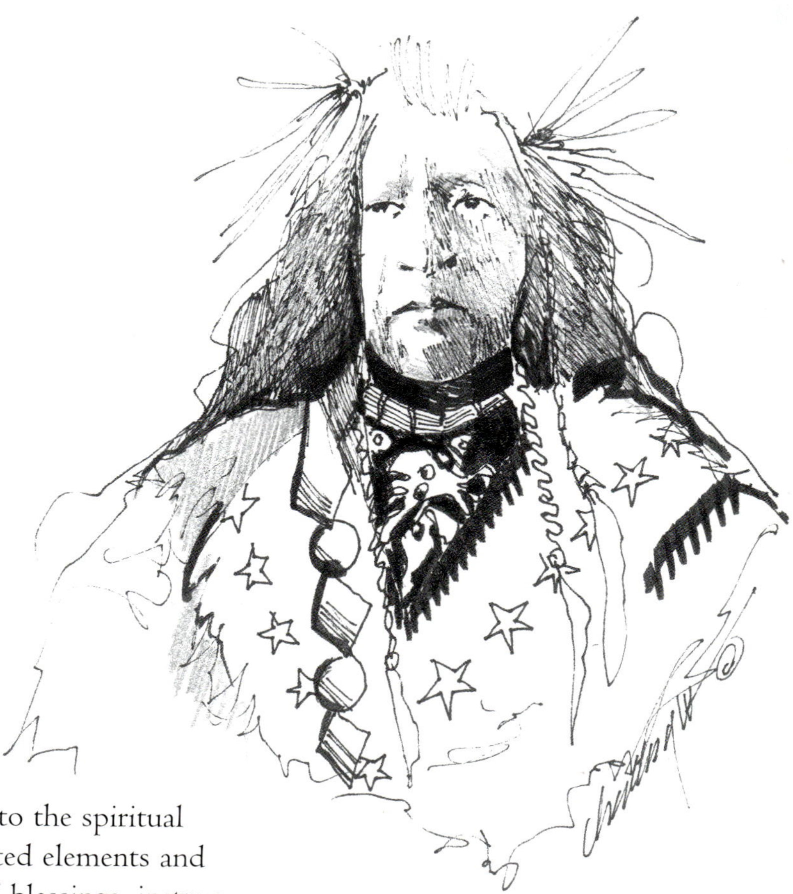

Sacred objects and the visions that define them are fundamental to the spiritual quest. The ceremonial objects and vestments fashioned from consecrated elements and imbued with power, through prayer and ritual, become the agencies of blessings, instruction, and knowledge. The dance place becomes the sacred center for this transformation, and the dance is its celebration. The sacred center integrates the heavens, the earth, and the underworld in a vertical nexus of divine intervention. The dance draws this column to earth and the sacred objects channel this power into the hands of the believer.

Any natural element—stone, pollen, a feather, a tree branch—accompanied by a simple gesture and integrated into a ceremony embraces the element in a reality that changes its value. In the Ghost dance, the ceremonies and attendant objects transcend these religious ties as well, defining fundamental principles of daily life. They represent a physical, social, economic, and political cohesion guaranteeing a consistent source of food and water, personal and family health, social well-being, and political stability.

Medicine, Mooney explains, is inseparable from the Native American religion.

> The doctor is always a priest, and the priest is always a doctor. Hence, to the whites in the Indian country the Indian priest-doctor has come to be known as the "medicine-man," and anything sacred, mysterious, or of wonderful power or efficacy in Indian life or belief is designated as "medicine," this term being the nearest equivalent of the aboriginal expression in the various languages. To "make medicine" is to perform some sacred ceremony, from the curing of a sick child to the consecration of the sun-dance lodge. Among the prairie tribes the great annual tribal ceremony was commonly known as the "medicine dance," and the special guardian deity of every warrior was spoken of as his "medicine."

The Sioux leader Crazy Horse had his *tunka* or medicine stone, a marble of polished sandstone bundled in sweet grass, wrapped in eagle down, and kept in a small pouch. After the murder of Crazy Horse, his mother passed this sacred medicine down to Kicking Bear, one of the leaders of the Ghost dance, who kept the bundle tied in his hair

OPPOSITE:
EARTH MEDICINE

PAGE 48:
POWER OF THE SUN

51

and out of sight behind his ear. As it had with Crazy Horse, the bundle gave Kicking Bear great power during battle.

"Many of the prairie tribes took stones or other objects which had special powers into a battle," says Challenger. "The Sioux liked small stones. These talismans are called *tunkan*. The word is short for *tunkasila* or 'grandfather,' which is also a Sioux word for God."

The *wotawe*, sacred war medicine of the Hunkpapa Sioux Chief Sitting Bull, was fashioned from a swath of muslin three feet long and over two feet wide and saturated in an orange-yellow dye. Dragonflies painted in green embellished the four corners, and an elk design graced the center. The elk was rendered in a green outline filled with red spots. The use of the *wotawe* required additional objects, including the tail of a deer, the aromatic root of the calamus (the plant used to make cane and rattan), and buffalo-hide wristbands. The *wotawe* was used for general protection and aided in remedying natural and man-made disasters confronting Sitting Bull's people.

Many sacred objects assist in defining the specific genesis of a tribal people. The historian Franklin Revard recalls researching the existence of an elaborate chart used by a "secret society" of Osage to explain the origins of their tribe. The use of the chart, according to Revard, required a special ceremony in which the female head of a clan first takes four sips of water, which symbolizes the river of life. The ceremony leader "then rubs cedar on the palms of his hands with which he rubs her from head to foot. If she belongs to the left side of the tribal circle, he first strokes the left side of her head, making three passes, pronouncing the name of the Great Spirit three times, repeating the process on her forehead, right side and back part of her head, making twelve strokes in all (a perfect number)."

The chart portrayed a river and, beneath it, the Morning Star, six stars together, the Evening Star, and the Little Star. Beneath these were the moon, a cluster of seven stars, and the sun. A peace pipe and a war hatchet were drawn beneath the seven stars. The artist had placed four parallel lines across the surface to indicate the four cosmic levels that the ancestors passed through on their way to earth.

"The stanza of the chart point to the different periods of evolution," explains Revard, "first when the children of the first period (former end) of the race were without human bodies and human souls. Then birds over the arch denote the evolution of human souls in bird bodies. Then the progress from the fourth to the first heavens, followed by descent to earth. The ascent to four and descent to three make up the sacred number seven. When they alighted, as the legend runs, it was on a beautiful day when the earth was clothed in luxuriant vegetation."

The sacred objects that appear throughout Native American history were often designed to promote a personal vision or assist in the struggle with European interlopers. A visionary of the late 1700s, known in history only as the Delaware Prophet, created a symbolic map that accomplished both. The symbolic parchment had been drawn on the tanned skin of a deer. The missionary Heckewelder, who traveled among the Delaware and had an opportunity to see the map and hear the Delaware Prophet speak of his vision, describes the parchment and cosmology as

about fifteen inches square, or, perhaps, something more. An inside square was formed by lines drawn within it, of about eight inches each way; two of these lines, however, were not closed by about half an inch at the corners. Across these

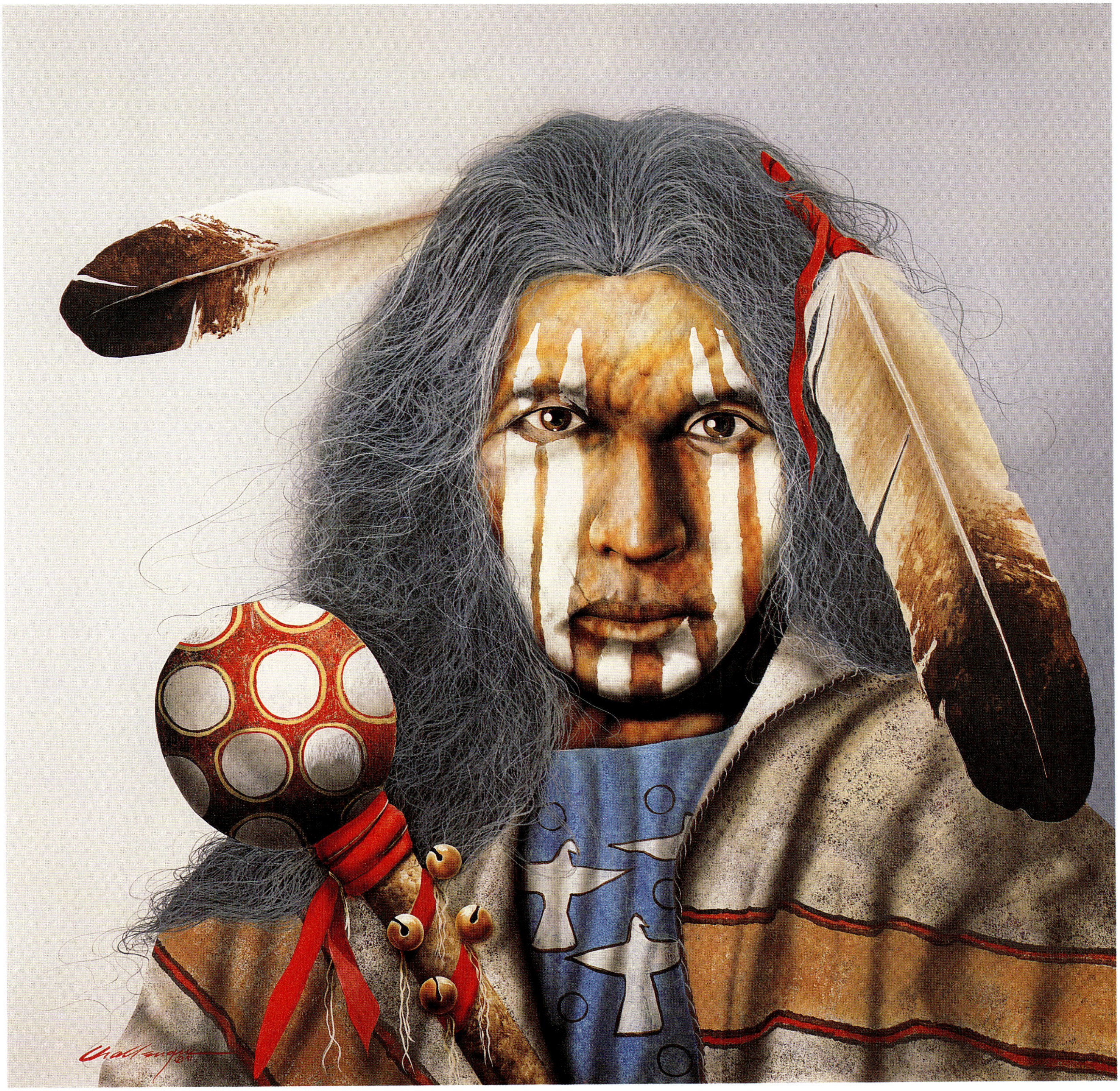

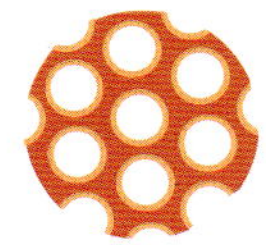

MEDICINE RATTLE

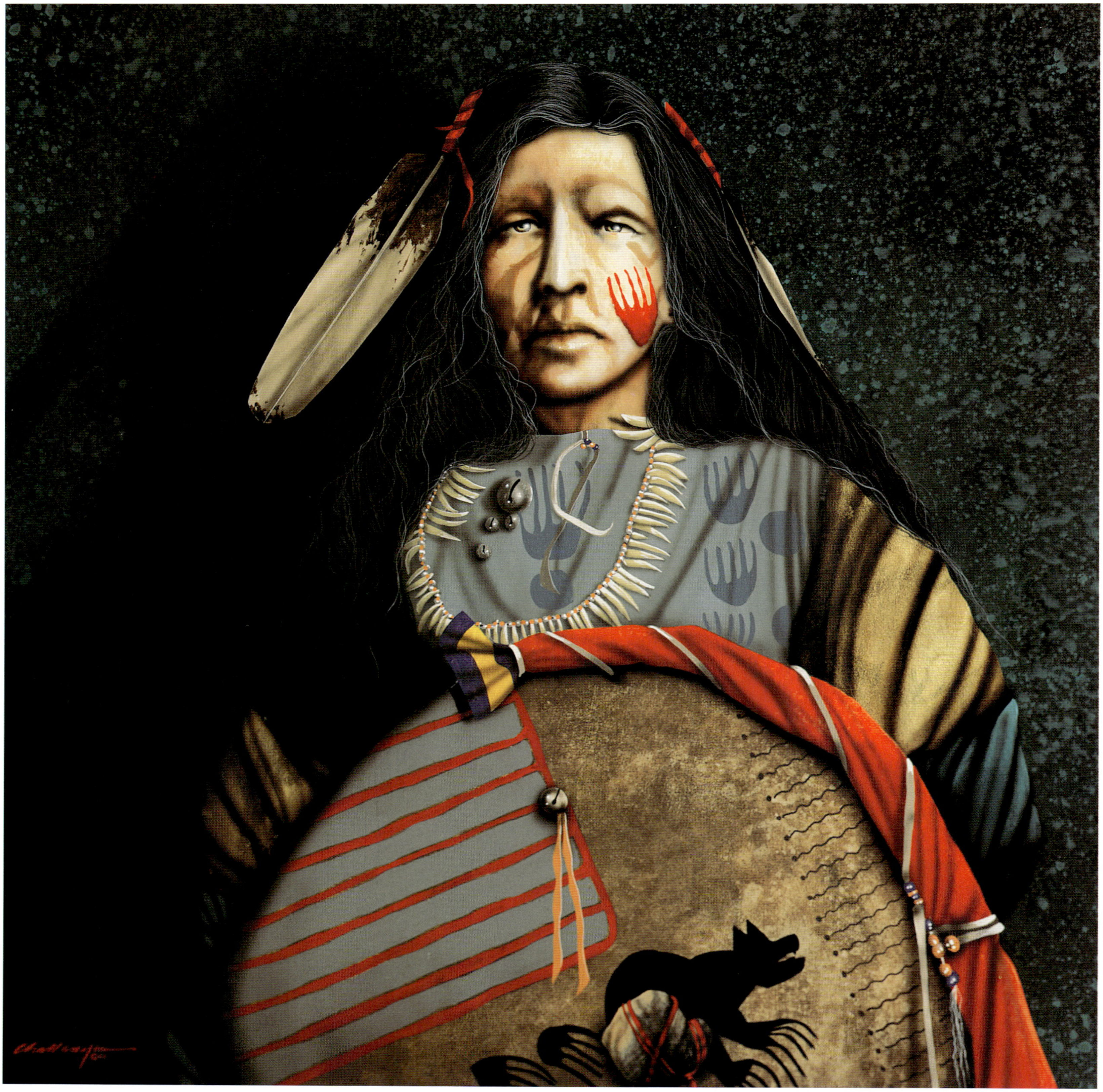

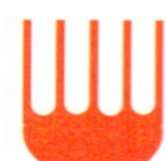

BEAR CLAN MEDICINE

inside lines, others of about an inch in length were drawn with sundry other
lines and marks, all of which was intended to represent a strong inaccessible
barrier, to prevent those without from entering the space within, otherwise
than at the place appointed for that purpose. . . . In explaining or describing
the particular points on this map, with his fingers always pointing to the place
he was describing, he called the space within the inside lines "the heavenly
regions," or the place destined by the Great Spirit for the habitation of the
Indians in future life. The space left open at the southeast corner he called the
"avenue," which had been intended for the Indians to enter into this heaven,
but which was now in the possession of the white people; wherefore the Great
Spirit had since caused another "avenue" to be made on the opposite side, at
which, however, it was both difficult and dangerous for them to enter, there
being many impediments in their way, besides a large ditch leading to a gulf
below, over which they had to leap; but the evil spirit kept at this very spot a
continual watch for Indians, and whoever he laid hold of never could get away
from him again, but was carried to his regions, where there was nothing but
extreme poverty; where the ground was parched up by the heat for want of
rain, no fruit came to perfection, the game was almost starved for want of pas-
ture, and where the evil spirit, at his pleasure transformed men into horses and
dogs, to be ridden by him and follow him in his hunts and wherever he went.

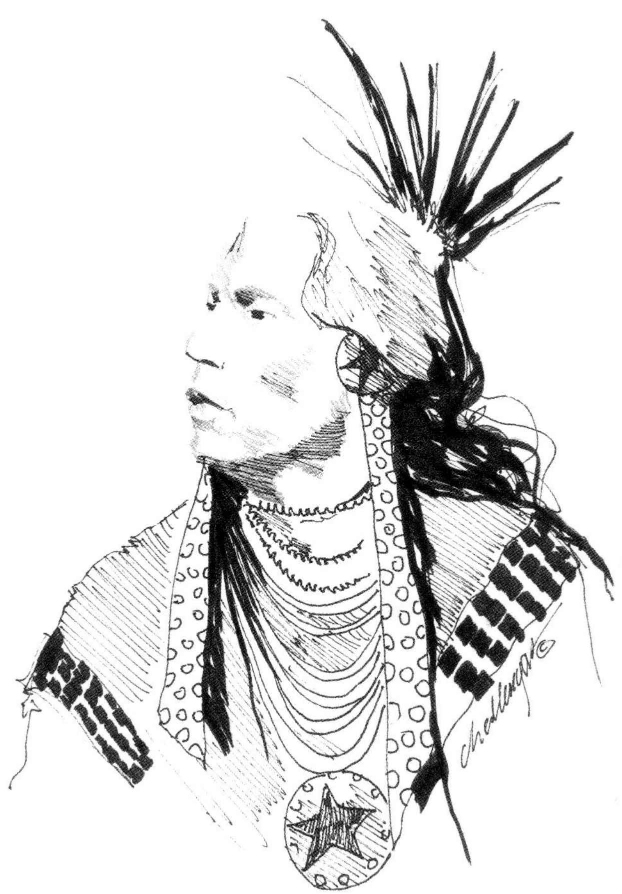

For much of Native American history, many Europeans and American settlers
attempted to disrupt and eliminate the Native American ceremonies and the use of sacred
medicine. Many simply remained passive voyeurs, rarely perceiving the dances and objects
as more than curious spectacles. Only on occasion were individuals able to draw analogies
to their own culture. Pioneer descendent Nora Lorrin tells of fellow Oklahoman John
Rice's experiences at the turn of the nineteenth century.

He has seen the actual service of the Indian medicine man, attired in his old
professional garb, attending the sick. The Medicine man had a cow head on his
head. It had the horns and also a tail on it. There were gourds and rattles, as
part of his paraphernalia and he would dance around the patient (who was a
woman) lying on a skin in the center of the tent, dancing, singing and rattling
his gourds. Then sometimes he would fill his mouth with water and spray it
toward the roof of the tent. Mr. Rice was only a boy of fifteen at the time
and raised the flap of the tent and watched the performance.
     He has seen the Scalp dance, the War dance, the Ghost dance, the Green
Corn dance (celebrating a feast), the Omaha dance and the Squaw dance. At
the Scalp dance, they have a scalp which is the center of attraction, and they
dance about it.
     The Omaha dance is a dance mimicking an attack with a bow and arrow;
creeping up on an enemy. He says that these dances are symbolical and tell a
story to anyone who understands them, much as folk songs do.

But the similarities between European American folk songs and Native American
ceremonies are few when compared with their differences. European culture utilized a

linear understanding of the world. The simple fables and morality plays were designed to promote puritanical social accord and define bad from good, right from wrong, the old way versus the current way. Church and State dictated the world's symbolism. Almost everything else remained neutral, existing only to be consumed, tolerated, or ignored. But the Native American existed in the world as it was originally created, and *everything* in it had meaning.

In this world, the buffalo grass was the hair of the good Mother—earth. The humble chickadee discovered the world. Dragonflies and butterflies were battle medicine. Trees, spiders, and turtles all held positions of power and importance. The evolution of the Ghost dance vocabulary gave this ideology full reign.

"The turtle embodies a tremendous amount of symbolism," says Challenger, "because, according to many tribes, the turtle supports the universe on its back. The turtle is the world swimming in an endless sea, the roundness of the shell is the sky, the flat underside is the earth, and the living turtle, enclosed inside, is all of living creation. Earthquakes occur whenever the turtle makes sudden movements. The prized medicine bowls of the Arapaho, Cheyenne, and Iroquois were turtle shells. In ceremonies, the turtle is sometimes addressed as the sacred Mother and the turtle silhouette often appeared on the shirts worn in the Ghost dance."

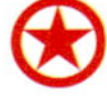

My children, my children,
Here is the river of turtles,
Where the various living things,
Are painted their different colors.
Our father says so,
Our father says so.

Birds could also be found throughout the Ghost dance symbolism. The eagle, the feathers of which were included in almost every aspect of the Ghost dance ceremony, is perhaps the most important bird in all of Native American culture and religion. In the Ghost dance doctrine, eagle feathers were seen carrying believers aloft and away from the dangers of the apocalypse. The feathers were used to embellish shields, spears, and arrows and were integral to ceremonial vestments. They were used as currency among many prairie tribes. Feathers were likened to the sun's rays, and wearing a feather manifested the nature of the Spirit on earth. The wing and tail feathers were considered most desirable and were used to scatter water blessed in prayer and to perform other sacred acts in Native American ceremonies. Whistles used in many important ceremonies were carved from the bone of an eagle. Prayers, songs, and sightings feature a spotted eagle, referring to the magnificent plumage of a first- or second-year bald eagle. An extraordinarily high flyer, the eagle is often associated directly with the Great Spirit.

"In order to obtain eagle feathers for ceremonies and medicine purposes, the birds had to be trapped," says Challenger. "But in order to do so, very specific rituals, prayers and actions had to be performed and followed because of the extreme sacred nature of the eagle. Two of the primary results desired from the preliminary ceremonies were to receive spiritual help to capture the eagle and to repel any consequences brought on by the anger of the eagle's spirits. In most of the prairie tribes of the plains, the eagle could only be captured live, then strangled to death with as little blood spilled as possible."

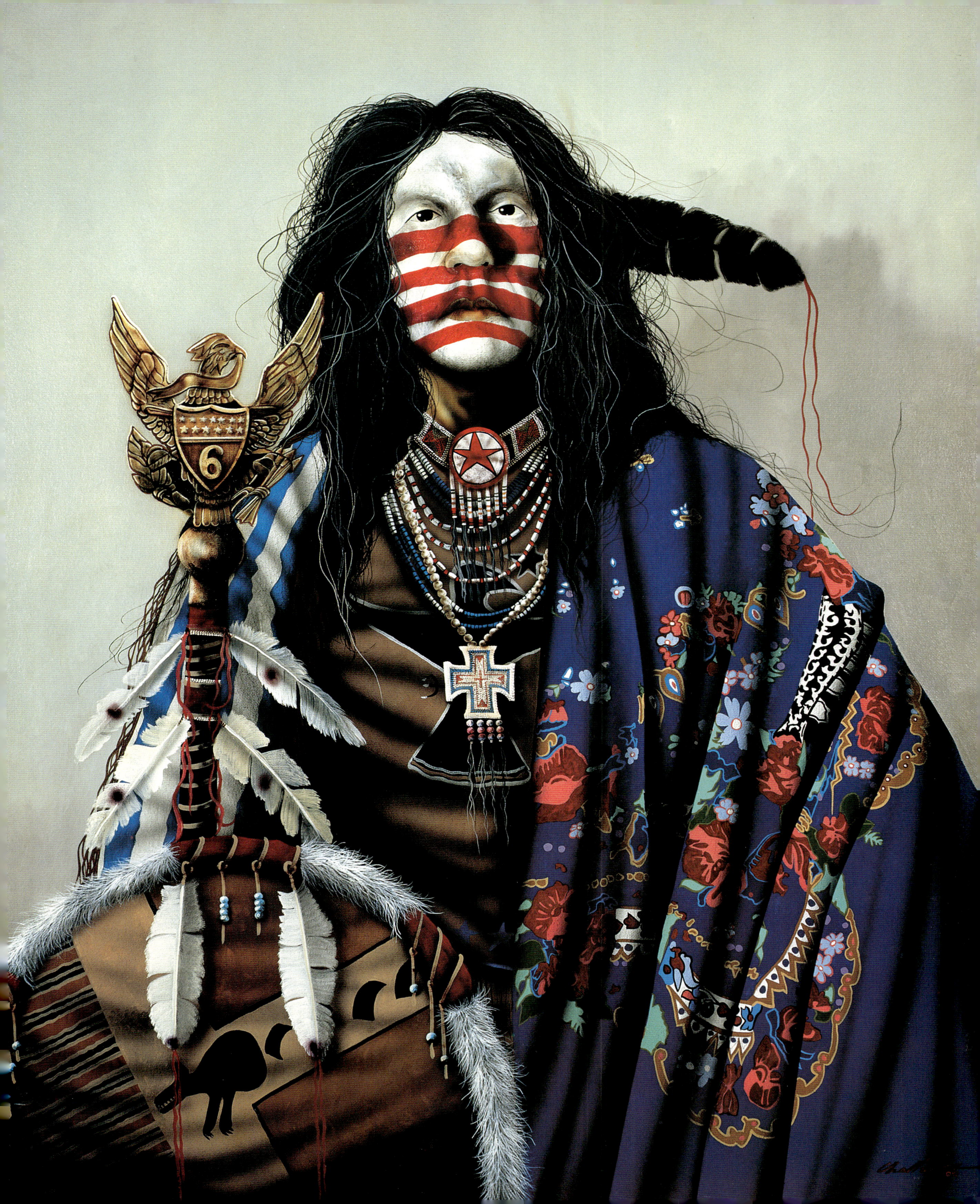

The Arapaho trapped eagles using pits. The hunter and his family would set up a camp in eagle country. His wife and daughters were instructed to refrain from using an awl, a pointed tool for making small holes in leather, while he hunted. Doing so might allow the eagle to impale the hunter with its talons. The eagle hunter would begin his ceremony with prayers, then dig a pit on the crest of the tallest surrounding hill. The excavated soil was then relocated so as not to alert the eagle. A roof of twigs, dirt, and grass was placed over the pit, and the bait—a piece of meat or tallow tied to a rawhide string—was positioned on top of the pitfall covering. The string was passed through the roof into the pit. The hunter might drape a coyote skin over sticks nearby to give the bait some authenticity. He would then continue the ceremony, singing the appropriate eagle songs all night and, just before dawn, climb the hill and enter the pit. He would bring a human skull with him to make himself invisible to the eagle. Once inside, the hunter would wait, holding onto the string to insure that nothing but an eagle would try to carry off the bait. The hunter refrained from eating, drinking water, or sleeping while in the pit, and he could not eat wild rose berries at any time during the four-day hunt or the eagle wouldn't take the bait.

Birds would gather around the pit, pecking at the bait or eating the seeds and insect larvae released during the digging. But once an eagle descended, the birds would fly away. The raptor would land to the side of the pit, then walk across the pit roof to snatch the bait. The hunter would thrust his hands through the thatching and grasp the eagle by the legs, pull it into the pit, and strangle it quickly. The hunter would place a small piece of pemmican, jerked and crumbled meat toasted over a fire, into the dead eagle's bill to entice other eagles to the bait. Once this was accomplished, the hunter would fix the roof,

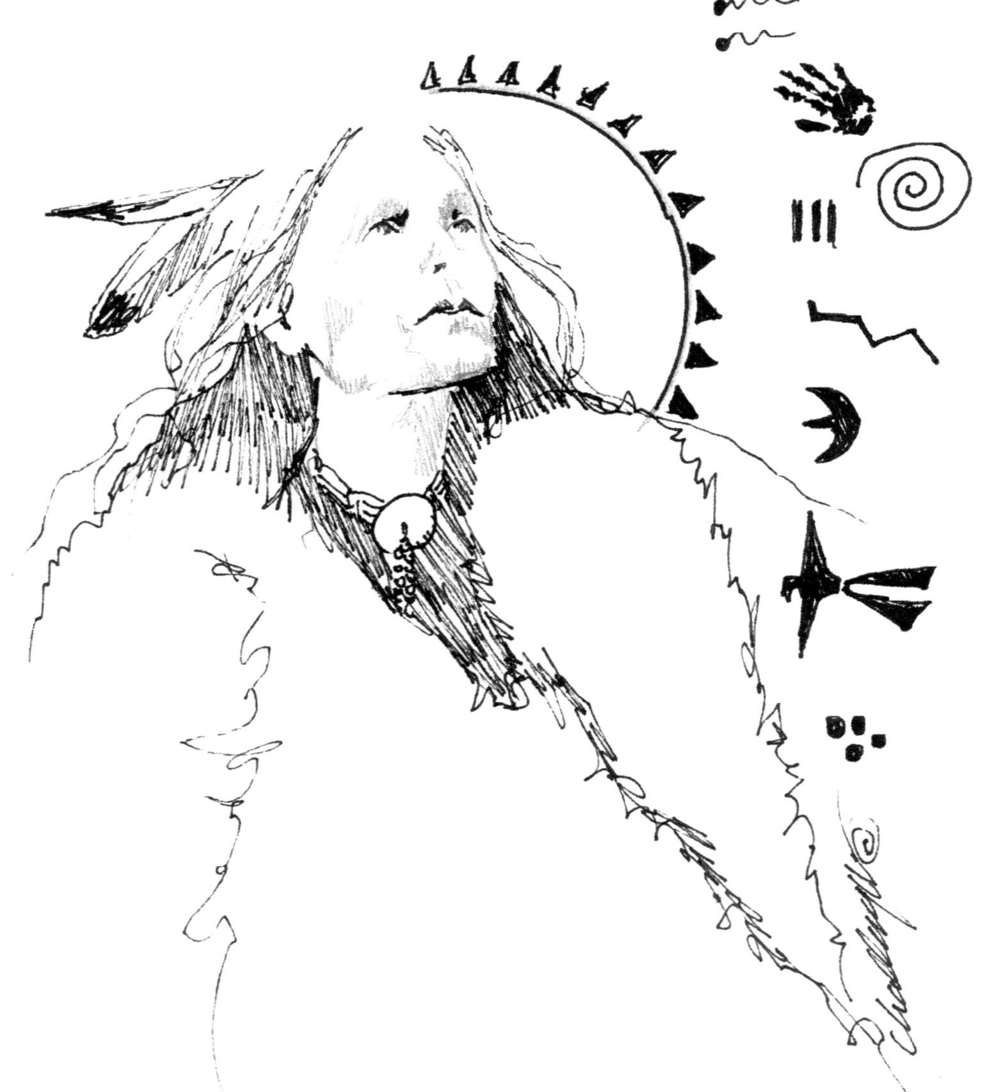

replace the bait, and wait for the next eagle. At night, he would return to camp to eat and
sleep, then be back in the pit before dawn. The hunt would end after four days, whether
the hunter had been successful or not.

Once he returned home, a lodge was built beside his tepee where the eagles were
strung along a pole balanced across two forked braces that were hammered into the
ground. The ceremony continued with prayers and additional preparations until complete,
then the eagles' bodies were dismantled and put to use.

The crow, the sacred bird of the Ghost dance, is the Arapaho messenger from the
spirit world. "Its black color," reveals Challenger, "is symbolic of death, but because of
this association, the crow is able to lead the spirits back from the darker world. Whenever
a crow is killed, the skin is treated and the bird is stuffed in a lifelike pose and carried in
the dance. The image of a crow appears on the shirts and other clothes of the Ghost
dancers and the feathers are worn on the dancers' heads."

The Arapaho believe the spirit world resides in the west, above the earth and separated from it by water. In their Ghost dance story of the crow, Mooney explains,

> the crow, as the messenger and leader of the spirits who had gone before, col-
> lected their armies on the other side and advanced at their head to the hither
> limit of the shadow land. Then, looking over, they saw far below them a sea,

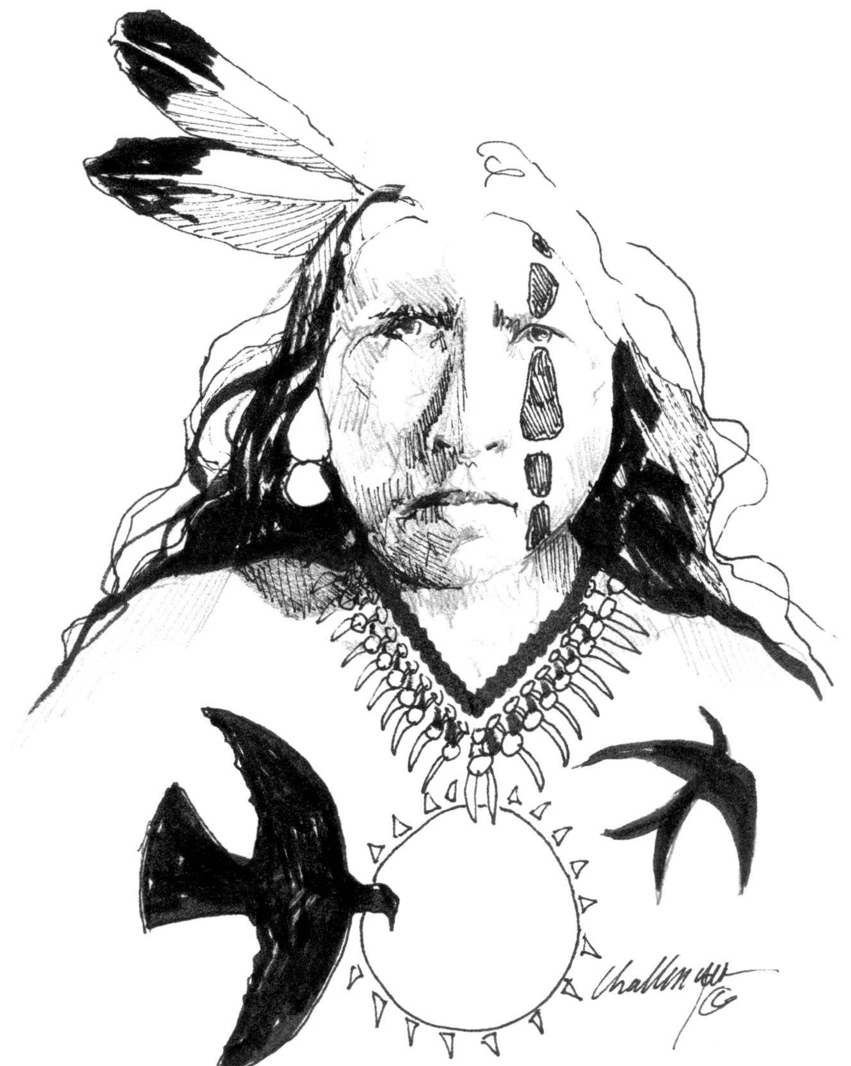

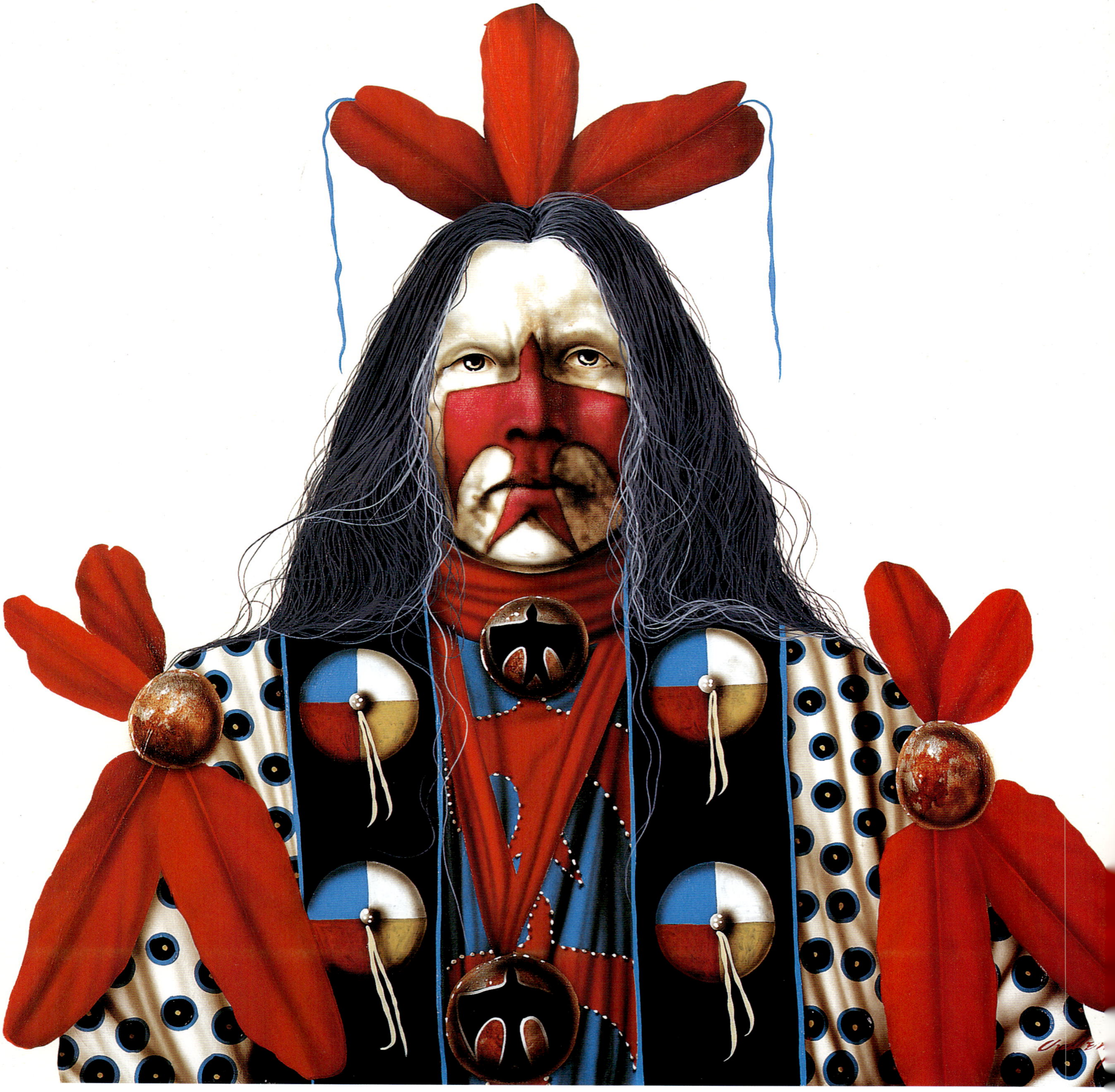

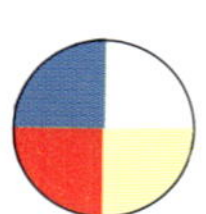

MESSAGE FROM
THE THUNDERBIRD

and far out beyond it toward the east was the boundary of the earth, where
lived the friends they were marching to rejoin. Taking up a pebble in his beak,
the crow then dropped it into the water and it became a mountain towering up
to the land of the dead. Down its rocky slope he brought his army until they
halted at the edge of the water. Then, taking some dust in his bill, the crow
flew out and dropped it into the water as he flew, and it became a solid arm of
land stretching from the spirit world to the earth. He returned and flew out
again, this time with some blades of grass, which he dropped upon the land
thus made, and at once it was covered with a green sod. Again he returned, and
again flew out, this time with some twigs in his bill, and dropping these also
upon the new land, at once it was covered with a forest of trees.

Once again the crow flew back to the base of the mountain and gathered together
the countless spirits of all those who had died. The sacred bird then led them across the
sea to the western boundary of the earth where they wait to rejoin the living at the dawn
of the new world.

> *The crow is making a road,*
> *He is making a road;*
> *He has finished it.*
> *His children,*
> *Then he collected them,*
> *Then he collected them on the farther side.*

The mythic Thunderbird can be found throughout the Ghost dance symbolism. The
Thunderbird hovers around the earth's highest elevations, and its domain is surrounded by
inaccessible terrain. A storm cloud racing across the earth becomes the Thunderbird's
shadow. The sound of thunder issues from its beating wings and its eyes shoot bolts of
lightning. For many tribes of the prairie, northwest coast, and central America, all thunder
and lightning emanate from this great bird, and its presence shadows the continent. Lake
Huron's Thunder Bay in Michigan and the area around Big Stone Lake in South Dakota
are considered Thunderbird nesting locations. Thunderbird eggs—enormous boulders—
crown the summit of Coteau des Prairies in South Dakota. Along the Red River, a singed
flat of grass in the shape of a giant bird spreading its wings remains burnt in testament to
the Thunderbird's one moment on solid ground. It can be found among the Ghost
dancers, painted on their ceremonial shirts or cut from a skin of rawhide, embellished
with beads and worn on the head.

"The Comanche," recalls Challenger, "have a story about a hunter who wounds an
enormous bird, which collapses into a draw. Fearful of approaching the bird alone, the
hunter locates help and returns to the place where the bird was felled as sounds of thunder and bolts of lightning emanate. As the hunter comes closer, to the draw, lightning
strikes and kills him. The remaining hunters, blinded by the flash, run quickly away, real-
izing with fear and dread that the angry creature lying in the draw is the Thunderbird."

> *The young birds,*
> *The young birds,*
> *The young Thunderbirds.*

Plants, as well as birds and animals, occupy an important place in the Ghost dance ceremony. The cedar tree, with its evergreen foliage, can be found in the center of many Ghost dance circles. Sometimes the tree is stripped of branches and reduced to a pole similar to a tepee brace. But often the tree is transplanted live to the circle and decorated with colored strips of cloth, eagle feathers, stuffed birds, wooden toys, and animal horns and claws. The tree is sacred in many Native American ceremonies and valued for its scent, particularly when dried, crumbled, and burned as incense. Its longevity and sturdiness make it useful in daily life. The wood is naturally tinted in the sacred color red.

"The Cherokee and the Yuchi believed the wood's red color came from the blood of a sorcerer," Challenger notes. "The sorcerer was defeated and beheaded by a hero and his head was hung from the top of a tree. But the head remained alive so the people kept hanging it in different trees. It still wouldn't die. So the medicine healer told the people to hang the head from the top of a cedar tree, and once they accomplished this, it finally died. The blood dripping down from the sorcerer's head gave the cedar wood its red hue."

The cedar tree, the cedar tree,
We have it in the center
When we dance,
When we dance.
We have it in the center.

Red became the most important color in the Ghost dance ceremony due in part to the sacred paint originally distributed by the Ghost dance visionary Wovoka. Acquired from the deposits around *Kurangwa,* the rusty ocher was ground into dust, mixed with water, and allowed to dry in small brick-red cakes. Mixing again with water or fat would create a brilliant red paint. Used to decorate the skin, Ghost shirts, and ceremonial objects, the paint contributed to good health, promoted longevity, and facilitated the dancers' visions.

The stars, moon, and sun are also important to Native American and Ghost dance medicine. Often, the Ghost dance ceremony lasted several days and ended on the fifth day just before dawn. A song to the Morning Star was sung on this last morning of the dance. The Morning Star is not actually a star but any one of several planets, depending on the season, that appears on the eastern horizon at dawn and is considered sacred by most of the prairie tribes. It appears in the form of a Maltese cross on the shirts worn in the dance. The Arapaho word for it means "a cross" and the Kiowa refer to it as "the great star."

My children, my children,
It is I who wear the morning star on my head;
I show it to my children,
Says the father,
Says the father.

According to the Cherokee, the sky opens and closes against the earth like a pair of scissors. At dawn and dusk, the sun slips in from the east as the sky opens and escapes out the west as it closes. The sun is considered a living entity by many tribes and is capable of

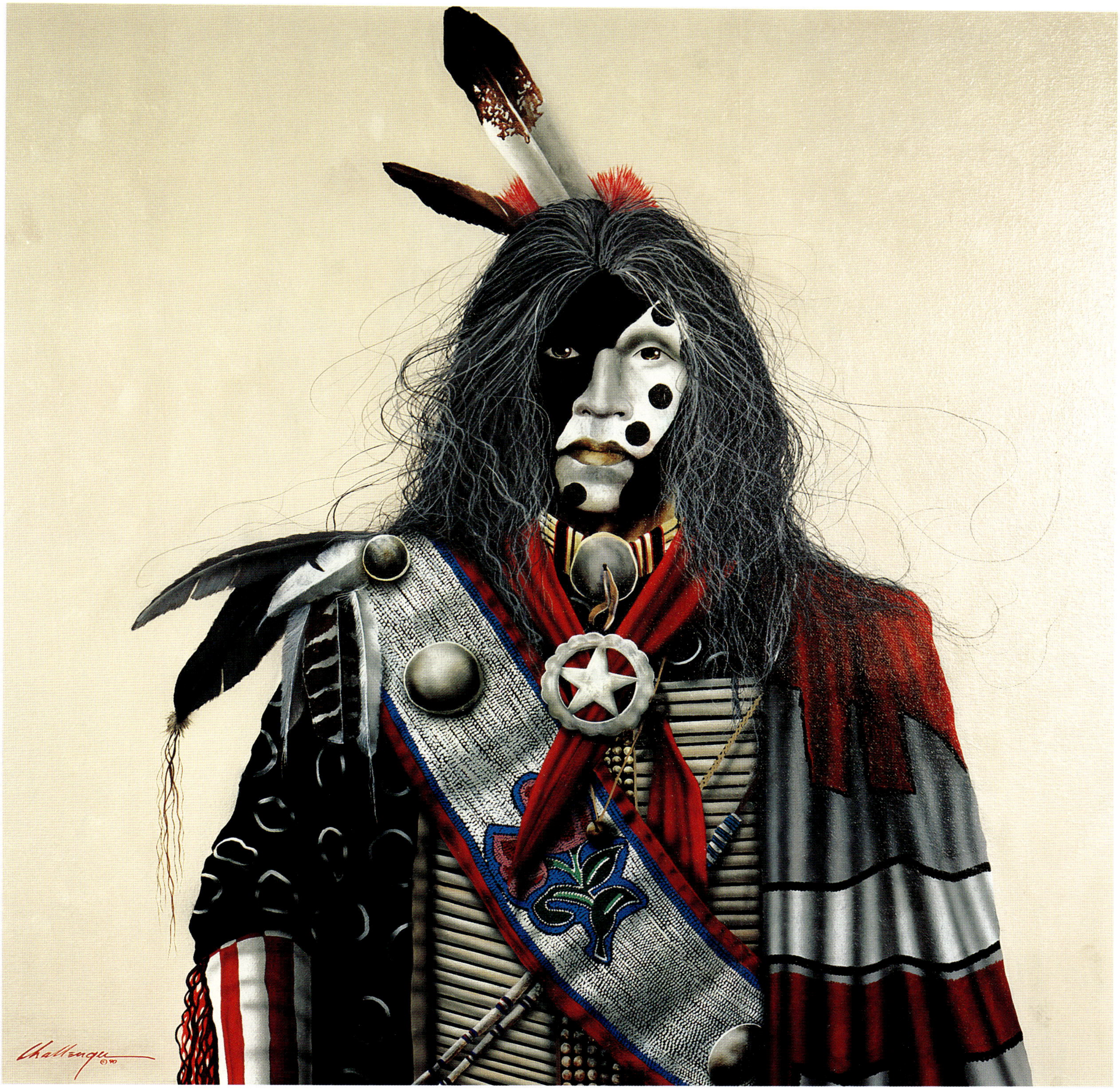

THE AWAKENING

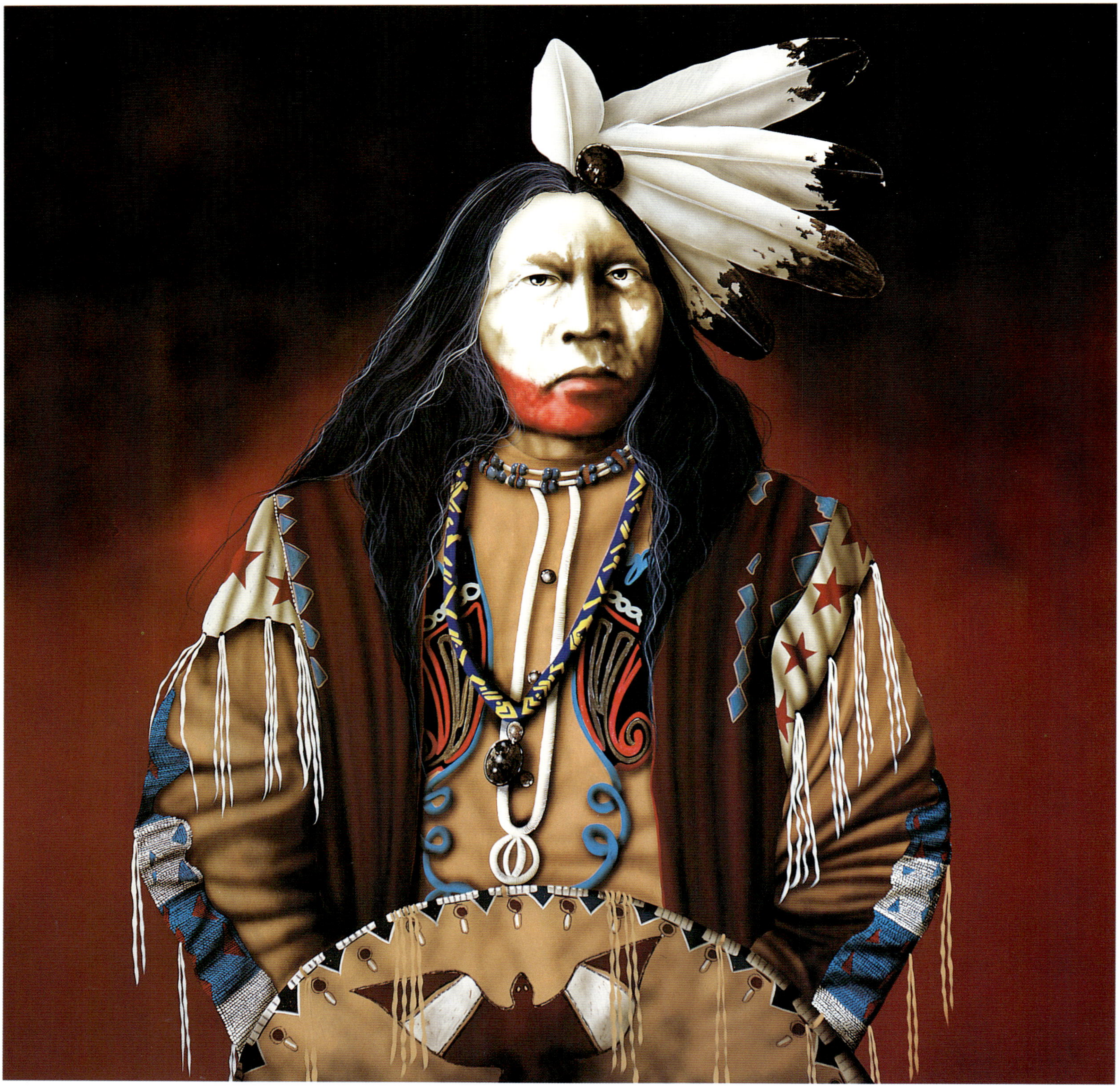

DAY OF THE RED DAWN

tremendous power. A solar eclipse represents a monster attempting to swallow the sun and doom the earth to everlasting darkness unless frightened away with loud prayer, rituals, and noises. Four solar eclipses occurred during the 1880s, and any one of them could have precipitated Wovoka's vision, which, as traditionally recorded, begins "when the sun died." As a consequence, the eclipse became an integral symbol in the Ghost dance ceremony.

Many tribes elevated an object to particular importance in the tribal vocabulary of symbols. Short Bull, one of the primary Sioux leaders of the dance, reveals four of these sacred symbols. "Our father in heaven has placed a mark at each point of the four winds. First, a clay pipe, which lies at the setting of the sun and represents the Sioux tribe. Second, there is a holy arrow lying at the north, which represents the Cheyenne tribe. Third, at the rising of the sun there lies hail, representing the Arapaho tribe. Fourth, there lies a pipe and nice feather at the south, which represents the Crow tribe."

"Many Ghost dance followers created their own personal sacred medicine, which they used or wore in the dance," Challenger explains. "Black Elk created a ghost stick by painting a whittled branch with the sacred red paint and tying a spotted eagle feather to it. Other dancers made their own ghost sticks and wore them in their hair when they danced."

Moon Head, one of the Caddo leaders of the Ghost dance, wore a remarkable creation of sacred medicine around his neck. "He wore a wide-brim hat," remembers Mooney, "with his hair flowing down to his shoulders, and on his breast, suspended from a cord about his neck, was a curious amulet consisting of the polished end of a buffalo horn, surrounded by a circlet of downy red feathers, within another circle of badger and owl claws. He explained that this was the source of his prophetic and clairvoyant inspiration. The buffalo horn was 'God's heart,' the red feathers contained his own heart, and the circle of claws represented the world. When he prayed for help, his heart communed with 'God's heart,' and he learned what he wished to know." Mooney remarks that Moon Head's companion "had a yellow sun with green rays painted on his forehead, with an elaborate rayed crescent in green, red, and yellow on his chin, and wore a necklace from which depended a crucifix and a brass clock-wheel, the latter, as he stated, representing the sun."

The Ghost dance created an opportunity to strengthen beliefs, reaffirm tribal icons, and experience new sacred moments. It required the individual to explore a personal commitment to traditional faith while providing the family or clan or tribe with hope in a collapsing world. The Ghost shirt, perhaps above all other things, may have provided dancers with the greatest opportunity to create this personal sacred medicine.

A Native American warrior typically went into battle naked above the waist. His protection was a feather, a bag of sacred powder, an animal claw, a bird's head, or some other small object woven into his hair or hidden in his shield. The object's facility to protect depended on its metaphysical power, not its size or physical ability to fend off weapons.

The Ghost shirt extended this protective medicine to all practitioners of the Ghost dance doctrine. The shirt was worn by men, women, and children and survives as perhaps the most recognized and creative invention of the Ghost dance religion.

During the ceremonial dance it was worn as an outside garment, but some evidence suggests it was also worn regularly beneath everyday dress. The shape, fringing, and feather adornments were typically the same on most shirts, but remarkable variation occurred in surface designs. Paintings of the sun, moon, stars, and visions from trances adorned the shirts. Eagle feathers were attached to many, and sometimes the fringe was painted the sacred color red. But whatever personal medicine appeared on the shirt, the purpose for all wearers remained the same—the Ghost shirt was believed to be impenetrable to bullets or weapons of any kind.

Black Elk recalls in his vision of the Ghost shirt:

I floated over the tepees and began to come down feet first at the center of the hoop where I could see a beautiful tree all green and full of flowers. When I touched the ground, two men were coming toward me, and they wore holy shirts made and painted in a certain way. They came to me and said: "It is not yet time to see your father, who is happy. You have work to do. We will give you something that you shall carry back to your people, and with it they shall come to see their loved ones."

I knew it was the way their holy shirts were made that they wanted me to take back. They told me to return at once, and then I was out in the air again, floating fast as before…

Then I fell back into my body, and as I did this I heard voices all around and above me, and I was sitting on the ground. Many were crowding around, asking me what vision I had seen. I told them just what I had seen, and what I brought back was the memory of the holy shirts the two men wore.

That evening some of us got together at Big Road's tepee and decided to use the ghost shirts I had seen. So the next day I made ghost shirts all day long and painted them in the sacred manner of my vision…

Conjured from the realm of dreams, the Ghost shirt was fashioned out of white cloth or buckskin and decorated with iconography pulled from personal visions. Simple in design or elaborately detailed, the Ghost shirt became the dancer's illustrated testimony.

"I think they wore the ghost shirt or ghost dress for the first time that day," recalls Mrs. Z. A. Parker, who watched the ceremony unfold along White Clay Creek in South Dakota.

I noticed that these were all new and were worn by about seventy men and forty women. The wife of a man called Return-from-scout had seen in a vision that her friends all wore a similar robe, and on reviving from her trance she called the women together and they made a great number of the sacred

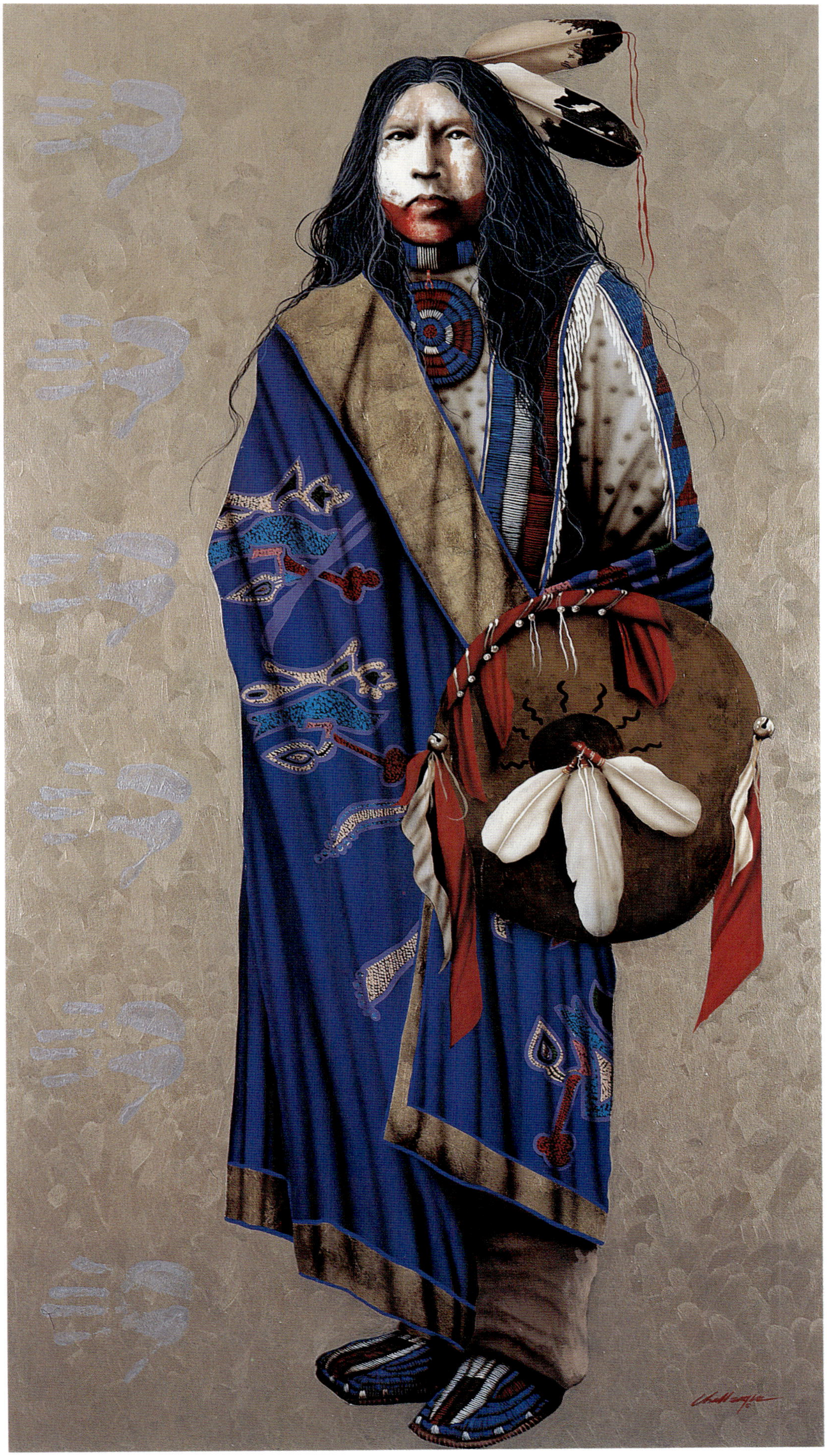

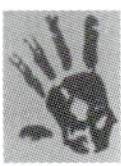

WARRIOR'S PRAYER

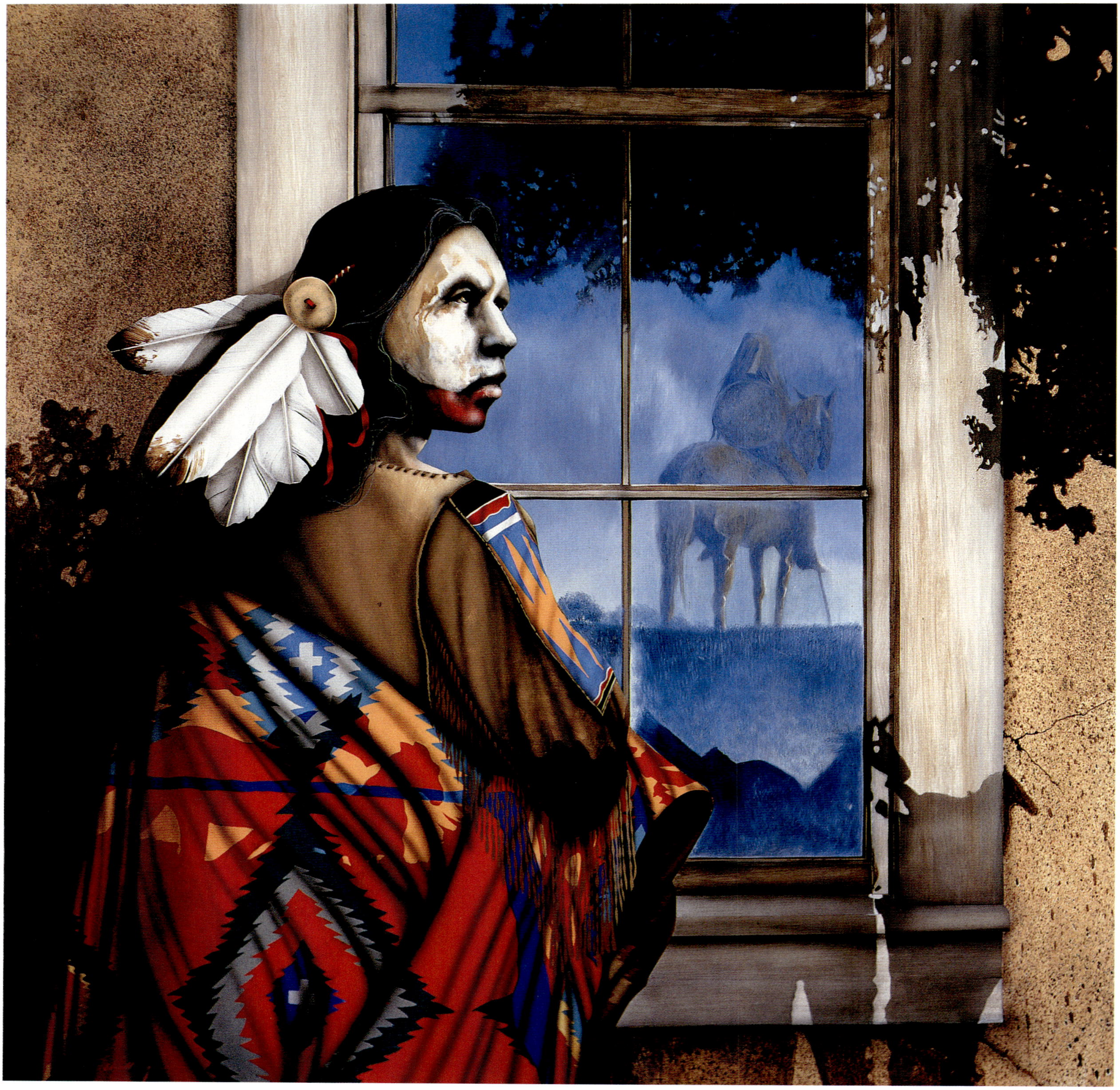

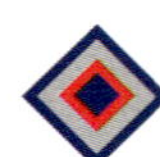

REFLECTIONS FROM THE SHADOW SPIRIT

garments. They were of white cotton cloth. The women's dress was cut like their ordinary dress, a loose robe with wide, flowing sleeves, painted blue in the neck, in the shape of a three-cornered handkerchief, with moon, stars, birds, etc., interspersed with real feathers, painted on the waist and sleeves. While dancing they wound their shawls about their waists, letting them fall to within three inches of the ground, the fringe at the bottom. In the hair, near the crown, a feather was tied. I noticed an absence of any manner of bead ornaments, and, as I knew their vanity and fondness for them, wondered why it was. Upon making inquiries I found they discarded everything they could which was made by white men.

    The ghost shirt of the men was made of the same material—shirts and leggings painted in red. Some of the leggings were painted in stripes running up and down, others running around. The shirt was painted blue around the neck, and the whole garment was fantastically sprinkled with figures of birds, bows and arrows, sun, moon, and stars, and everything they saw in nature. Down the outside of the sleeve were rows of feathers tied by the quill ends and left to fly in the breeze, and also a row around the neck and up and down the outside of the leggings. I noticed that a number had stuffed birds, squirrel heads, etc., tied in their long hair. The faces of all were painted red with a black half-moon on the forehead or on one cheek.

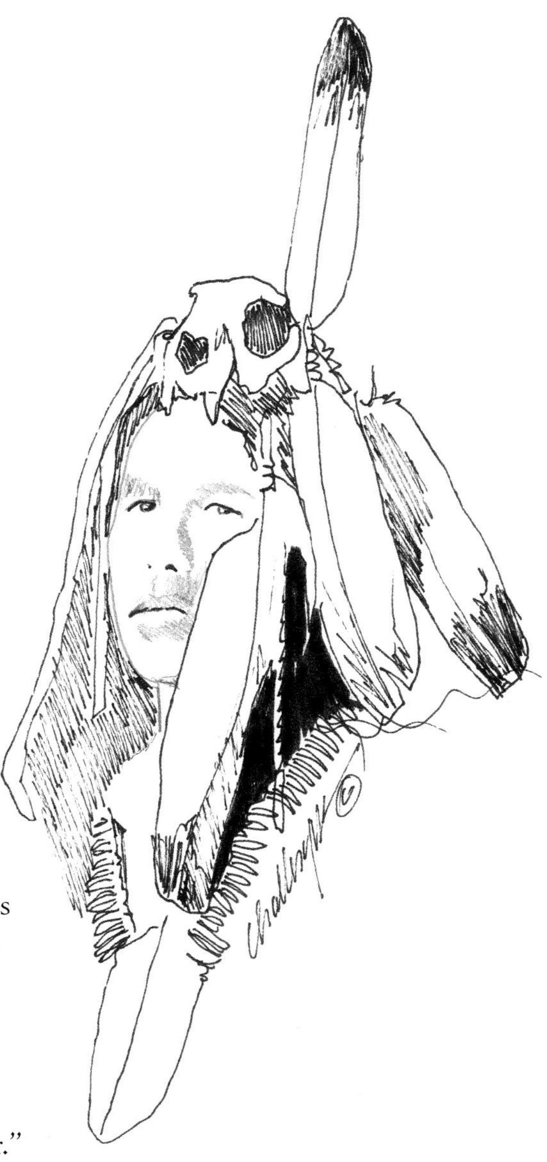

The Sioux Ghost dancers had particular need for the protective medicine the shirts were meant to provide. "They paint the white muslins they made holy shirts and dresses out of with blue across the back, and alongside of this is a line of yellow paint," recalls George Sword, describing the Sioux Ghost shirts. "They also paint in the front part of the shirts and dresses. A picture of an eagle is made on the back of all the shirts and dresses. On the shoulders and on the sleeves they tied eagle feathers. They said that the bullets will not go through these shirts and dresses, so they all have these dresses for war."

    The Sioux, like almost all of the Native American tribes, had been driven unwilling-ly onto reservations by the late 1800s. The constant presence of munitions and military in their daily lives eliminated any sense of security or well-being. A threatening undercur-rent of armed force influenced every individual movement, every tribal decision, and every major ceremony performed on the reservation premises. It is not unreasonable to expect a people under constant pressure to adopt protective measures. The Ghost shirt was an attempt to provide this protection. Despite George Sword's testimony regarding "dresses for war," translated over one hundred years ago from the original Teton Dakota dialect, the overwhelming military presence required the Ghost dancers to dress for protection *against* war. With the exception of a belief in an apocalyptic future beyond any mortal person's control, the Ghost dance message promoted peaceful coexistence, family cohesion and faith. Ghost dance practitioners desired only to return to simple freedoms and undis-turbed prayer. Instead, they were met with a massacre.

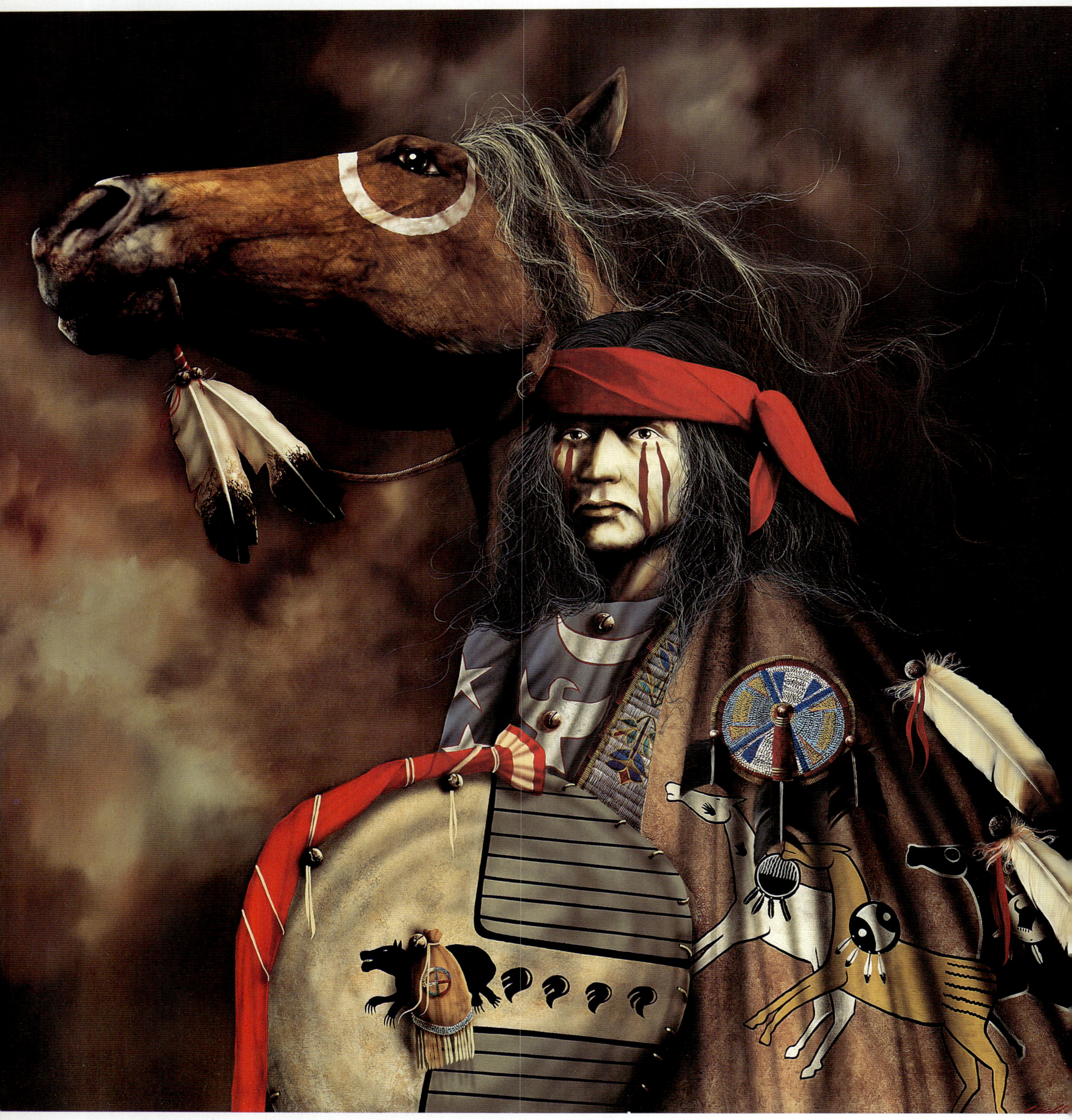

MOON OF THE FALLING LEAVES

THE GHOST DANCE ERA

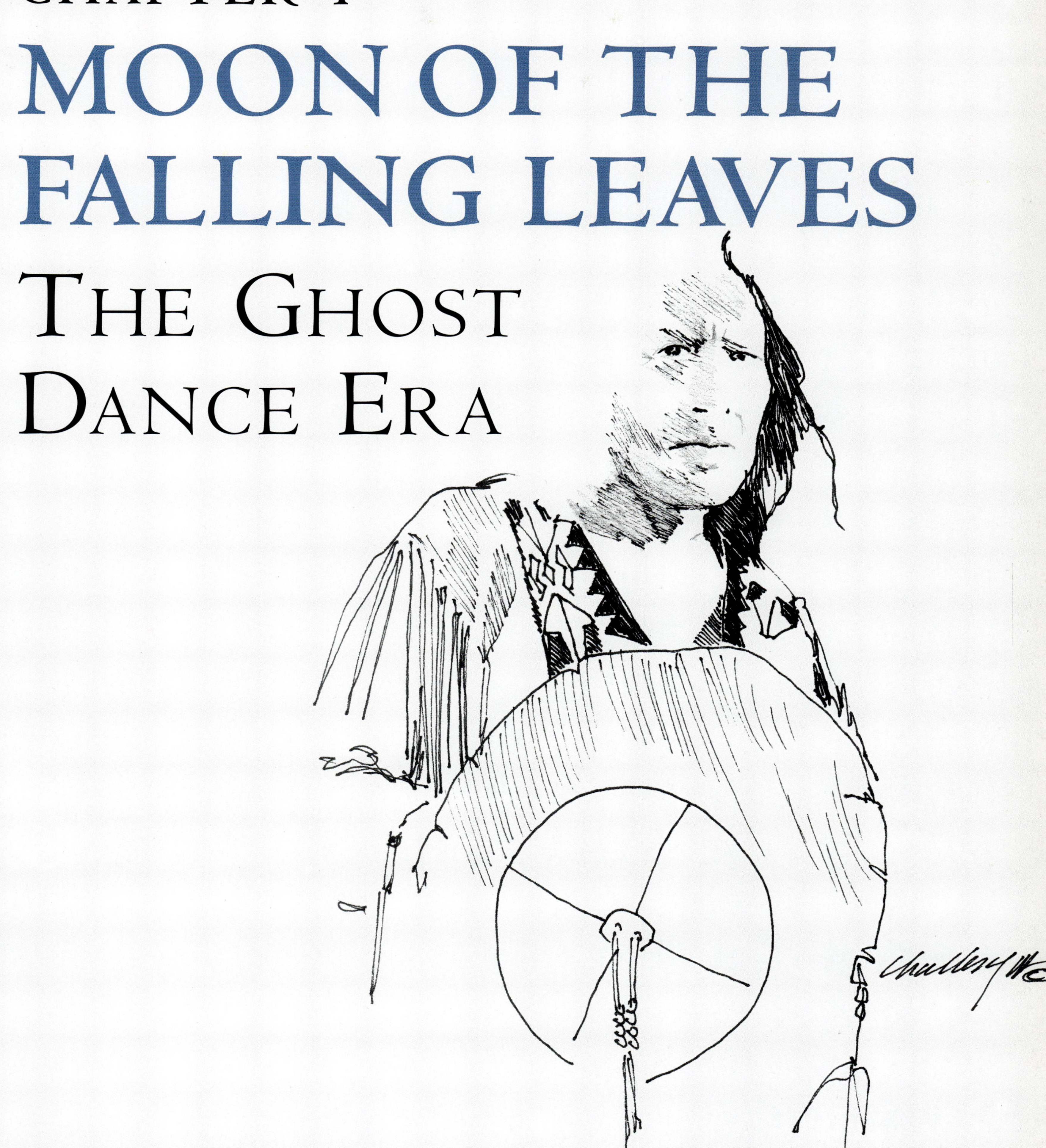

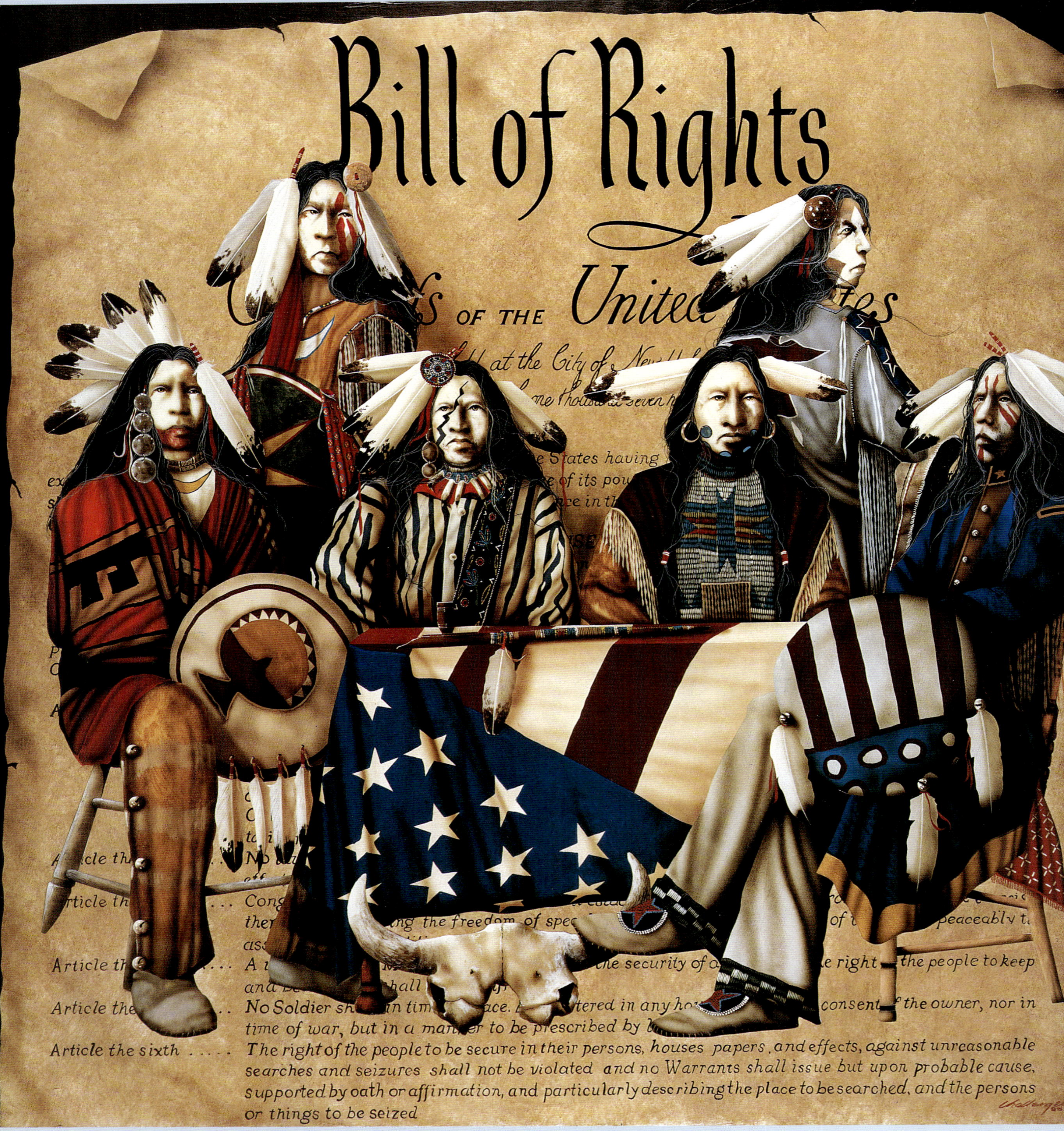

Bill of Rights
OF THE United States
at the City of New York
thousand seven
States having
of its pow
ce in the
Article the ... No
Article the ... Cong
the freedom of spec peaceably t
ass
Article the ... A the security of a right the people to keep
and shall
Article the ... No Soldier sh in time ace. tered in any ho consent of the owner, nor in
time of war, but in a man er to be prescribed by
Article the sixth ..... The right of the people to be secure in their persons, houses papers, and effects, against unreasonable
searches and seizures shall not be violated and no Warrants shall issue but upon probable cause,
supported by oath or affirmation, and particularly describing the place to be searched, and the persons
or things to be seized

The sound is fading away.
It is of five sounds.
Freedom.
The sound is fading away.
It is of five sounds.

In the American East and Midwest of the 1880s, literature, science, and financial power reigned. Within this cosmopolitan dominion, built upon the violent appropriation of Native American lands, the world began to spin much faster as the nineteenth century collapsed. Freud's theories on the human psyche, Louisa May Alcott's *Little Women,* Charles Darwin's *The Origin of Species,* and the Ku Klux Klan were already familiar territory to the denizens of the age, dubbed "Victorian" after the then-current Queen of England.

But the American West remained an auspicious victory only in the *minds* of America's European descendants. Constructing a life in this vast expanse, unstabilized by the tenets of the Manifest Destiny, presented a harsh reality for both Native people and the encroaching emigrant population.

The Cheyenne Chief Good Bear remembers the hardships of life in this wilderness:

Once in Northern Country we had no meat to eat in our camp. It was bitter cold and our children cried from hunger. To comfort them, a kettle of water with a few stones in it was set on the fire to boil. The children thought it was a kind of soup, drank some, and became quiet for a time. Our men who had gone after game came back, saying: Neither deer nor buffalo were in sight. I could no longer see the hunger of my people, and although a cold snowstorm was raging, I took my bow, arrow, and knife to seek after game. Four days I thus hunted, without eating. The fourth day I spied two Indians at some distance, standing still in the snow. Foe or friends? I came closer to them and shouted, "Who are you?" No answer or movement on their part. I held my arrow ready on the bow walking to them. They were Pawnee Indians, made no sound or motion. Finally, as I touched them they felt stone hard, standing there frozen to death. I was cold and near the same fate myself, but I dragged myself further. At last I spied a deer foundering in the snow, and I shot him. I was so hungry that there was no thought of cooking some of the meat. I opened the animal, took out the liver and kidneys, and devoured them as they were. Then I dragged the deer as far as my strength permitted, then being not far from our camp, I cut out a large piece. With that I soon reached my lodge where I was greeted with joy, for I had been given up for lost and frozen.

THE BILL OF RIGHTS

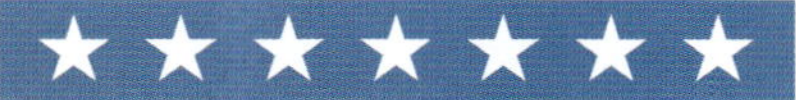

PAGE 70:
WAR PONIES

73

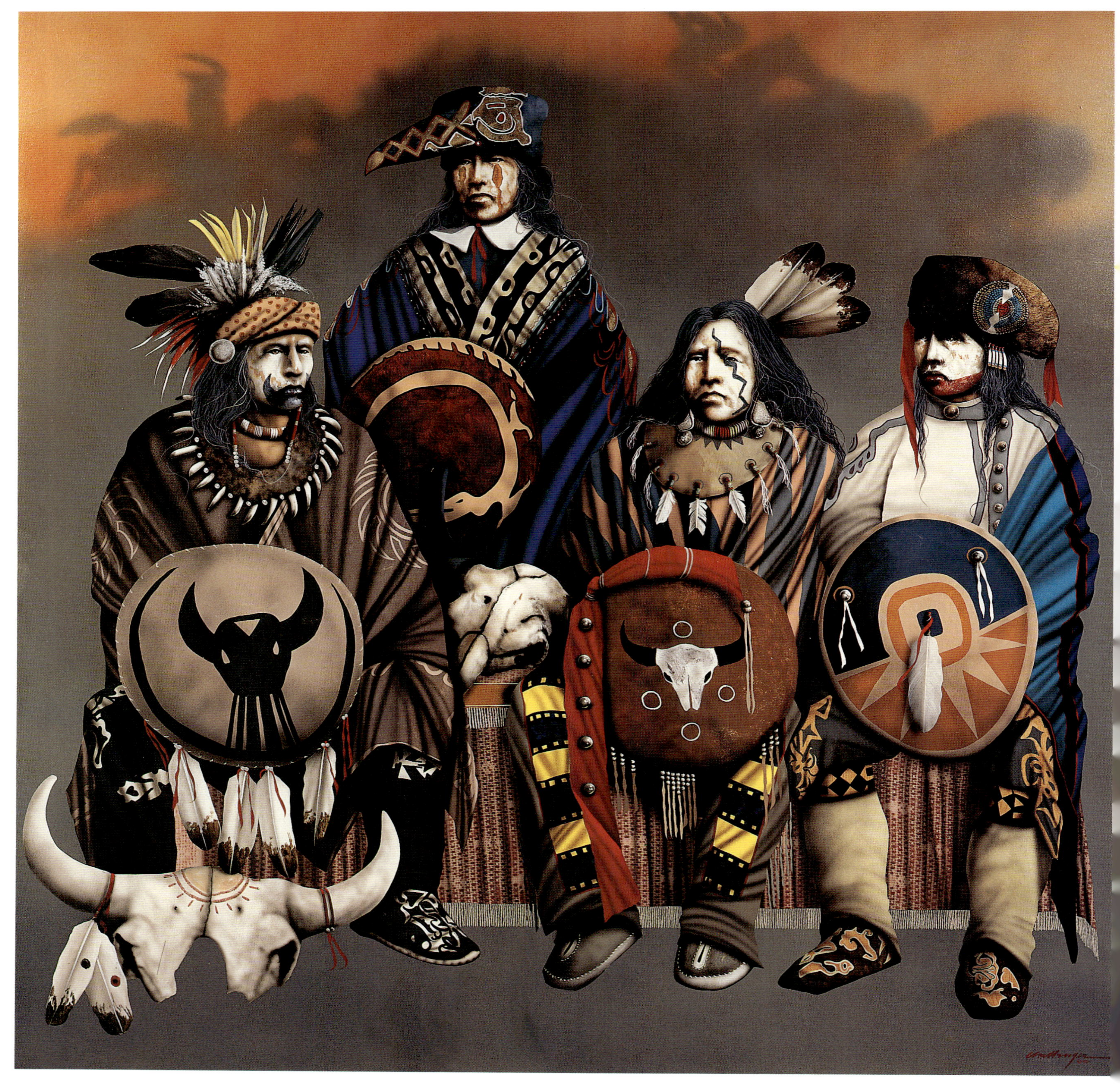

ROAMS THE PLAINS NO MORE

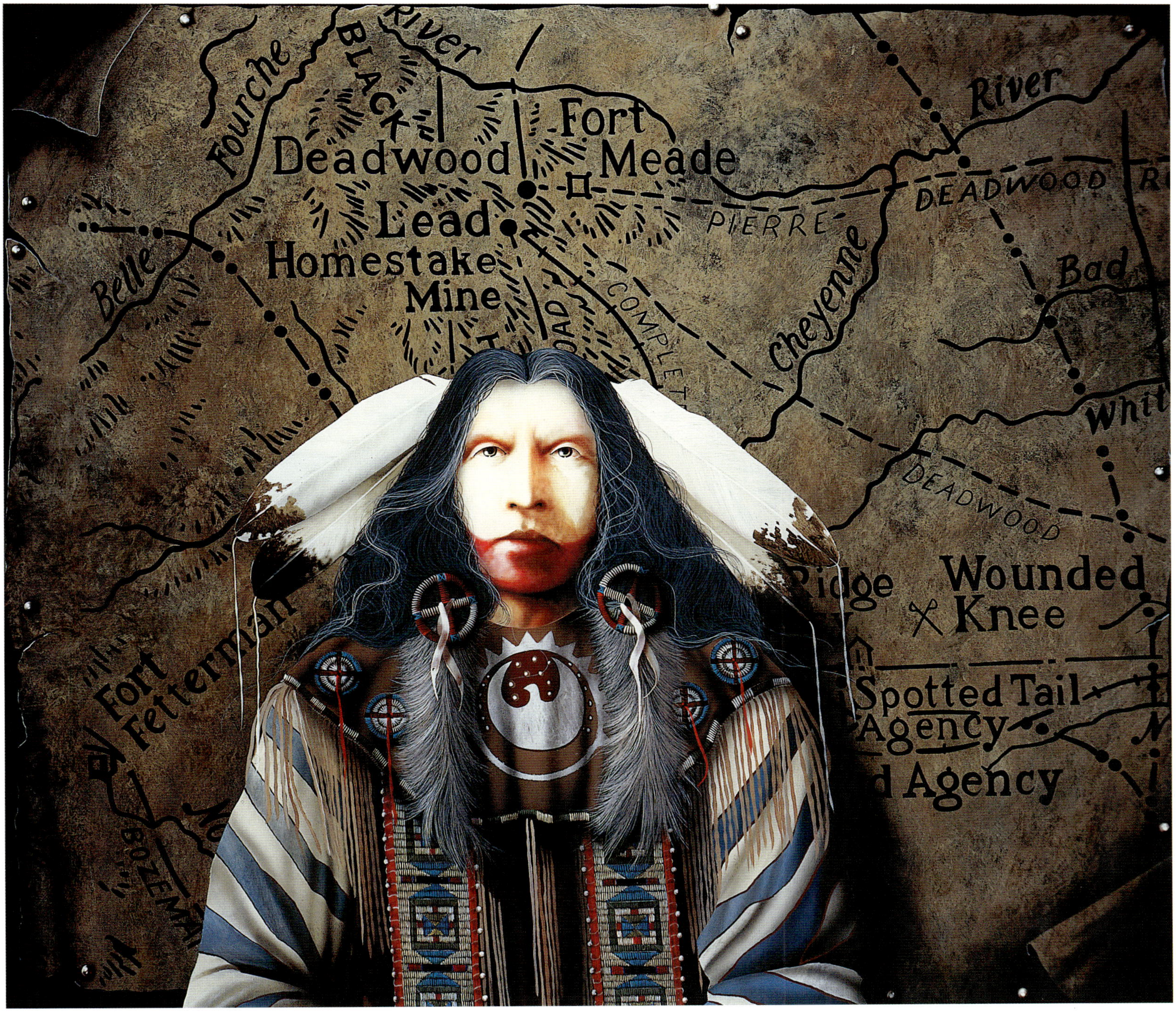

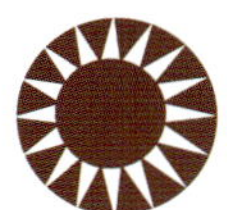

PROMISED LAND

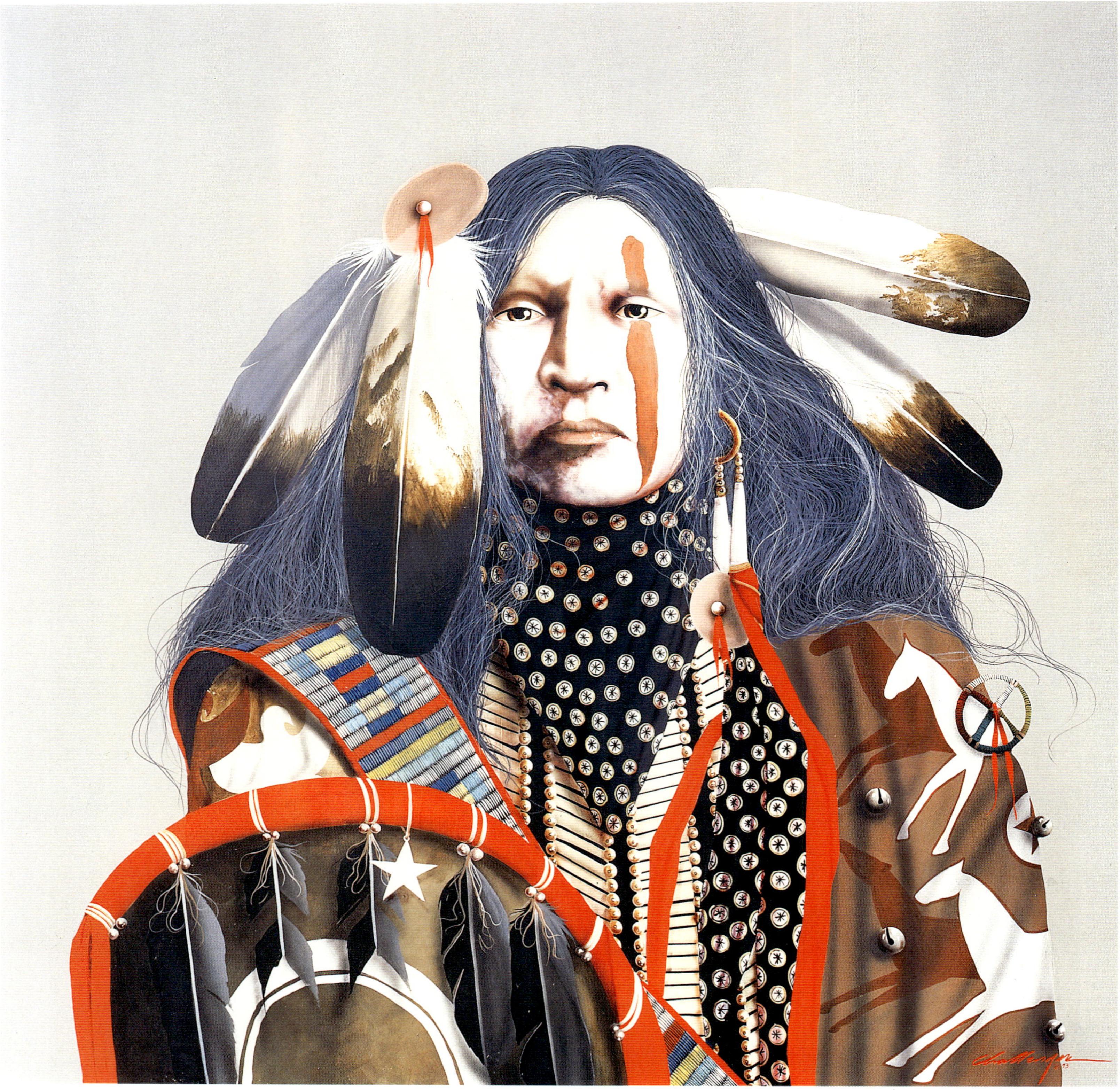

STRENGTHENED BY HIS PAST

But the hardships of western habitation ultimately ceased to be an equalizer for Native American and pioneer cultures. As campaigns to eradicate the "wild" from the American wilderness gained momentum, any obstruction to the complete settlement of the West collapsed. Expansionism moved westward in full force, and with it came a real and constant threat to the survival of Native Americans across the country. Hunger began to dominate their daily lives.

The slaughter and subsequent disappearance of the buffalo can be counted as one of the primary catalysts for starvation among the Native American people. Dependent in great part on the animal for food and shelter, Native Americans watched most of their self-sufficiency expire with the bison. It took just a few years for settlers, migrating across the plains, to eliminate an estimated 60 million buffalo in an extermination campaign unrivaled by any other event of its kind in history. According to a Smithsonian Report entitled *Extermination of the American Bison,* by 1889 the buffalo population had been reduced to 541 animals. Antelope and deer were also shot down for sport, with much of the meat and hides left to scavengers. Skins for new clothing and tepees were no longer available. Government-issue canvas, muslin, and dried beef became poor substitutes.

The Kiowa people were one tribe out of many devastated by the loss. "The change was so swift and terrible in its effects that they could not believe it real and final," reveals Mooney. "It seemed to them like a dream of sorrow, a supernatural cloud of darkness to punish their derelictions, but which could be lifted from them by prayer and sacrifice. Their old men told of years when the buffalo was scarce or had gone a long way off, but never since the beginning of the world of a time when there was no buffalo. The buffalo still lived beyond their horizon or in caves under the earth, and with its return would come back prosperity and freedom."

"The United States government spent the great part of the nineteenth century manipulating, coercing, bribing, and cheating Native Americans out of their land," laments Challenger. "Once the reservations were established, the government continued to reduce the land allotments further whenever the land and its resources were perceived as valuable. The desire for new grazing pastures, the discovery of gold, or the want of fertile soil would force Native Americans back to the negotiating table where they invariably lost. The government's machinations were meant to control larger and larger tracks of land and resources and reduce Native Americans to powerless dependents." But it was the tremendous influx of emigrants that ultimately sealed the fate of the Native population. In the end, they were simply outnumbered.

Whether coercion succeeded or failed, the U.S. government would ultimately break treaty agreements and prevail over Native American territory. Creating homestead allotments on confiscated land enabled the U.S. population to explode across the West. The Oklahoma territories, despite having become the destination for the Cheyenne's "Trail of Tears" in the early 1800s and christened "Indian country," was not exempt from settlement. Once large tracts of land were negotiated out of Native American hands, the government organized "runs" in which thousands of settlers literally raced across the countryside staking claims to acreage.

"I made the run into the Cheyenne Country from Cloud Chief," recalls pioneer E. E. Blake,

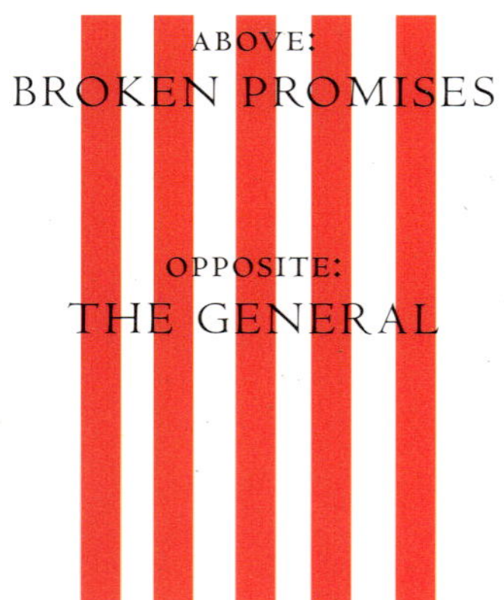

but when I arrived the whole country was taken. You could not ride a horse over that country as fast as you could drive an ox team and wagon.

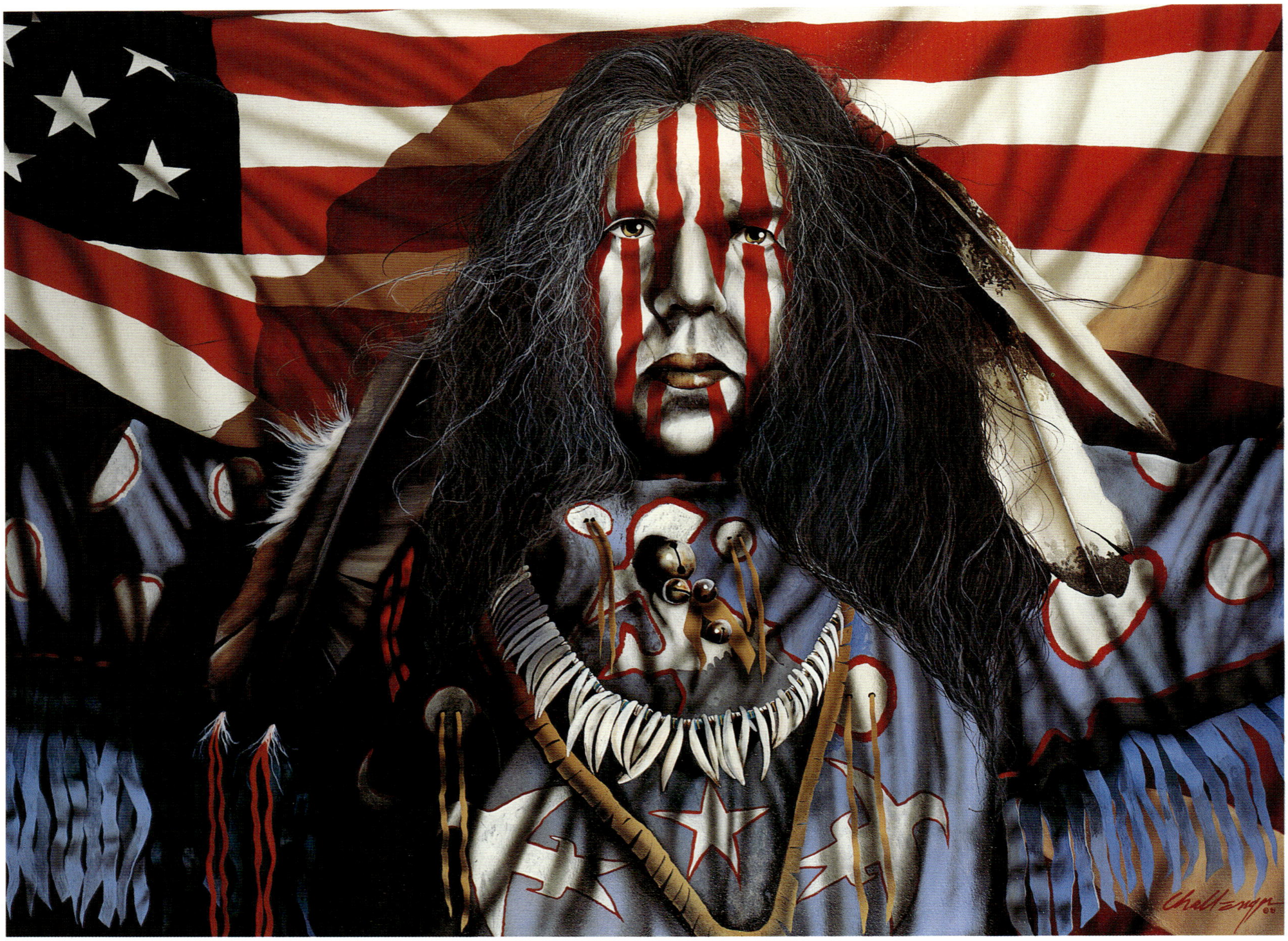

In the Potawatomi opening I rode a beautiful black pony. I had a rope for a saddle, as something to hold on to, as I was not a good rider. We made the run from the banks of the river not far from Shawnee. The river was full of horses and was about two feet deep. There must have been a hundred thousand at the opening. I began to feel a little uneasy before the shot was fired signaling to go, as the crowd back of us kept crowding, and this made it dangerous so that we were easily apt to get hurt, as many were injured in the runs by others running into them, or other mishaps.

After the run, there was not a drop of water left in the river. It had all been thrown out of the stream by horses running across it.

I also made a run in the Tecumseh opening; there was about as large a crowd there as the Potawatomi opening. U.S. Marshal Smith was killed in the opening. He had a fine saddle horse and was a good rider, but his horse fell on

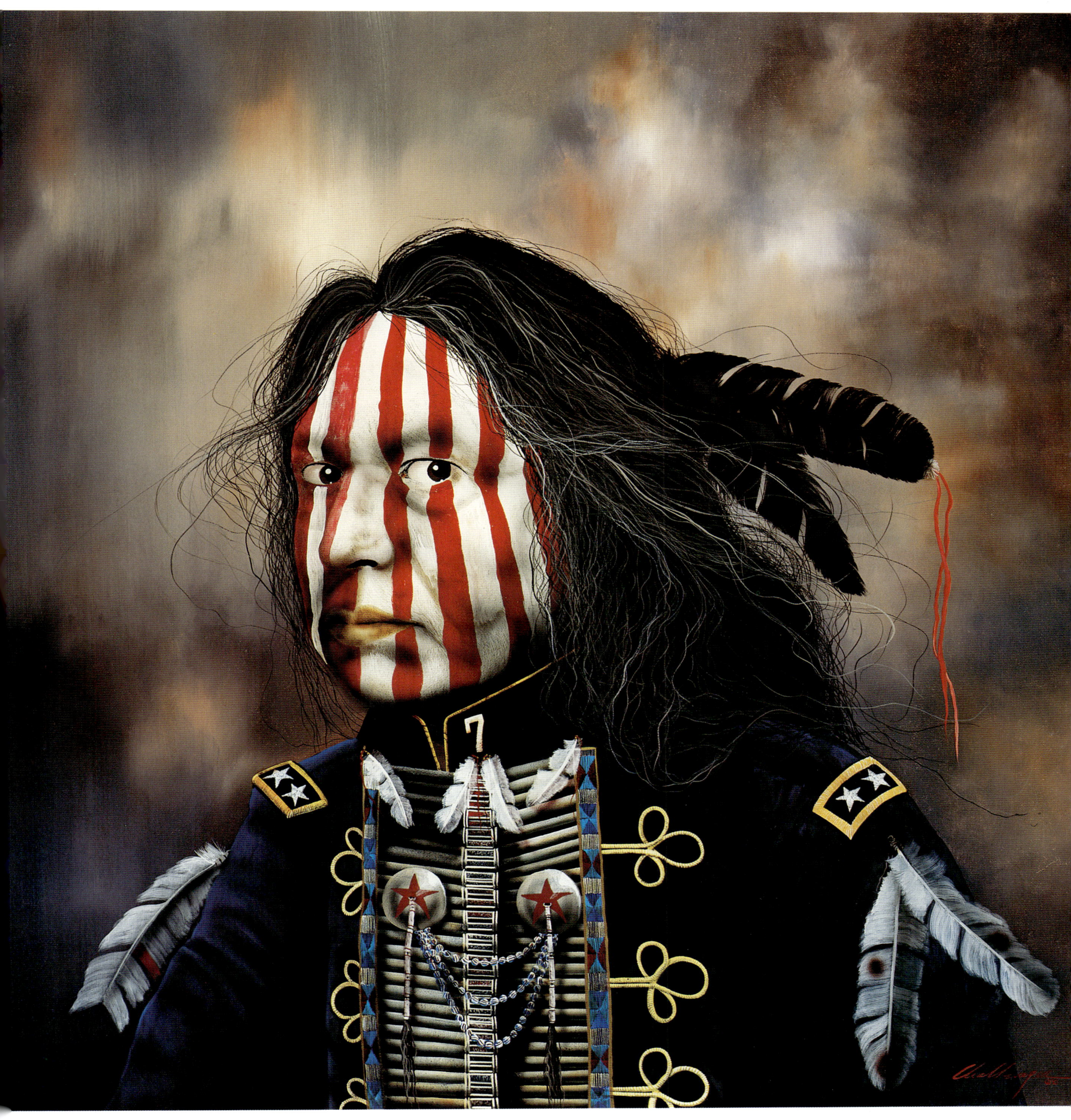

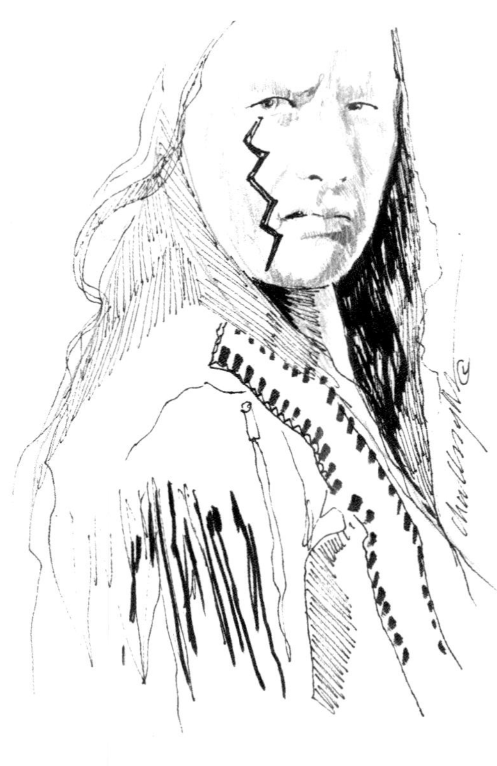

top of him. The horse's feet were up in the air and he was pinned underneath. As I was back of Marshal Smith, pushed by the crowd, my horse in the excitement jumped over his horse. He was struck in the face and was killed.

The narrative of western expansion—innocent pioneers and their loved ones driving covered wagons packed with all their worldly possessions, passing through vast prairie lands and rugged terrain, then suffering the attacks and brutality of an evil Native population—has been embraced as truth for over one hundred years. It is a simplified image of expansionism and one that vanishes in the darkness of the California gold rush—a period that best illustrates the collapse of Native American populations during the nineteenth century.

An estimated one hundred fifty thousand Native Americans peaceably occupied the westernmost territory of the country until gold was discovered glittering within the waters of California's American River. News of the find reached north to Canada, across the Atlantic to Europe, and deep into South America, bringing thousands of gold seekers. The mad stampede for precious metals and the attendant mining processes devastated the natural resources, driving off and killing game and turning salmon-rich rivers into sludge troughs. In order to create a cheap work force to support mining efforts, California law declared that any unemployed Native American could be prosecuted as a vagrant. The punishment for this vagrancy was little more than legalized slavery. An auction was held and the "vagrant's" labor, up to four months' worth, was sold to the highest bidder. Children were not exempt. The court system provided no recourse as California law stated that Indians, blacks, and mulattos were not allowed to testify for or against a white person.

The elimination of California natives, by both disease and murder, continued indiscriminately and with impunity throughout the mid–1800s. Native women were targeted for assault, and men who attempted to come to their aid were killed. Bounties were paid for Native American scalps and severed heads. By the late 1800s, an estimated one hundred twenty thousand Native Americans had been slaughtered in California. It was the worst devastation of a Native population in the history of the United States. But it would not be the end of the violence.

The conditions on many of the reservations by the 1880s were formidable. Unable to hunt for food, many tribes depended on government rations, which consisted of army hardtack, sugar, and bacon. Pay allotments, programs that turned self-sufficient communities into "domestic dependent nations," disrupted the natural evolution of Native American culture. Most tribes had traditionally lived communally and shared ownership of the land. The injection of land tenure, free enterprise, and unreasonable agriculture practices changed the fundamental balance of the Native American way of life. Many reservations were reduced to the worst sectors of a territory where dry land farming and controlled grazing were impossible.

Reservation proximity to encroaching settlements and the large numbers of participants in reservation ceremonies, particularly the Ghost dance, created tremendous unease among settlers and emigrants despite the peaceful intentions of the dances. Settler M. B. Louthan remembers that "the Comanches, who were blanket Indians out west of us, staged a big Ghost dance which made us more or less nervous…Notwithstanding that conditions relative to the Indians had greatly changed, we new comers had heard many superstitions and legends about their ceremonial dances and we couldn't keep from being afraid when we knew they were staging one."

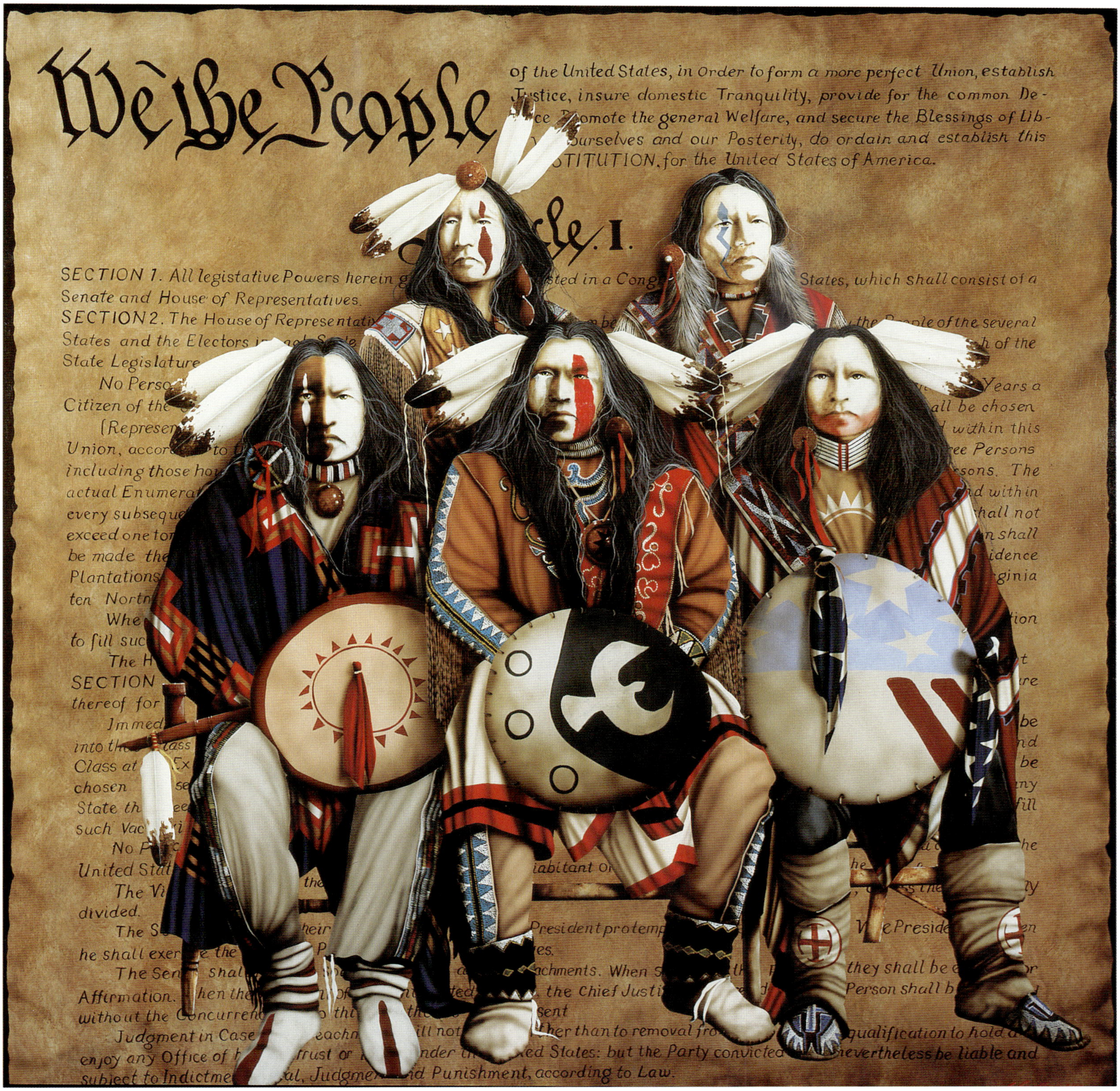

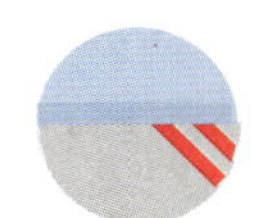

WE THE PEOPLE

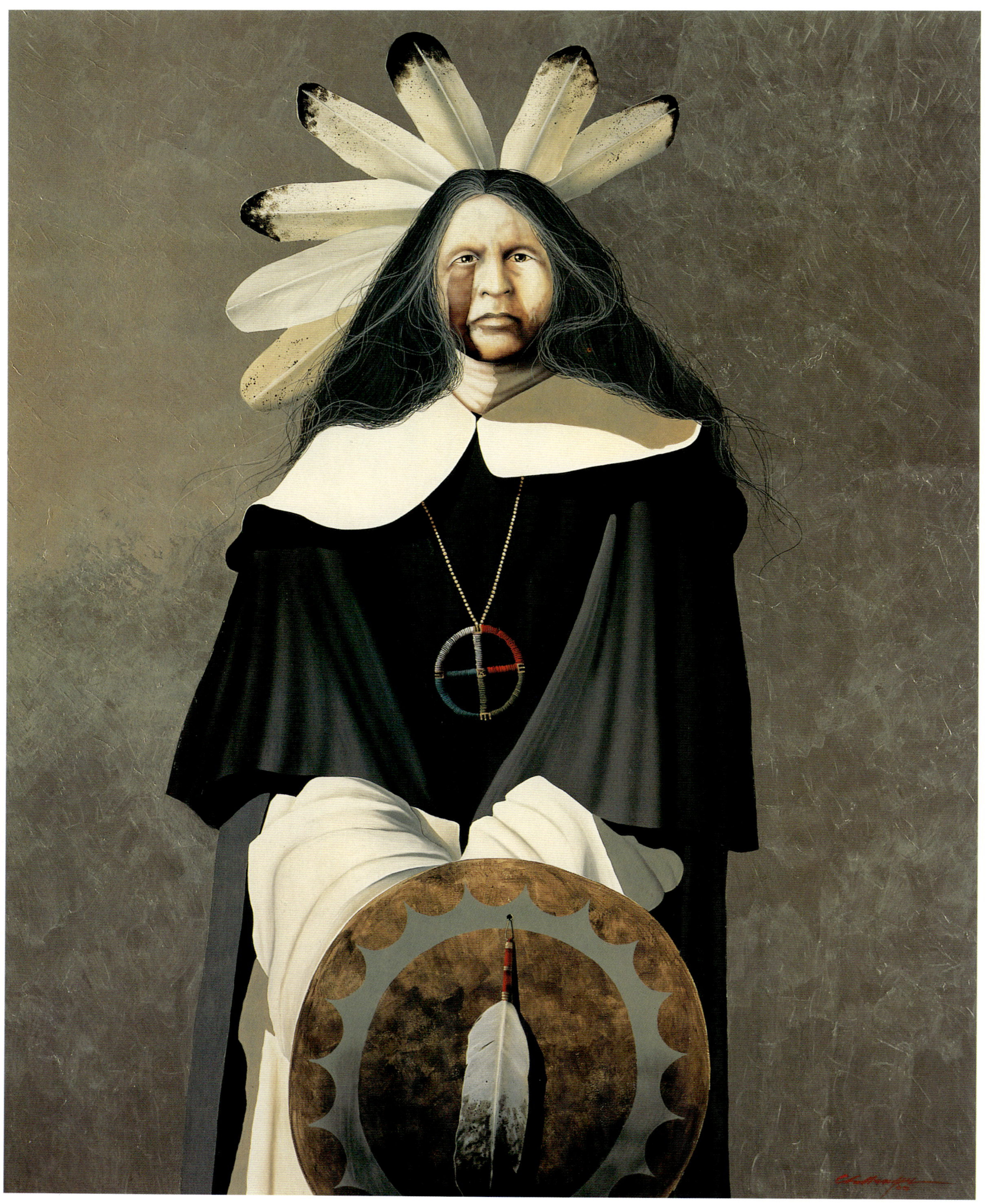

The rampant disparity between the true meaning of Native American practices and their gross misinterpretation only made matters worse. "Other disturbances among Indians," recalls pioneer E. E. Blake,

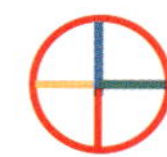

were when some agitators got among the Sioux, Cheyenne and Arapahoes. They began holding their Messiah dances. It was a legend that the country would be covered with a wave of mud. This was in 1888 or 1889. They began to gather up around Calumet, Oklahoma, where they held their dances, and where they danced from twenty-four to thirty-six hours at a time; or until they were worn out, or until they fell by fainting. Others would keep on dancing and paid no attention to those lying on the ground. They danced in a circle to the right clock wise, very compact, with a space in the center of the circle, where drum beaters and pedal beaters sat. Some among the crowd chanted songs, while some of the more agile of the group danced by themselves in single file within the circle, holding one arm high into the air, which they continued so long as they danced. Those who fainted and fell to the ground usually died, and they believed the Great Spirit had taken them.

While others, who fell from exhaustion and who finally came to, claimed they had seen the Great Spirit and they conceived the idea that they should wipe out the lives of all the white people. Additional troops were brought into Fort Reno around this time. Oklahoma City people became very much alarmed over the situation. Usually they were on guard near Lake Overholser awaiting the Indians when they arrived to make their attack. Soldiers and citizens at El Reno were on guard out west of El Reno to prevent any hostilities.

Citizens' militia groups, inflamed by sensational newspaper accounts of the Ghost dance, volunteered to provide protection from the "impending" Indian revolt. The Sioux, one of the most fervent proponents of the dance, were particularly targeted. A loosely organized militia of Minnesota citizens contacted the Secretary of the Interior with an offer to eliminate the "threat" in exchange for ammunition, horses, a bounty of three hundred dollars, a fifty-dollar-per-month salary, and food.

"The troubles in the Sioux country now began to attract public attention," explains Mooney, "and there was suggestion of military interference. The newspaper liar has reached an abnormal development in Oklahoma, and dispatches from Guthrie, El Reno, and Oklahoma City were filled with vivid accounts of war dances, scalping parties, and imminent outbreaks, mingled with frantic appeals for troops."

Journalistic integrity was an alien concept in the 1880s. Newspapers, capitalizing on their readers' apprehensions, created sensational stories about the Ghost dance and consequently sold more newspapers. The more fearful the public, the more likely it was to purchase the "news" on a daily basis to update the degree of its safety. "In proportion as Wovoka and his doctrines have become subjects of widespread curiosity," laments Mooney,

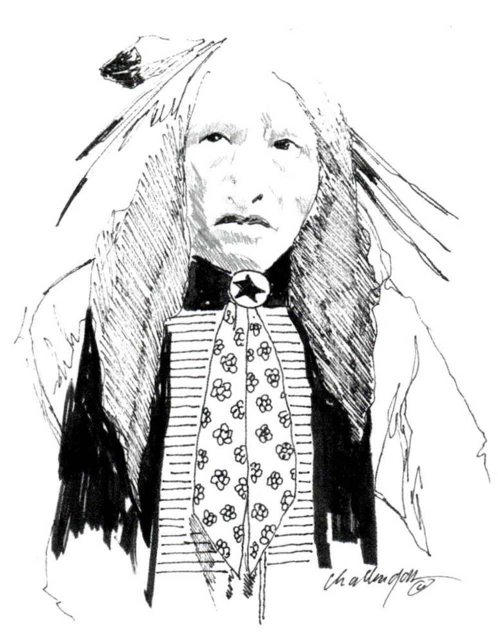

so have they become subjects of ignorant misrepresentation and deliberate falsification. Different writers have made him a Paiute, a half-blood, and a Mormon white man. Numberless stories have been told of the origin and

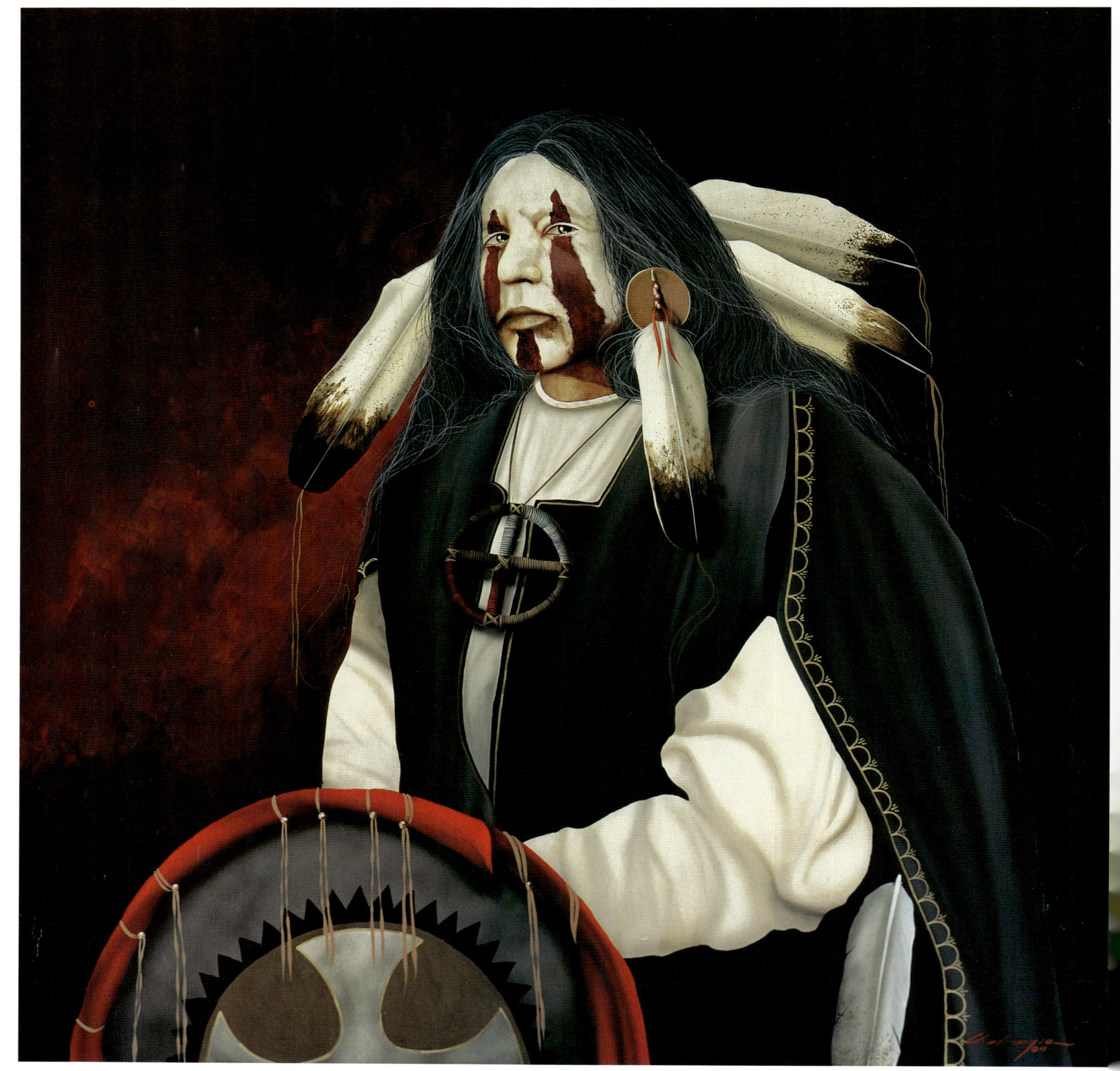

COLUMBUS DAY

character of his mission and the day predicted for its final accomplishment.
The most mischievous and persistent of these stories has been that which
represents him as preaching a bloody campaign against the whites, whereas his
doctrine is one of peace…He has been denounced as an impostor, ridiculed as
a lunatic, and laughed at as a pretended Christ, while by the Indians he is
revered as a direct messenger from the Other World…Notwithstanding all that
had been said and written by newspaper correspondents…not one of them had
undertaken to find the man himself and to learn from his own lips what he
really taught. It is almost equally certain that none of them had even seen a
Ghost dance at close quarters—certainly none of them understood its meaning.

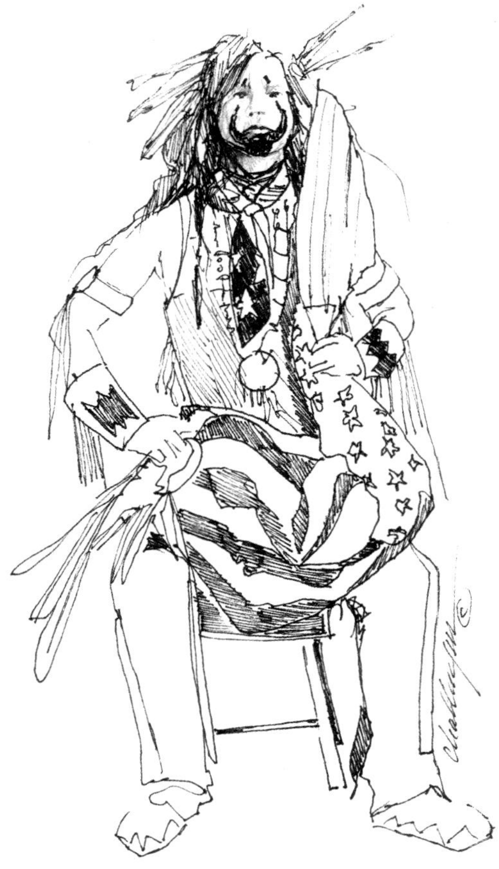

In addition to the negative media campaign, the Ghost dancers had to contend with
civil disturbances from emigrant settlements expanding all around them. "I also attended
the Pi Cody Indian dances," settler Guy Cox recalls. "Several of my boy friends and I went
to Pi Cody's dance one night. They were dancing in the open. The Indians were friendly
to us. There was a white man who was drunk there at the dance. The Indians were doing a
Ghost dance, so this white man got a sheet around his head and joined in the dance, dancing in a circle, until finally, the Indians discovered him there and they gave him a kick and
put him out of the circle."

The increasing contact with Native American communities engaged in the Ghost
dance amplified settler apprehension and finally caught the attention of the U.S. government. Unsure of what to make of the dance and how to quell participation in it, officials
began intervention tactics designed to disrupt the ceremonies without provoking a violent
response. But Ghost dancers remained defiant, ignoring the government interference and
drawing together in even greater numbers to perform the ceremonies.

The Sioux Ghost dance, subjected to media exposure, drew the strongest government
ire for the way it seemed to attract and sway the nation's attention. This attention validat-
ed settler apprehensions and provided the government with a focal point for action. By
reacting specifically to the Sioux Ghost dance "threat," the government could pinpoint its
response to a prevailing national issue dominant in the minds of voters. Officials, unable
to comprehend the meaning of the dance and unwilling to accept diversity in religious
beliefs, selected to aggressively oppose the Sioux Ghost dance, making it their final—and
fatal—stand against Native American religious freedom.

It would be a decision with tragic consequences, shadowing Native American and
U.S. relations for the next one hundred years.

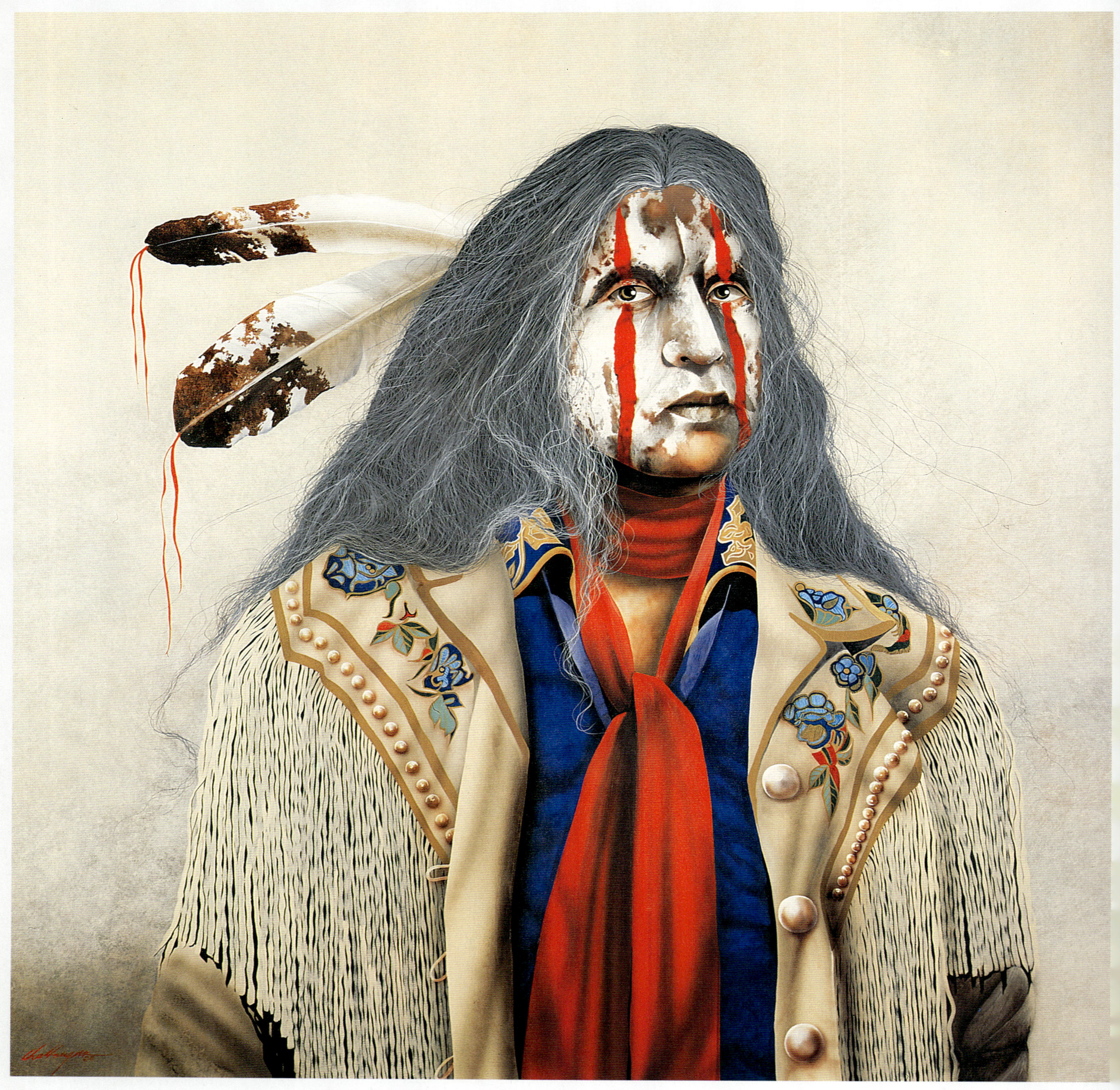

CHAPTER 5

NECKLACE PEOPLE IN THE CRIMSONING SNOW

THE SIOUX AND THE END OF THE DANCE

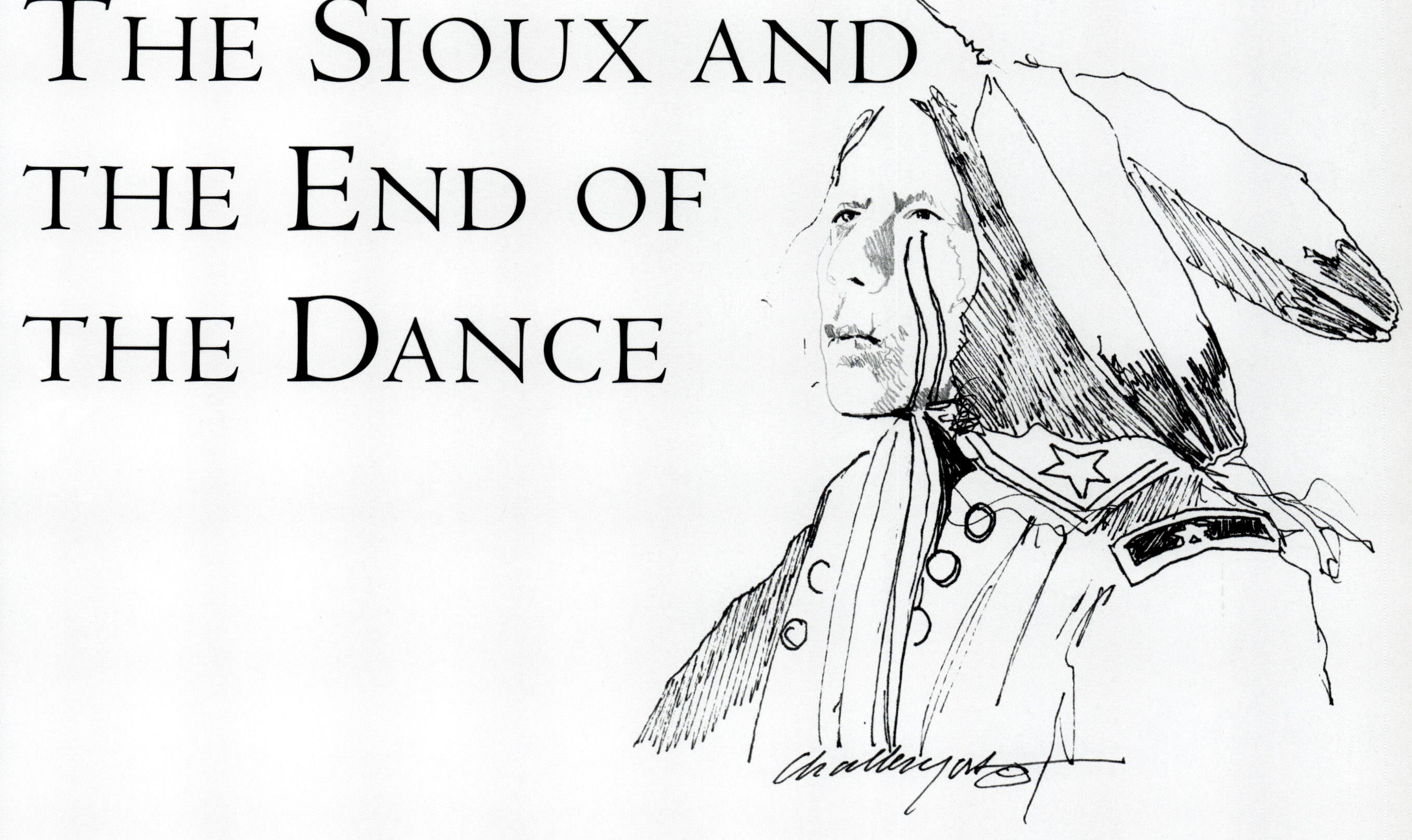

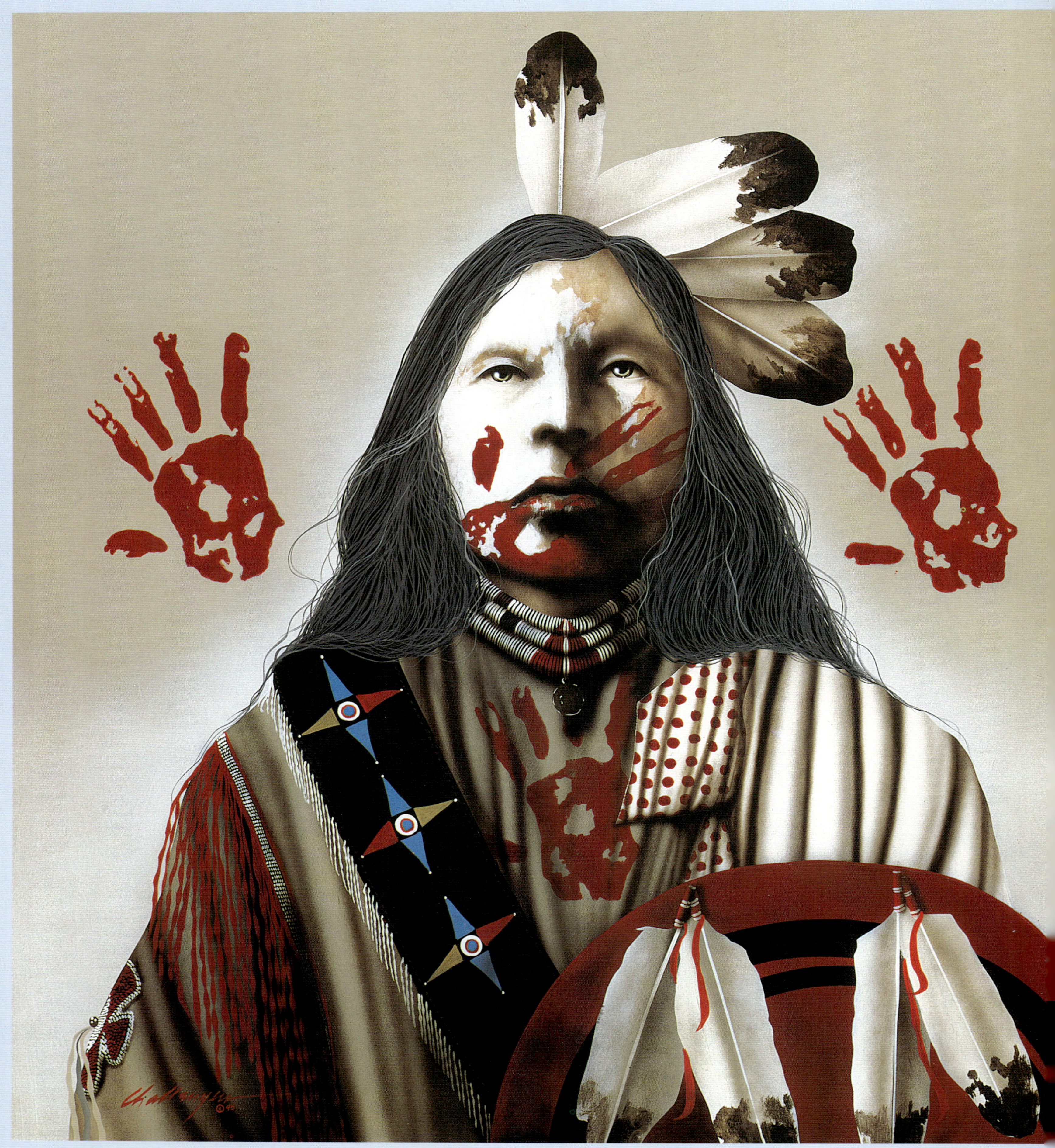

My son, let me grasp your hand,
My son, let me grasp your hand,
Says the father,
Says the father.
You shall live,
You shall live,
Says the father,
Says the father.
I bring you a pipe,
I bring you a pipe,
Says the father,
Says the father.
By means of it you shall live,
By means of it you shall live,
Says the father,
Says the father.

The Sioux tribe of the 1800s consisted of seven great divisions or villages and together formed the largest tribe in the United States. They call themselves *Oceti Sakowin*— seven council fires—in honor of these divisions. The Kiowa call them "the necklace people," an elegant allusion to the Cheyenne, Arapaho, Shoshoni, Comanche, and Caddo names for the Sioux, "the throat cutters."

"The Sioux village names translate as the leaf shooters, the leaf village, swamp village, end village, upper end village, village of the Spirit lake, and prairie village," explains Challenger. "This last, the prairie village or Teton, accounts for over two-thirds of the entire Sioux tribe and is subdivided into seven additional villages. The Hunkpapa or 'those who camp at the opening of the camping circle,' the Brules or 'burnt thighs,' the Minikanzu or 'those who plant by the water,' the Sans Arcs or those 'without bows,' the Sihasapa or 'black feet,' the Ohenonpa or 'two kettles,' and the Ogalala as in 'to scatter dust in the face.'"

Throughout the nineteenth century, the Sioux would remain the most prominent and powerful tribe in the country, exceeding twenty-five thousand members, despite the wars, reduced food supplies, and forced relocation they would ultimately face. Their history illustrates that once they took possession of the horse, the vast expanse of prairie lands became their world. The Sioux lived and hunted freely from the Rocky Mountains east to Minnesota, north to the Yellowstone River in North Dakota and south to the Platte in Nebraska. Seemingly endless resources of buffalo, horses, and range land elevated the Sioux to the wealthiest and proudest tribe found on the plains.

"In 1815," Challenger recalls, "the United States began to bring the Sioux tribe under

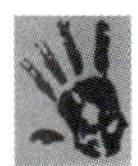

89

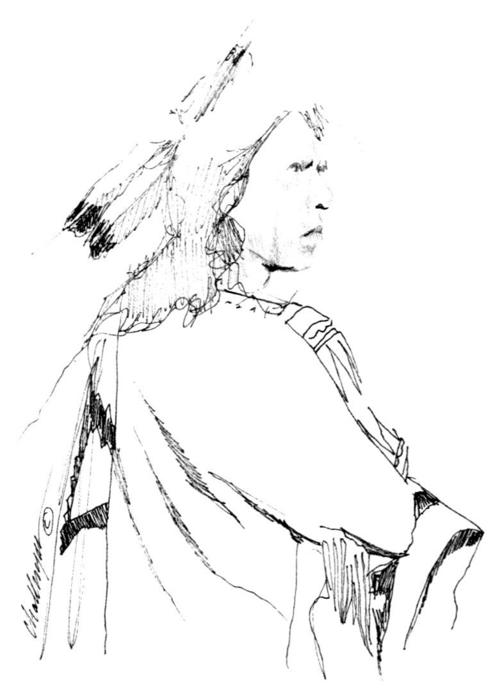

government jurisdiction. This program and its negotiation tactics repeatedly reduced Sioux land to significantly smaller and smaller parcels. By 1865, the reservation included only the state of South Dakota west of the Missouri River. Agencies were set up to administer a 'welfare' system to this nation of newly dependent people. Food and currency rations, livestock, doctors, teachers, and additional necessities were promised in exchange for this land deal. Railroads were surveyed and military posts were established in and around this new territory. The Sioux were also permitted to continue hunting the buffalo across the animal's range and beyond the perimeters of the new reservation as long as buffalo existed."

Unfortunately for the Sioux, the agreement was not honored. The railroads carried with them a continuous stream of emigrants who proceeded to wipe out the buffalo population. "It is hard to overestimate the magnitude of the calamity, as they viewed it," Commissioner Morgan of Indian Affairs testified in the late 1800s, "which happened to these people by the sudden disappearance of the buffalo and the large diminution in the numbers of deer and other wild animals. Suddenly, almost without warning, they were expected at once and without previous training to settle down to the pursuits of agriculture in a land largely unfitted for such use."

Then gold was discovered in the reservation's Black Hills, and prospectors filled the countryside, ignoring treaty rights. The Sioux, refuting the invasion, met and championed the offenses of Custer. Despite the general's defeat, the Sioux lost an additional third of their land including the gold rich hills. A short six years later, additional demands were made on Sioux land that tribal leaders stringently opposed. "All complained," recalled Bishop W. H. Hare, missionary among the Sioux at the time, "that many of the engagements solemnly made with them in former years when they had surrendered valued rights had been broken, and here they were right. They suspected that present promises of pay for their lands would prove only old ones in a new shape (when milk cows were promised, cows having been promised in previous agreements, the Indians exclaimed, 'There's that same old cow'), and demanded that no further surrender should be expected until former promises had been fulfilled."

But Congress prevailed, and in 1889, the Sioux saw almost eleven million acres, half the reservation, slip through their grasp. Their remaining land was divided into five smaller and separate territories. Here, in a country of little soil, a short growing season and dry climate, they were expected to raise crops, graze cattle, and accept rations. As 1890 approached, the Sioux saw their cattle succumb to disease and crops wither from the worst drought in many years. Bishop Hare remembers that "the Indian crops were a total failure. There is ample evidence that, during this period, the rations issued lasted, even when carefully used, for only two-thirds the time for which they were intended."

It was no surprise that the Sioux were running out of food. Congress has reduced their rations. "The fact that they had not received sufficient food is admitted by the agents and the officers of the government who have had opportunities of knowing," General N. A. Miles revealed in his 1891 *Report of the Secretary of War.* "The majority of the Sioux were under the charge of civil agents, frequently changed and often inexperienced...They claimed that the government had not fulfilled its treaties and had failed to make large enough appropriations for their support; that they had suffered for want of food, and the evidence of this is beyond question and sufficient to satisfy any unprejudiced intelligent mind."

Treaty terms were once again ignored. "While the Indians were urged and almost forced to sign a treaty presented to them by the commission authorized by Congress, in which they gave up a valuable portion of their reservation which is now occupied by white people," General Miles wrote to Senator Dawes in Washington, "the government has failed to fulfill its part of the compact, and instead of an increase or even a reasonable supply for their support, they have been compelled to live on half and two-thirds rations, and received nothing for the surrender of their lands, neither has the government given any positive assurance that they intend to do any differently with them in the future."

Disease began to diminish the population. "The measles prevailed with great virulence in 1889, the grippe in 1890," recalls Bishop Hare. "Whooping cough also attacked the children. The sick died from want…The people said their children were all dying from diseases brought by the whites, their race was perishing from the face of the earth…"

A Native American delegation from the Sioux territories traveled west in the fall of 1889 to learn about the Ghost dance. Upon their return that spring, the delegates informed their people of the doctrine and the new world it promised to bring. The message spread through the community and generated tremendous enthusiasm. In response, Colonel Gallagher, agent for the Pine Ridge Sioux reservation, had three members of the delegation arrested, placed behind bars, and questioned. They were held for several days but refused to discuss their pilgrimage. Once released, the delegates rejoined their fellow travelers and began to lead the reservations in the dance.

"The Sioux reservations each had agencies and staff assigned to maintain order and distribute rations," explains Challenger. "The Pine Ridge, the Rosebud, the Standing Rock, and the Cheyenne River agents were concerned about the dancing, but all stated to their superiors that they believed the Sioux had no intentions of promoting anything but the peaceful Ghost dance ceremony. The agent McLaughlin at the Standing Rock agency appeared to have a good relationship with the Sioux. He was adamant in his statements regarding the Sioux's intentions. He insisted that in no way were the Ghost dancers hostile nor were they planning any hostile acts. He felt that if the U.S. government would just treat them fairly, there would no longer be a need for concern on anyone's part."

Despite the apparent confidence, agency apprehension grew with the number of Sioux tribal members embracing the doctrine. In August of 1890, approximately two thousand Ghost dancers gathered on the Pine Ridge reservation, just twenty miles from the agency. Colonel Gallagher called on reservation police to approach the dancers and order them to stop dancing. The dancers ignored the orders. Gallagher gathered additional police and arrived at the ceremony in person, demanding that the dancing cease. Several dancers then raised guns to their shoulder, aimed them at the Colonel, then informed him that they were willing to die in defense of their religion. The agent backed down and the ceremony continued.

Similar police action increased across the Sioux reservations as agents attempted to arrest Ghost dance leaders in the hopes of extinguishing the movement's flame. The Pine Ridge agent resigned, and his replacement, Agent Royer, was quickly ordained "Young-man-afraid-of-Indians" by the Sioux. By all accounts, Royer was an incompetent racked with fear. After encountering the Ghost dancers, Royer requested military intervention, insisting that over half his reservation residents were dancing and out of his control. This initial report went unnoticed. He continued to send exaggerated reports accompanied by frantic pleas for military assistance. His alarm was finally noted by the War Department, which instructed him to send an overview of conditions to Fort Robinson, Nebraska, the closest military post. In Royer's telegraph to the fort's commanding officer, he stated that "the Indians were wild and crazy" and a minimum of one thousand soldiers would be necessary to bring them under control.

By November of 1890, almost three thousands troops were deployed throughout the Sioux reservations. The presence of the military force threw many of the residents into a panic, and a mass exodus began. Many people left the reservations and headed for the Bad Lands and the *Oonagazhee*—the sheltering place. This sanctuary consisted of a plateau of several square miles thrust above the surrounding countryside. The stronghold held two springs of water and spread flat and level to the edges, then dropped hundreds of feet to the land below.

Meanwhile, agents for the Sioux reservations had been instructed by the Indian Office to submit lists of Sioux leaders who should be arrested and separated from the tribe. The use of the military for this purpose was available if the Indian Office felt it necessary. The name of Sitting Bull, a prominent member of the Teton Sioux, was at the top of the blacklist. Upon his arrest, Sitting Bull was shot and killed as he called for his people to protect him. The skirmish lasted only several minutes but resulted in fourteen deaths.

Big Foot, leader of a band of people camped along the Cheyenne River, was apprehended next and then released. Instructed to lead his band of people to the Cheyenne River agency, he reluctantly agreed. Then, at the first available opportunity, he and his people ignored the orders and began moving towards the *Oonagazhee.*

When Big Foot and his people arrived, they found the plateau abandoned. The day before, with military forces pressing the plateau, the members of the stronghold had surrendered, then descended from their sanctuary and began to make their way toward the Pine Ridge agency. When the Seventh Cavalry caught up with Big Foot's slow-moving caravan, Big Foot rode toward the cavalry's commander, Major Whiteside, carrying a white flag. The Sioux leader requested a conference, determined to negotiate a surrender beneficial to his people, but was denied and his unconditional surrender demanded. Not wanting to risk his people's lives against the heavily armed cavalry, Big Foot submitted. With Big Foot's band under military control, the Seventh began to police the approximately three hundred and seventy Sioux toward the Pine Ridge agency. Within just twenty miles of their destination, they were ordered to stop and set up camp along Wounded Knee Creek.

How shall I begin my songs
In the blue night that is settling?

In the great night my heart will go out,
Toward me the darkness comes rattling.
In the great night my heart will go out.

Grassy hummocks lull and crest across Wounded Knee, a pleasant valley made delicate by the meandering creek of its namesake. But on the morning of December 29, 1890, the peaceful valley was transformed into an armed detainment camp by the Seventh Cavalry. In addition to the infantry stationed around the small Sioux encampment, four

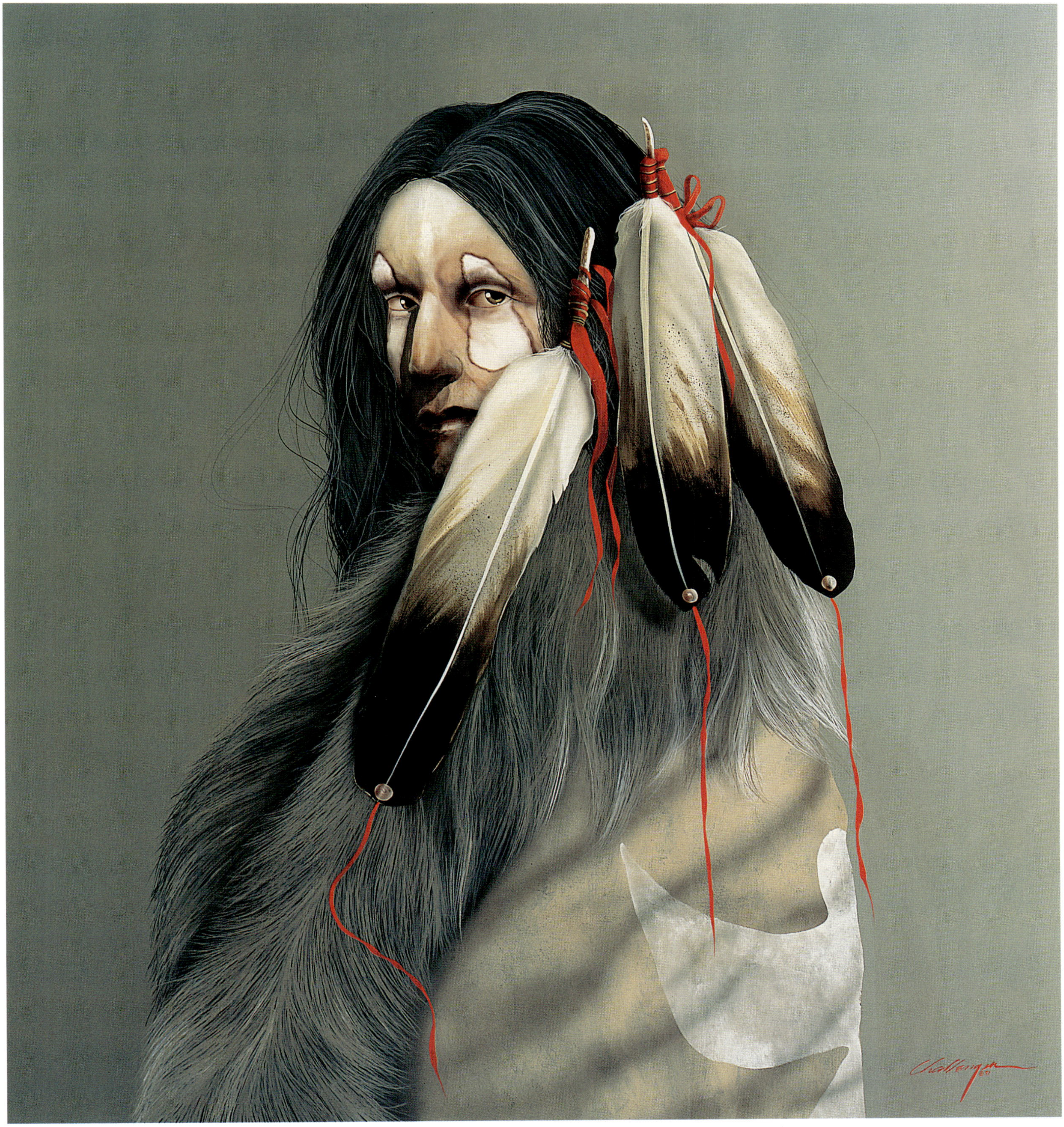

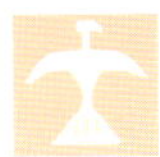

NO MORE PROMISES

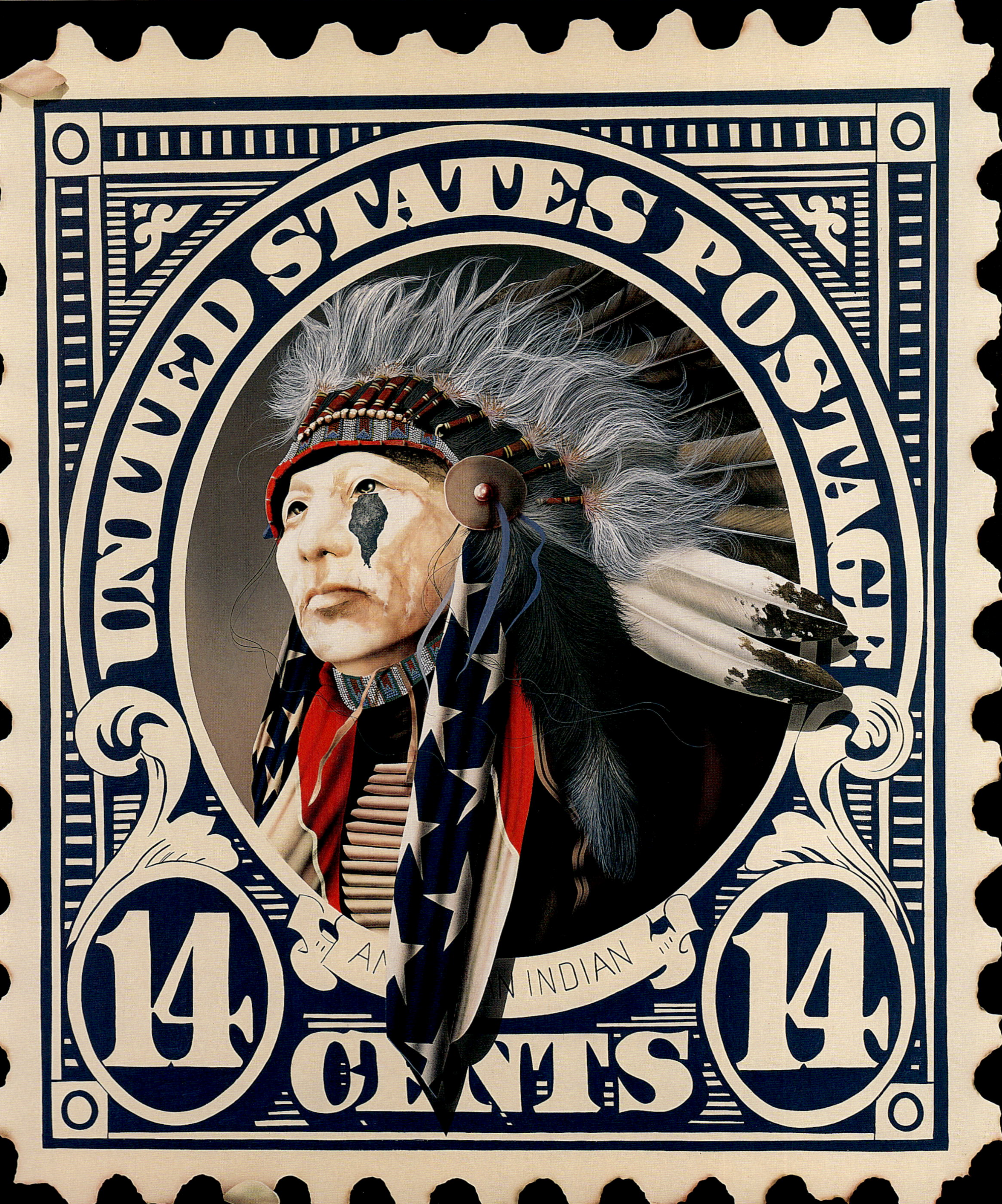

UNITED STATES POSTAGE
14
14
AMERICAN INDIAN
CENTS

Hotchkiss guns, heavy mounted artillery, were positioned above the camp and directed into its center. The infantry's instructions were to confine Big Foot's band to the camp, assure that no one escaped, relieve all Sioux of their weapons, escort them to the Pine Ridge agency, load them onto trains, and ship them south or east until the Ghost dance movement subsided.

"In the center of the camp the Indians had hoisted a white flag as a sign of peace and a guarantee of safety," Mooney reports. "Behind them was a dry ravine running into the creek, and on a slight rise in front was posted the battery of four Hotchkiss machine guns, trained directly on the Indian camp. In front, behind, and on both flanks of the camp were posted the various troops of cavalry, a portion of two troops, together with the Indian scouts, being dismounted and drawn up in front of the Indians at the distance of only a few yards from them. Big Foot himself was ill of pneumonia in his tipi…"

Despite his illness, Big Foot called a council, and the Sioux men, approximately one third of the camp, gathered in a circle around the leader's tent. Almost all of them wore their Ghost shirts. But before the council meeting could begin, soldiers approached the circle and instructed the men to return to their own tepees and retrieve their weapons. Twenty men cooperated and returned with two guns. The military, convinced that the Sioux were hiding more weapons, ordered troops to station themselves within ten yards of the Sioux council circle while an additional detachment rummaged through the tepees, disrupting the interiors, dumping out Sioux belongings, and upsetting the women and children. This only succeeded in producing a cachet of forty old and useless rifles and elevating the tension between the soldiers and the Sioux men.

Many of the women, grouped a short distance away and distraught over the soldiers treatment, donned their own Ghost shirts and dresses. The medicine man, Yellow Bird, began to move among the men, eagle-bone whistle to his lips, reminding the Sioux of their power in the Ghost shirts. Reaching to the ground, Yellow Bird brought up a handful of dust and blew it into the air.

The passage of time has complicated the moment following Yellow Bird's simple gesture, giving history many versions. But what actually happened in that moment matters little when compared to the events it inspired. A single shot was fired, out of anger or accident, and the bullet struck down an officer. The soldiers immediately responded with heavy gunfire into the crowd of Sioux men, killing nearly half of them instantly. One of the soldiers raised his barrel to Big Foot's forehead and pulled the trigger. The surviving men attacked the soldiers and, according to Mooney, "for a few minutes there was a terrible hand to hand struggle, where every man's thought was to kill. Although many of the warriors had no guns, nearly all had revolvers and knives in their belts under their blankets, together with some of the murderous warclubs still carried by the Sioux. The very lack of guns made the fight more bloody, as it brought the combatants to closer quarters."

Within minutes, the Hotchkiss guns began to fire indiscriminately, delivering almost fifty exploding shells per minute into the camp where many women and children huddled in terror. Parents fled with their children under their arms as soldiers gave chase, shooting at them as they ran across the plain. Yellow Bird collapsed, a bullet through his head, as his four-year-old son looked on. "My father ran and fell down and the blood came out of his mouth, and then a soldier put his gun up to my white pony's nose and shot him, and then I ran and a policeman got me."

"There was a woman with an infant in her arms who was killed as she almost touched the flag of truce," eyewitness American Horse remembers,

> and the women and children of course were strewn all along the circular village until they were dispatched. Right near the flag of truce a mother was shot down with her infant; the child not knowing that its mother was dead was still nursing, and that especially was a very sad sight. The women as they were fleeing with their babes were killed together, shot right through, and the women who were very heavy with child were also killed. All the Indians fled in these three directions, and after most of all of them had been killed a cry was made that all those who were not killed or wounded should come forth and they would be safe. Little boys who were not wounded came out of their places of refuge, and as soon as they came in sight a number of soldiers surrounded them and butchered them there.

"In a few minutes," Mooney laments, "two hundred Indian men, women, and children, with sixty soldiers, were lying dead and wounded on the ground, the tipis had been torn down by the shells and some of them were burning above the helpless wounded, and the surviving handful of Indians were flying in wild panic to the shelter of the ravine, pursued by hundreds of maddened soldiers and followed up by a raking fire from the Hotchkiss guns, which had been moved into position to sweep the ravine." Very few escaped as they tried to run on foot, unable to reach their ponies and ride away, cut down by the heavy artillery and soldiers on horseback. "All the men who were in a bunch were killed right there," recalls American Horse, "and those who escaped that first fire got into the ravine, and as they went along up the ravine for a long distance they were pursued on both sides by the soldiers and shot down, as the dead bodies showed afterwards. The women were standing off at a different place from where the men were stationed, and when the firing began, those of the men who escaped the first onslaught went in one direction up the ravine, and then the women, who were bunched together at another place, went entirely in a different direction through an open field, and the women fared the same fate as the men who went up the deep ravine."

Many of the Native Americans who had been forced to relinquish their stronghold atop the *Oonagazhee* were camped close by at the Pine Ridge agency. When they heard the guns less than twenty miles away, a resistance force mounted up and headed to the Sioux camp. "I heard shooting off toward the east," recalls Black Elk,

> and I knew from the sound that it must be wagon-guns [cannon] going off. The sounds went right through my body, and I felt that something terrible would happen...
>
> I saddled up my buckskin and put on my sacred shirt. It was one I had made to be worn by no one but myself. It had a spotted eagle outstretched on the back of it, and the daybreak star was on the left shoulder, because when facing south that shoulder is toward the east. Across the breast, from the left shoulder to the right hip, was the flaming rainbow, and there was another rainbow around the neck, like a necklace, with a star at the bottom. At each shoulder, elbow, and wrist was an eagle feather; and over the whole shirt were red streaks of lightning...

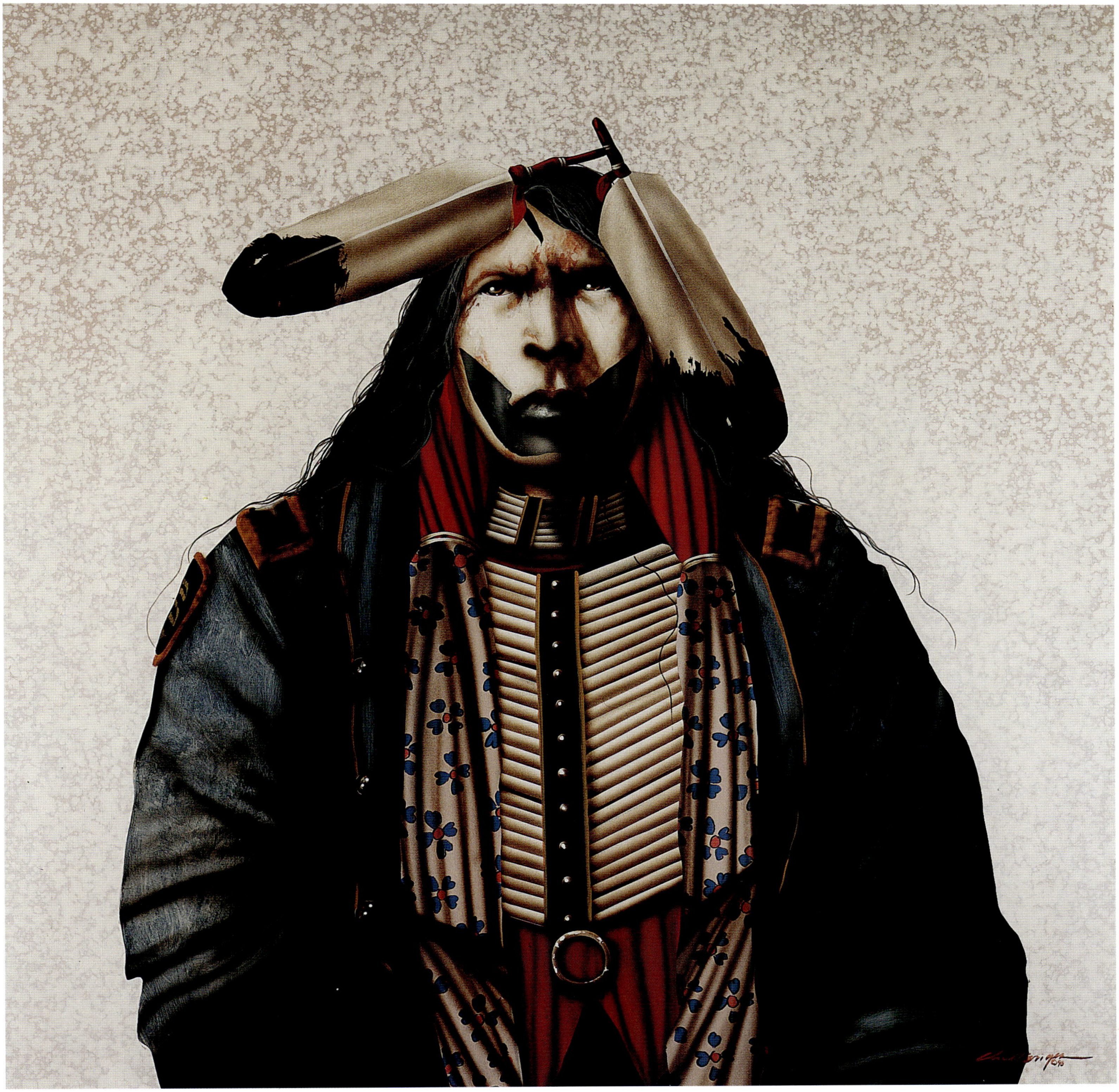

PONY SOLDIER

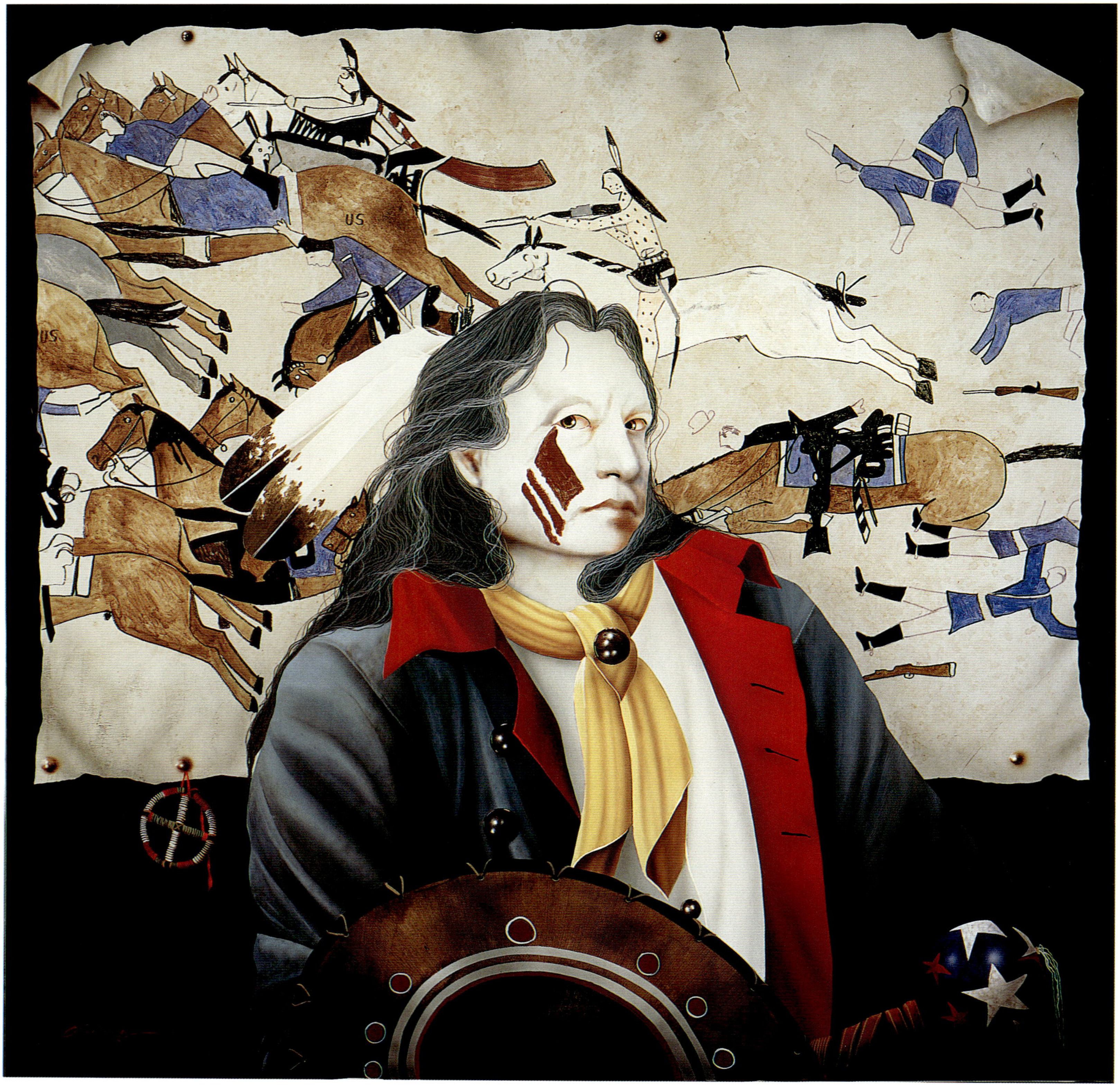

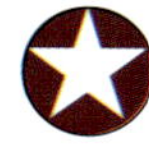

WEAR WITH HONOR

We rode fast, and there were about twenty of us now. The shooting was getting louder…We stopped on the ridge not far from the head of the dry gulch. Wagon guns were still going off over there on the little hill, and they were going off again where they hit along the gulch. There was much shooting down yonder, and there were many cries, and we could see cavalrymen scattered over the hills ahead of us. Cavalrymen were riding along the gulch and shooting into it, where the women and children were running away and trying to hide in the gullies and the stunted pines.

Black Elk and his fellow warriors came upon a group of women and children crowding together as several soldiers shouldered their guns and prepared to shoot.

Then I rode over the ridge and the others after me, and we were crying: "Take courage! It is time to fight!" The soldiers who were guarding our relatives shot at us and then ran away fast, and some more cavalrymen on the other side of the gulch did too. We got our relatives and sent them across the ridge to the northwest where they would be safe.

I had no gun, and when we were charging, I just held the sacred bow out in front of me with my right hand. The bullets did not hit us at all…

By now many other Lakotas, who had heard the shooting, were coming up from Pine Ridge, and we all charged on the soldiers. They ran eastward toward where the trouble began. We followed down along the dry gulch, and what we saw was terrible. Dead and wounded women and children and little babies were scattered all along there where they had been trying to run away. The soldiers had followed along the gulch, as they ran, and murdered them in there. Sometimes they were in heaps because they had huddled together, and some were scattered all along. Sometimes bunches of them had been killed and torn to pieces where the wagon guns hit them.

Black Elk and his men pushed the infantry back until the small but powerful band of twenty could no longer hold off the hundreds of soldiers. Once the shooting ended, the band took cover and watched the soldiers march up Wounded Knee Creek and out of sight.

It was a good winter day when all this happened. The sun was shining. But after the soldiers marched away from their dirty work, a heavy snow began to fall. The wind came up in the night. There was a big blizzard, and it grew very cold. The snow drifted deep in the crooked gulch, and it was one long grave of butchered women and children and babies, who had never done any harm and were only trying to run away.

Three days after the battle, on the first day of 1891, troops returned to Wounded Knee to bury the dead. "The bodies of the slaughtered men, women, and children were found lying about under the snow, frozen stiff and covered with blood," Mooney writes. "Almost all the dead warriors were found lying near where the fight began, about Big Foot's tipi, but the bodies of the women and children were found scattered along for two miles from the scene of the encounter, showing that they had been killed while trying to

"A long trench was dug and into it were thrown all the bodies, piled one upon another like so much cordwood, until the pit was full, when the earth was heaped over them and the funeral was complete. Many of the bodies were stripped by the whites, who went out in order to get the 'ghost shirts,' and the frozen bodies were thrown into the trench stiff and naked."

Dick Fool Bull remembers witnessing the aftermath as his family made its way into the Pine Ridge agency:

Old Unc said, "You children might as well see it; look and remember."

There were dead people all over, mostly women and children, in a ravine near a stream called Chankpe-opi Wakpala, Wounded Knee Creek. The people were frozen, lying there in all kinds of postures, their motion frozen too. The soldiers, who were stacking up bodies like firewood, did not like us passing by. They told us to leave there, double-quick or else. Old Unc said: "We'd better do what they say right now, or we'll lie there too."

So we went on toward Pine Ridge, but I had seen. I had seen a dead mother with a dead baby sucking at her breast. The little baby had on a tiny beaded cap with the design of the American flag.

"And so it was all over," remembers Black Elk.

I did not know then how much was ended. When I look back now from this high hill of my old age, I can still see the butchered women and children lying heaped and scattered all along the crooked gulch as plain as when I saw them with eyes still young. And I can see that something else died there in the bloody mud, and was buried in the blizzard. A people's dream died there. It was a beautiful dream.

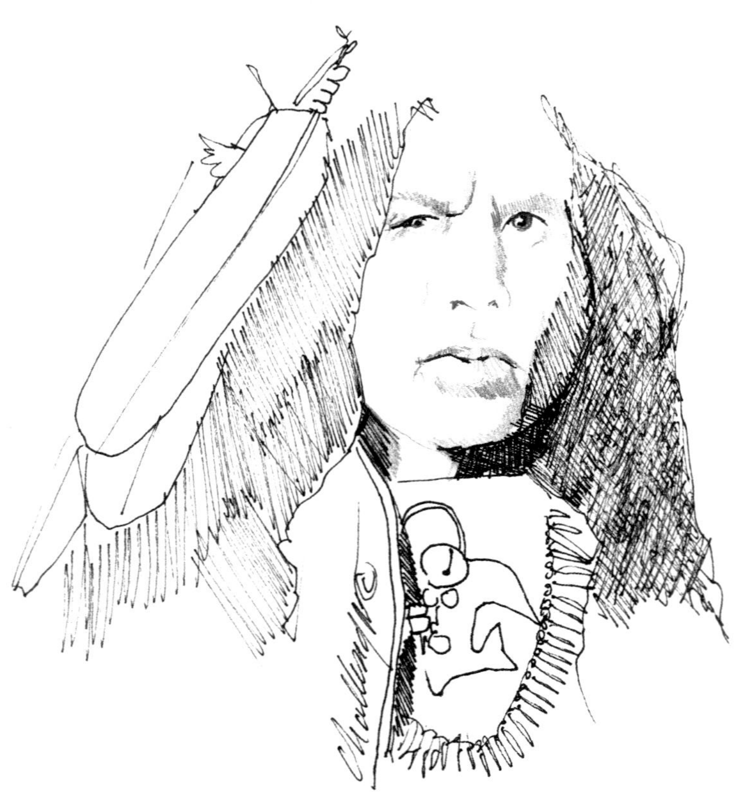

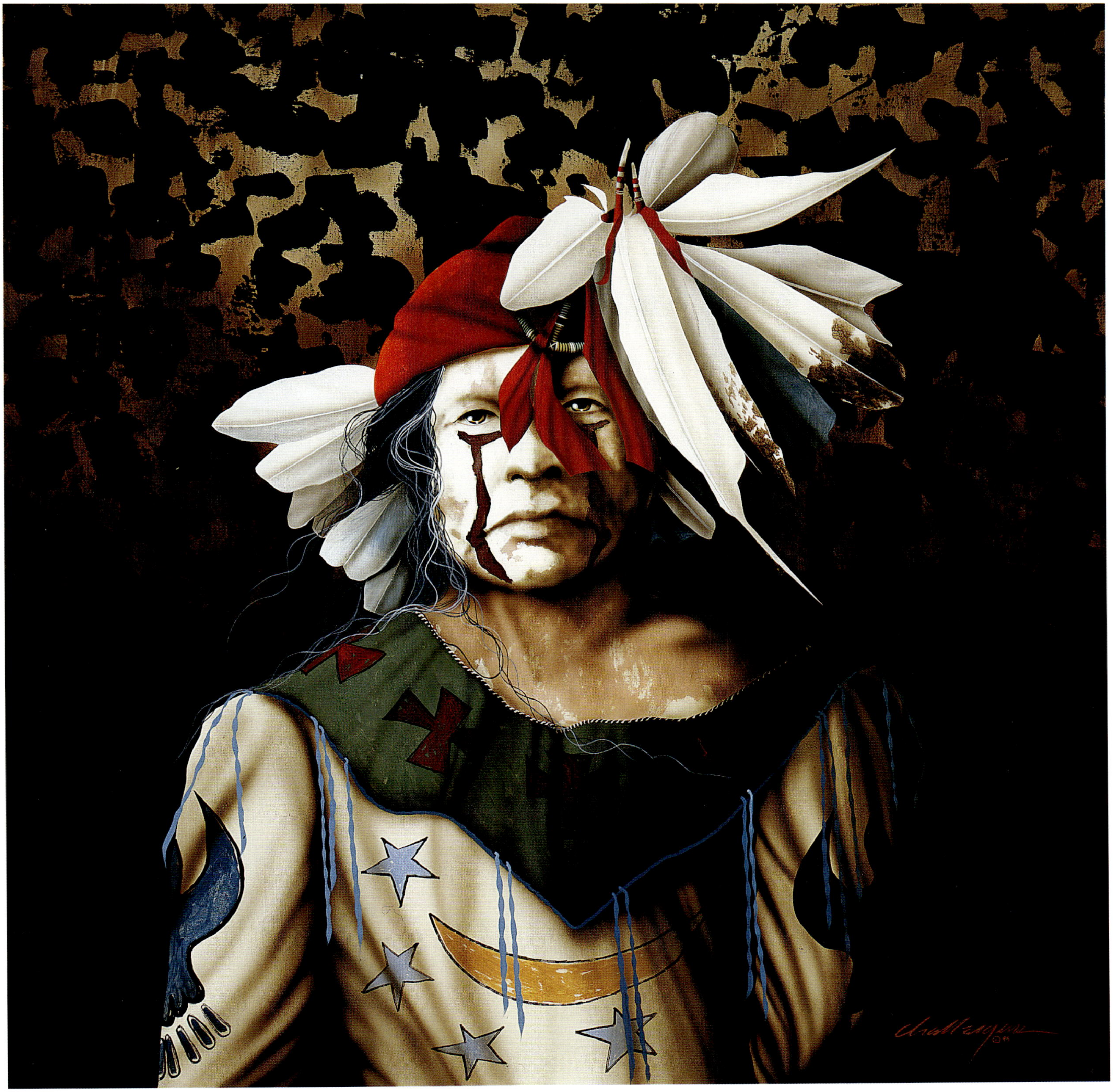

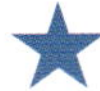

SANCTUARY

CHAPTER 6

WALKING IN A SACRED MANNER

HEROES OF THE GHOST DANCE

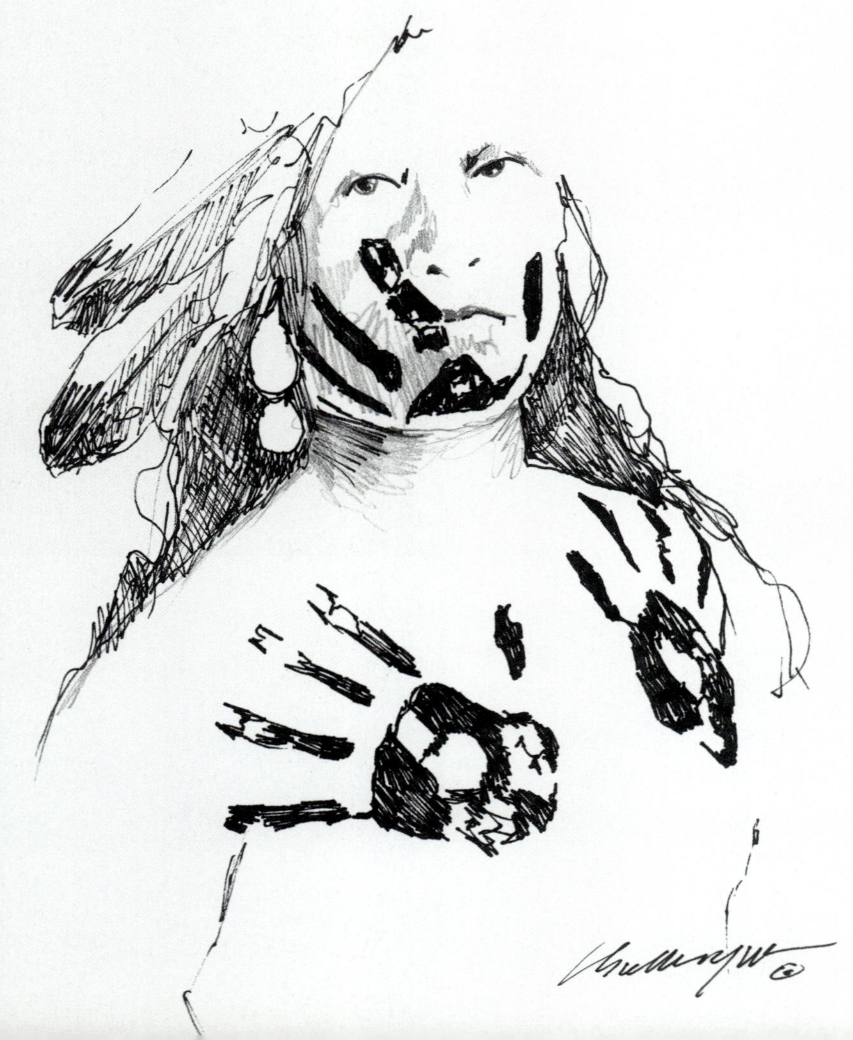

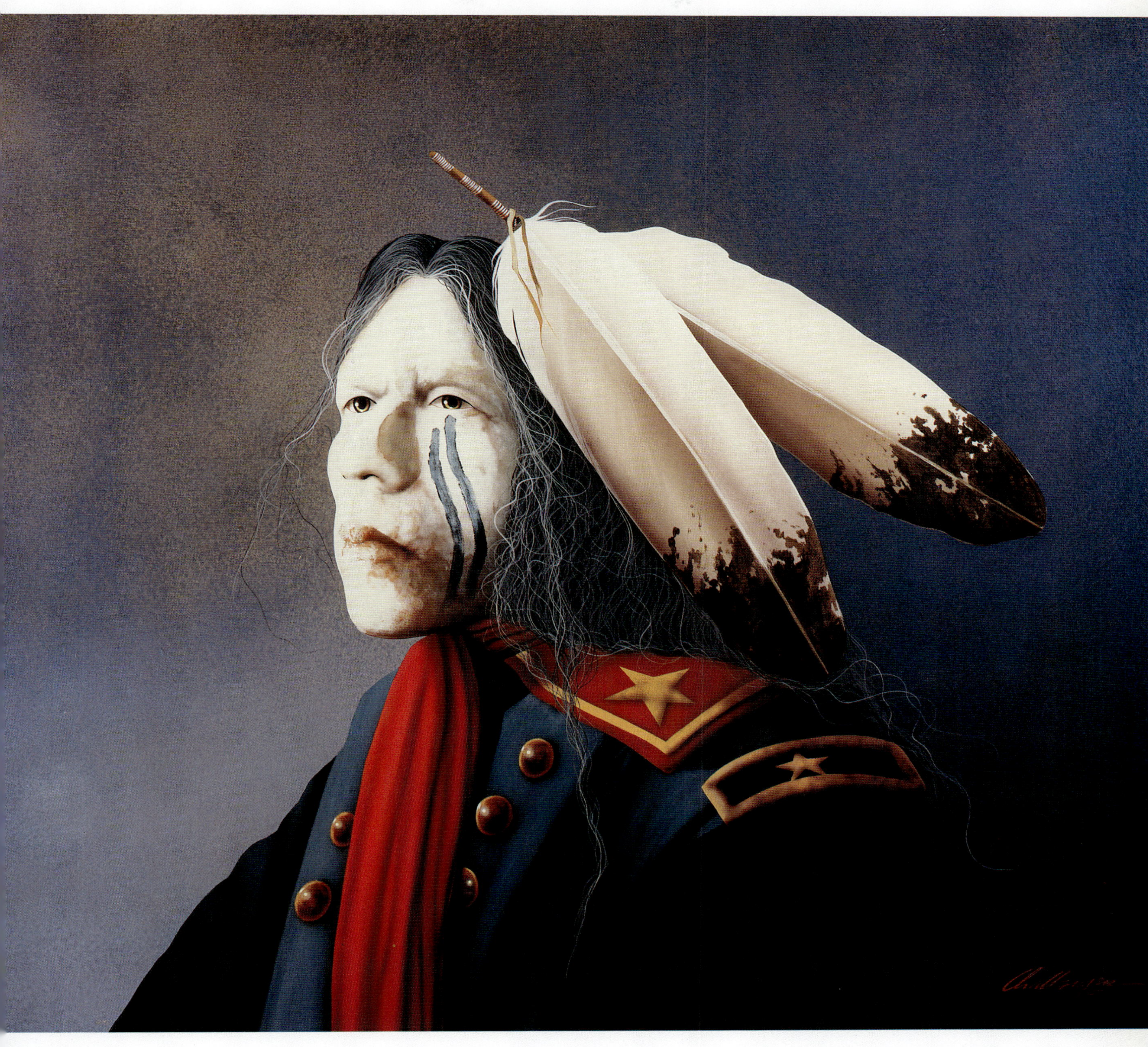

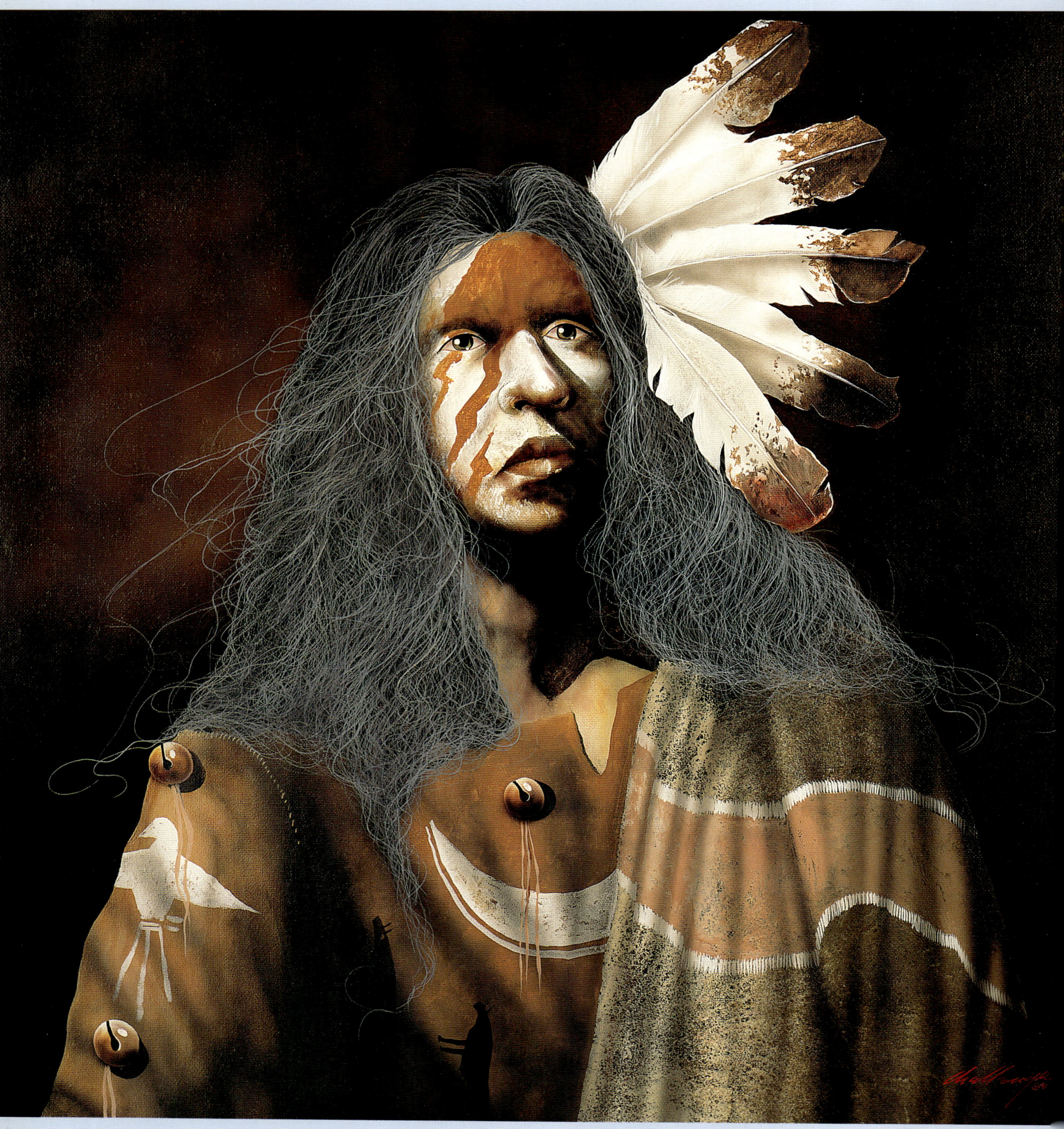

The Ghost dance history vibrates with the loss of great leaders. It is ironic that many of them died defending their religious beliefs against a government founded on free expression and liberation from tyranny. The leaders of the Ghost dance, their noble qualities and brave actions, and the admirable practitioners they led embody some of the most compelling forces to have shaped America's past.

"Many Native Americans should be given the status of heroes," insists JD Challenger, "but history has not done so. Heroes must be willing to make personal sacrifices, put their lives on the line for what they believe in, and protect their families and way of life at any cost. I don't think anything describes so many of our Native American leaders better than this."

The visionary Black Elk braved great odds during the Wounded Knee massacre, rescuing an infant from the onslaught by wrapping it in a shawl for protection. He continued to fight, then returned to the child between attacks and eventually delivered it to safety. Black Elk survived Wounded Knee despite taking a bullet across the abdomen. Injured, he tied a blanket around his waist to keep his intestines from exiting the wound. He rested for several weeks, then rode out again, engaged in skirmishes, and helped rescue the wounded. Black Elk continued to fight despite insurmountable odds until a final surrender was unavoidable.

The Sioux warrior Red Cloud, Ogalala leader of over six thousand Native Americans on the Pine Ridge reservation, was a primary force in disseminating the Ghost dance doctrine. In addition, he stringently opposed the constant pressure to cede Sioux land. Red Cloud, concerned for the diminishing rights of his people, held a council in the fall of 1889 that included the leaders Young Man Afraid, Little Wound, and American Horse. With cooperation from additional Sioux leaders, Red Cloud assembled a delegation to investigate the teachings of Wovoka. The council meeting and the delegates' journey to Mason Valley would ultimately create some of the key leaders of the Ghost dance including Kicking Bear, Short Bull, Good Thunder, Broken Arm, Flat Iron, and Yellow Breast.

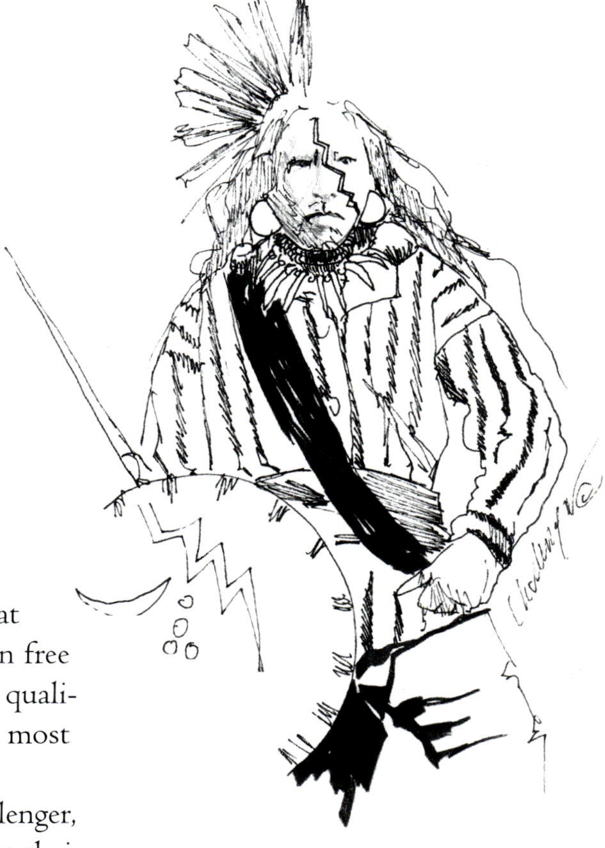

PAGE 98:
A NATIONS VOICE

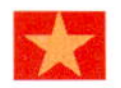

OPPOSITE:
FAST THUNDER

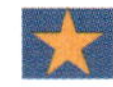

These Ghost dance leaders join a historic legion of Native Americans opposed to the European way of life and the relinquishment of tribal lands. Smohalla, the Dream prophet of the Columbia River, differentiated between his people, who were the first people made by God, and the intruders, who included the Canadian French, the American colonists he called "Boston men," the English "King George men," the priests, the African Americans, and "the Chinamen," whom God made last. "All these are new people," Smohalla believed. "Only the Indians are of the old stock. After a while, when God is ready, he will drive away all the people except those who have obeyed his laws.

"Those who cut up the lands or sign papers for lands will be defrauded of their rights and will be punished by God's anger. Moses was bad. God did not love him. He sold his people's houses and the graves of their dead. It is a bad word that comes from Washington. It is not a good law that would take my people away from me to make them sin against the laws of God."

Many Native American leaders had a clear understanding of European culture, pondering its values and questioning its paradoxes. This understanding would account for their ultimate lack of faith in what it had to offer them. But the European American understanding of Native American culture undoubtedly left much to be desired. The discrepancy involving the meaning of *Nakai'-dokli'ni*, the name of the Apache medicine healer, is a good example of the degree to which European Americans misunderstood the Native American language, religious doctrines, ceremonies, and culture. "The name of the medicine-man is written also Nakay-doklunni or Nockay Delklinee," Mooney explains, "and he was commonly called Bobbydoklinny by the whites. Dr. Washington Matthews, the best authority on the closely related dialect of the Navaho, thinks the name might mean 'spotted or freckled Mexican,' "Nakai, literally 'white alien,' being the name for Mexican in both dialects." Many European Americans believed this indicated that *Nakai'-dokli'ni* was not Native American. Not so, says Mooney. "The name would not necessarily indicate that the medicine-man was of Mexican origin, but might have been given, in accordance with the custom of some tribes, to commemorate the fact that he had killed a freckled Mexican."

Native American leaders were not afraid to speak out against efforts to change their culture and reduce their lands. Smohalla, in his address to the U.S. military officer Major MacMurray, proclaimed "You ask me to plow the ground! Shall I take a knife and tear my mother's bosom? Then when I die she will not take me to her bosom to rest.

"You ask me to dig for stone! Shall I dig under her skin for her bones? Then when I die I can not enter her body to be born again.

"You ask me to cut grass and make hay and sell it, and be rich like white men! But how dare I cut off mother's hair?

"It is a bad law, and my people can not obey it. I want my people

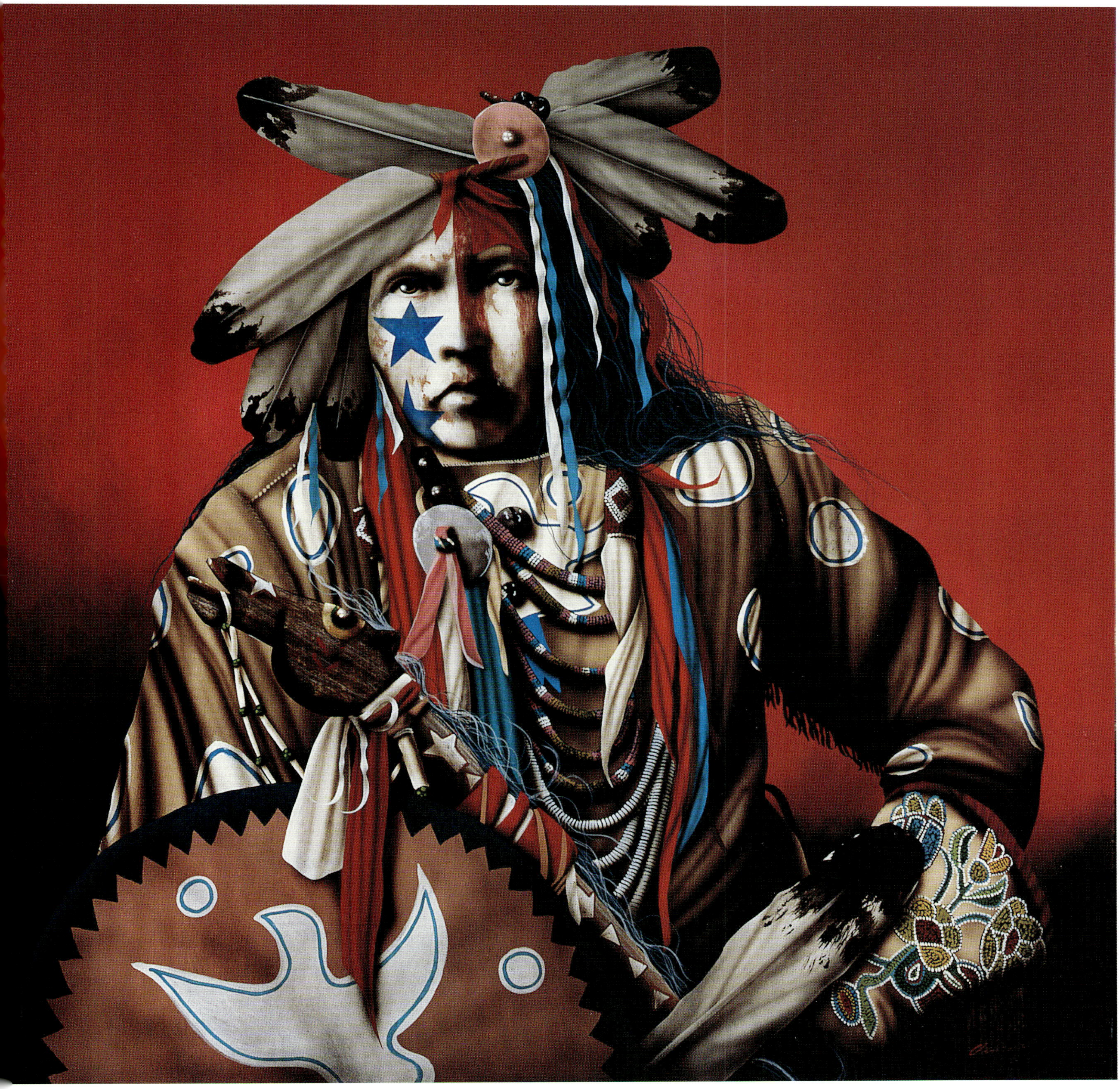

FIRE THUNDER

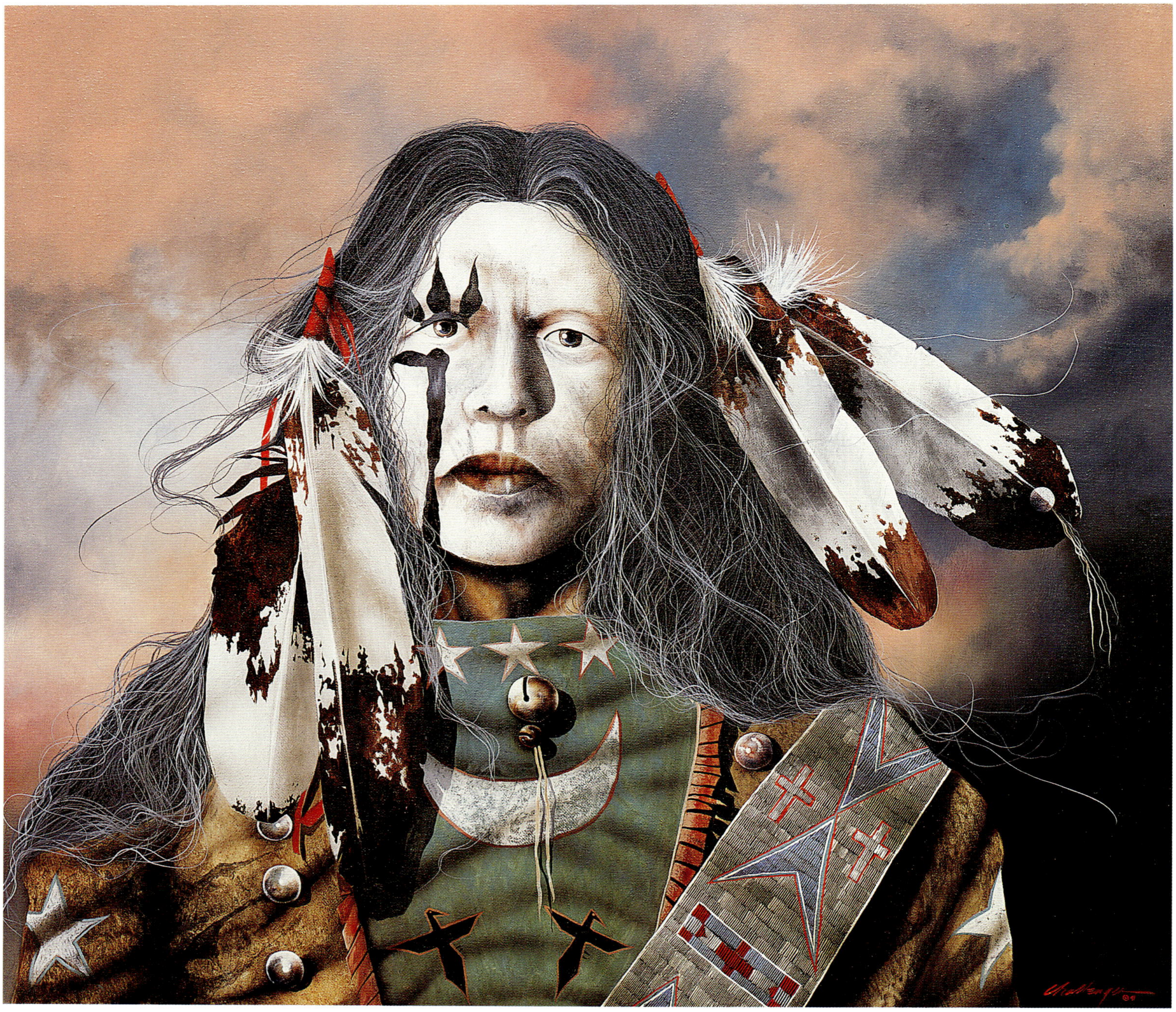

SKY HAWK

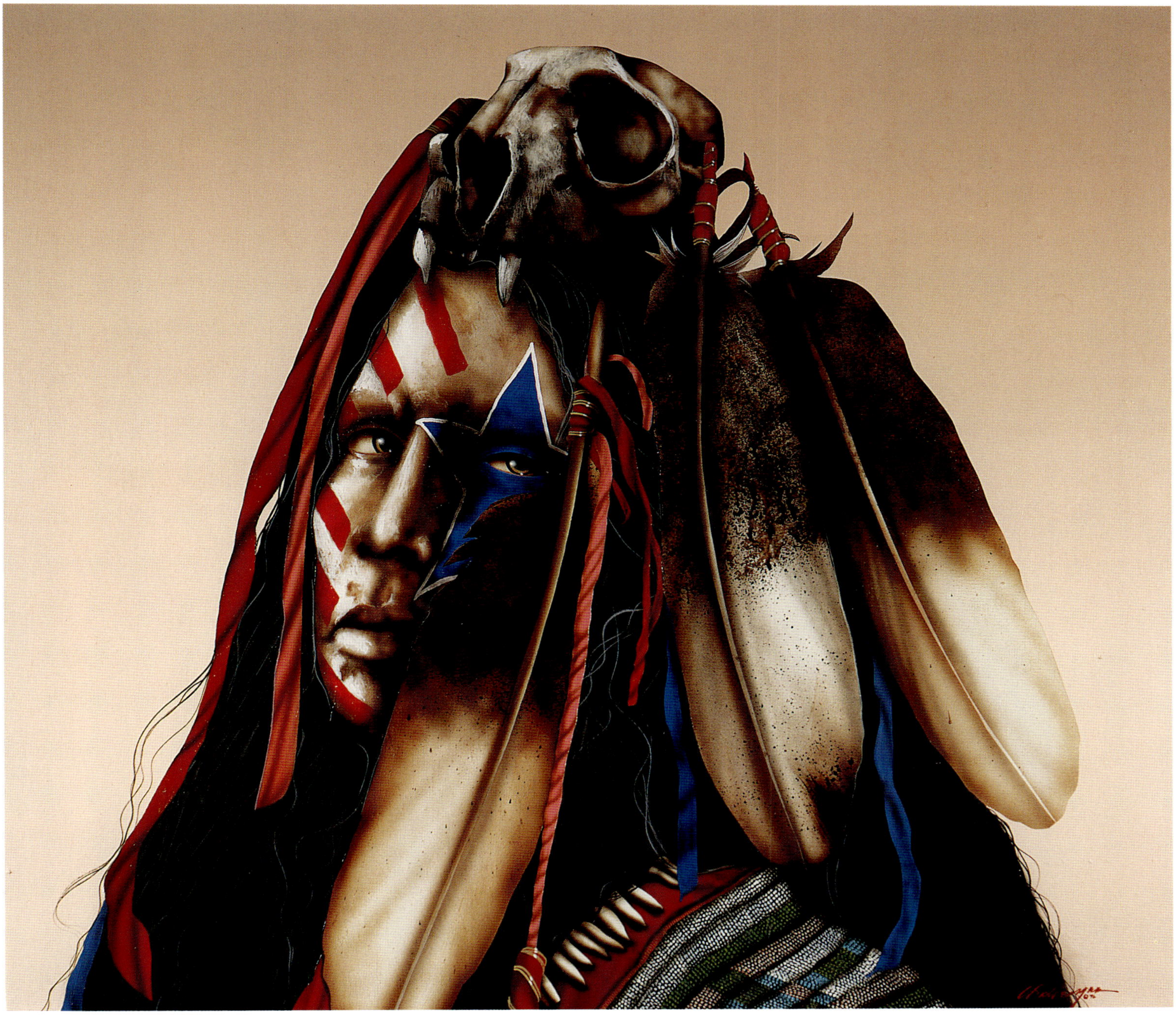

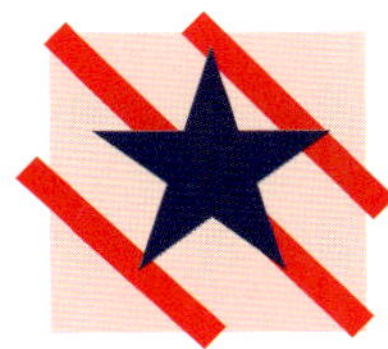

SWIFT BEAR

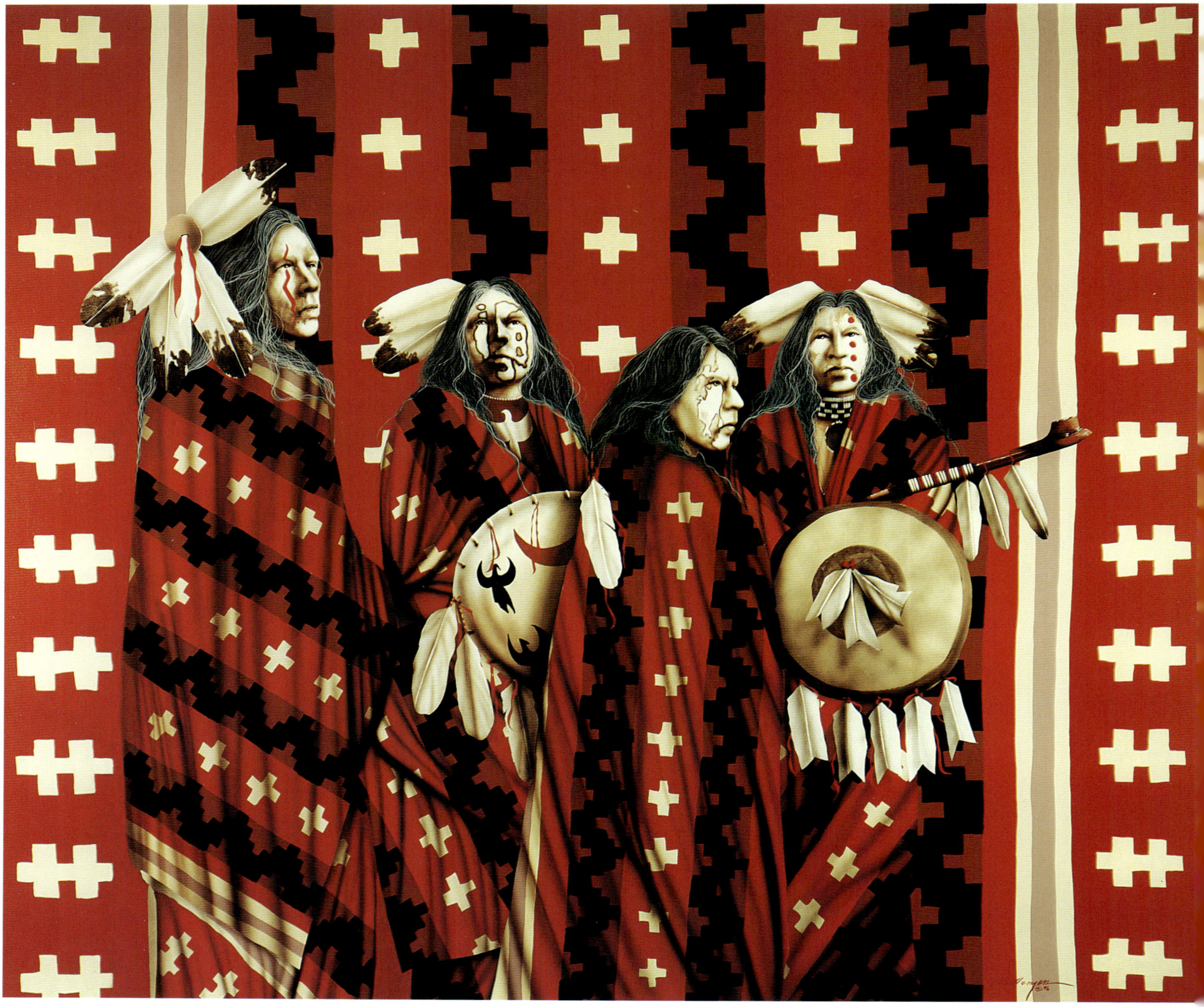

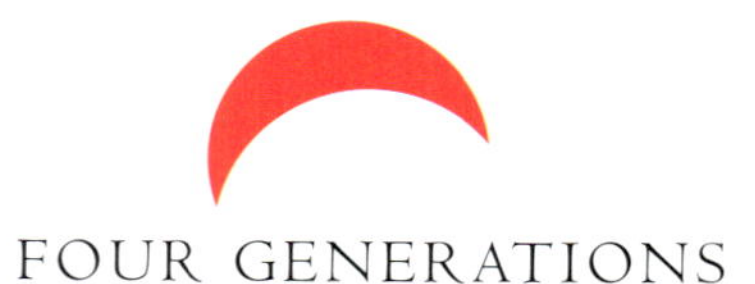

FOUR GENERATIONS

to stay with me here. All the dead men will come to life again. Their spirits will come to their bodies again. We must wait here in the homes of our fathers and be ready to meet them in the bosom of our mother."

These proud men derived a fierce dedication to their beliefs from a strict tradition of military and social order. Many tribes, including the Sioux, Cheyenne, Kiowa, and Arapaho, adhered to a precise hierarchy designed to promote responsibility, provide protection, and define identity within the tribe. Uninformed European Americans, ignoring the subtleties that define different tribal systems, lumped them all into what has been referred to as the Dog Soldiers. Despite order differences, each tribe strove to produce strong, dedicated, and proud members of tribal society.

The Arapaho, a tribe significant in their devotion to the Ghost dance, called their order "Warriors." The organization consisted of eight degrees and included almost all the tribe's men of or above the age of seventeen. Each level had a particular insignia that defined rank, and a specific dance corresponded to each of the first six degrees.

Members of the lowest degree of Arapaho Warriors were called the Fox men and included young men under twenty-five years of age. They were without privilege and were given no specific responsibilities other than to perform the Fox dance.

The second degree, the Star men, consisted of men thirty years of age and constituted the battle troops. Their ceremony was called the Star dance.

The Club men, the third degree made up of men in their prime, were of particular importance. This degree included four leaders responsible for charging the enemy and bashing him with an ornamented club, then returning to the tribe's front line. This action, meant to humiliate the enemy, brought great honor to the leaders due to its extreme danger. The accompanying members of the Club men carried carved and decorated sticks that were sharpened to a point at one end. During particularly heated moments in a battle, the Club men would drive their sticks into the ground and fight beside them until killed or a retreat was ordered.

The Spear men, the fourth degree of the Arapaho Warrior organization, were responsible for tribal order, policing the village, and insuring that the chief's instructions were carried out. Their duties included the enforcement of tribal code. During a hunt, the Spear men prevented anyone from killing a buffalo until the appropriate ceremonies were completed. Their leaders carried piked lances painted black or wrapped in otter skin, a batlike club, and a rattle fashioned from a buffalo's scrotum. It was the rattle carrier's responsibility to cast the rattle into the enemy's defenses and charge.

The remarkable Crazy men constituted the fifth degree and included men over fifty who had graduated through the ranks and were no longer expected to fight. They were represented by a bow and symbolic blunt arrows. The Crazy men's responsibilities included religious and ceremonial duties, and their dance, appropriately named the Crazy dance, featured many peculiar details. They were joined in the dance by other members of the tribe including women and children. Some of the dancers wore buffalo capes, slipping the

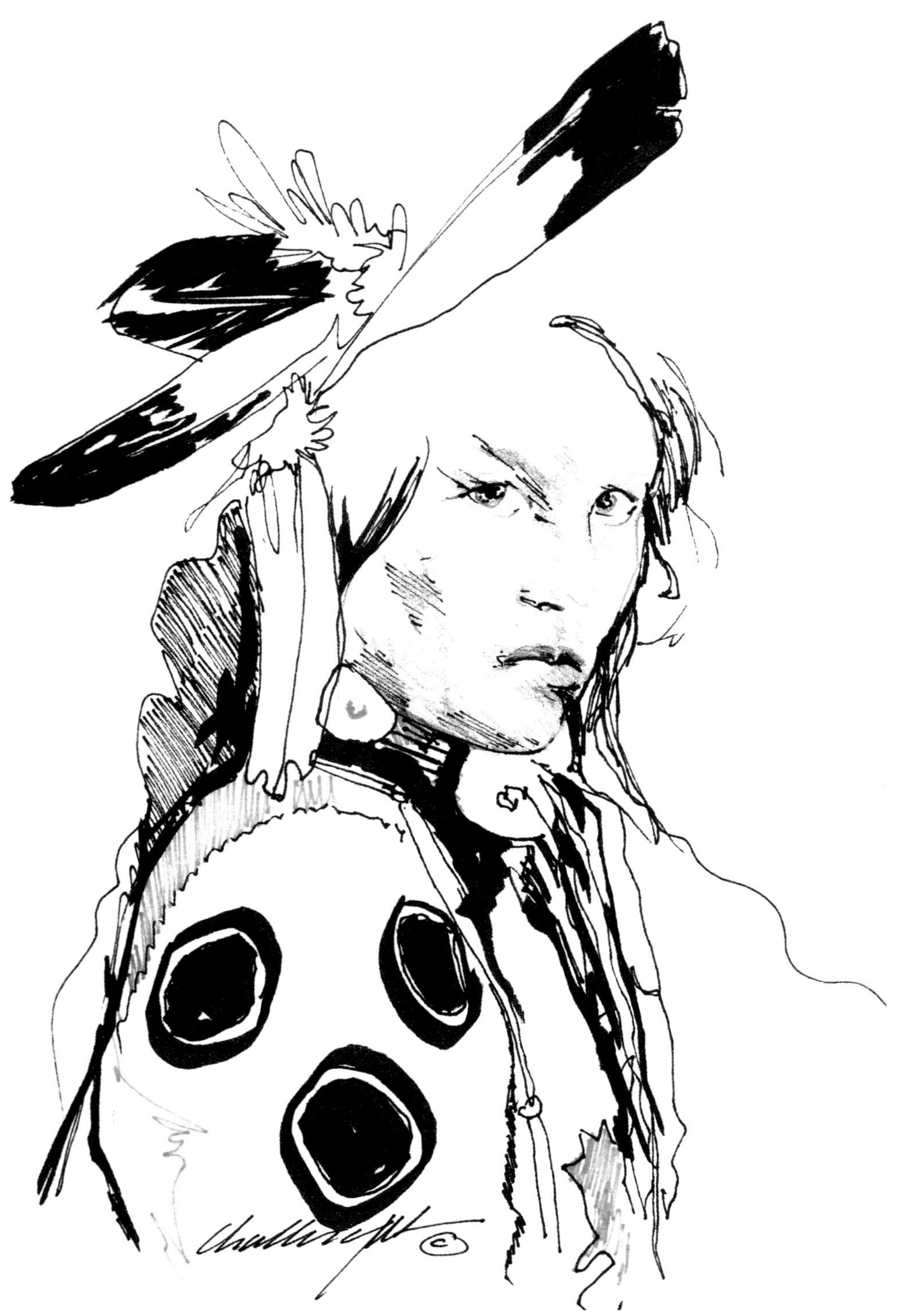

head and horns over their own head. Others created costumes designed to represent deer, birds, and mountain lions. In addition, the dance required participants to portray a bear, two foxes, seven wolves, and two medicine wolves.

The dance featured the wild and contrary actions of the dancers who deliberately performed the exact opposite of whatever they were told to do. The two leaders, decorated in white clay and with ears full of buffalo hair, blew whistles and shot their blunt arrows into the crowd. The dancers would careen around a dance fire, stomping and trampling the flames until the fire was out. Their performance imitated that of the fire moth, which in the Arapaho language means "crazy," as it flies closer and closer to a flame until consumed by the blaze.

The Dog men, sixth degree of the order, provided the tribe with leaders of the battle. Like the Club men, they would thrust their lances into the ground as a prelude to

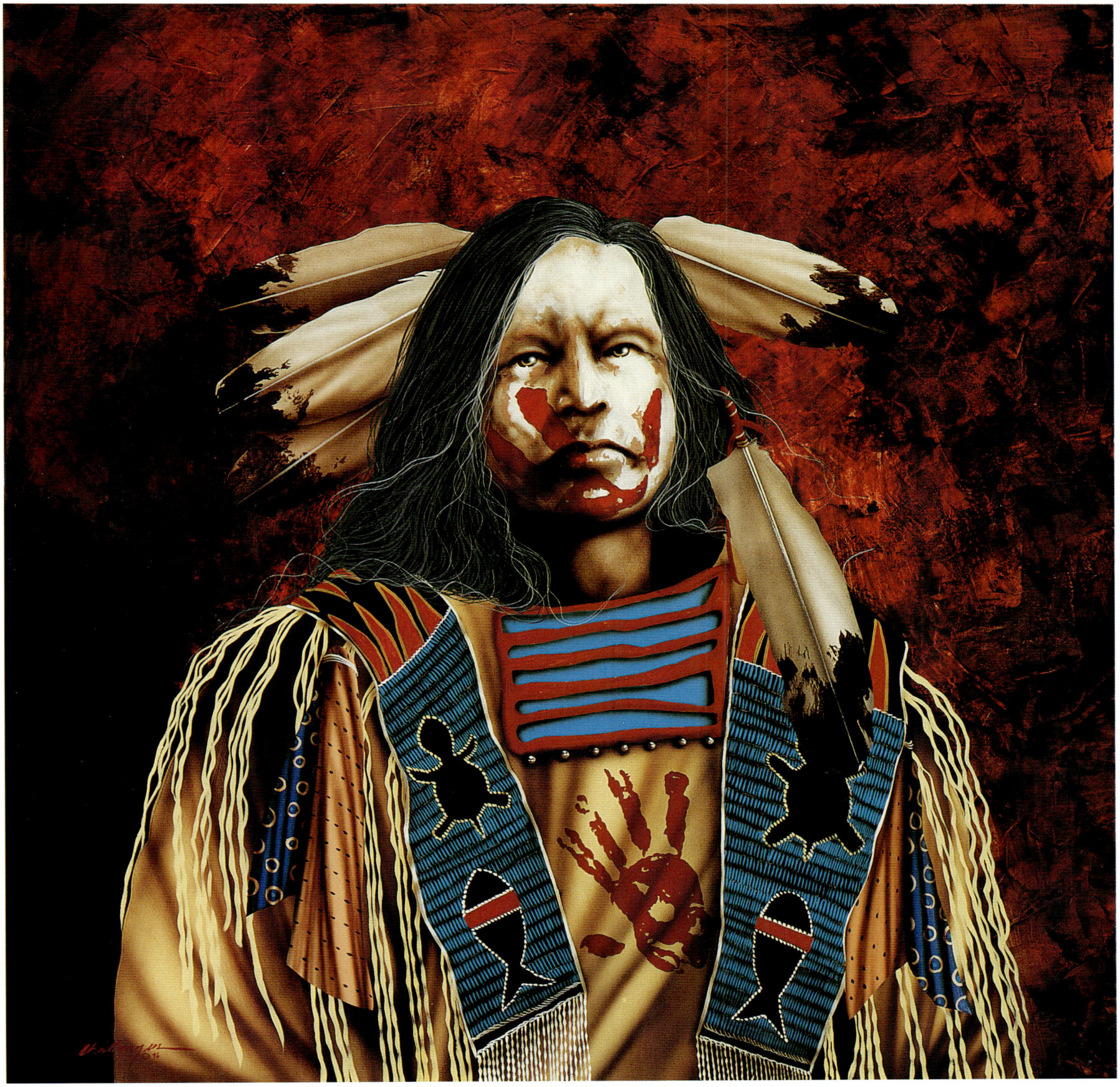

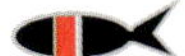

LAST WARRIOR

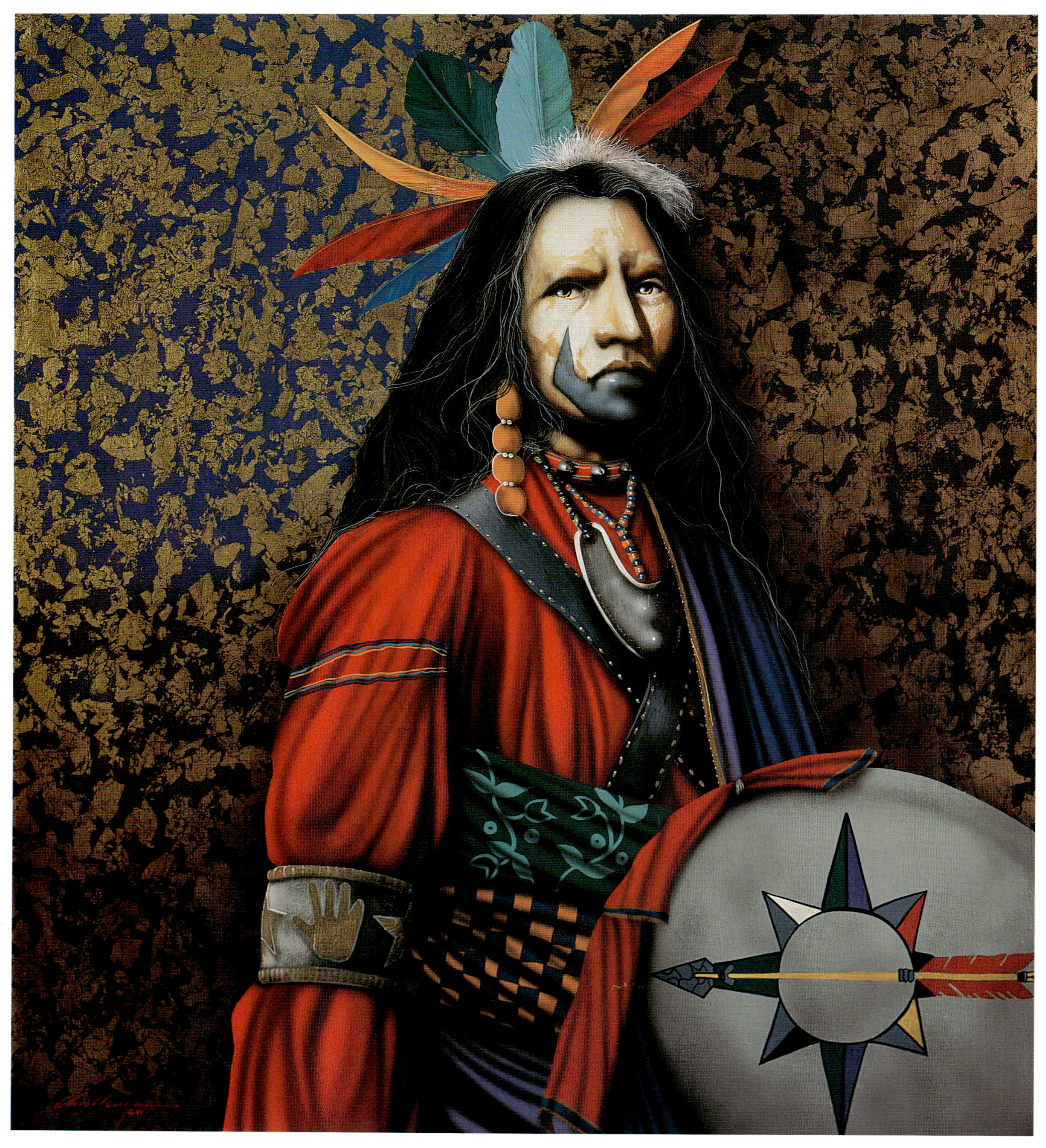

IN THE FOOTSTEPS OF THE GRANDFATHER

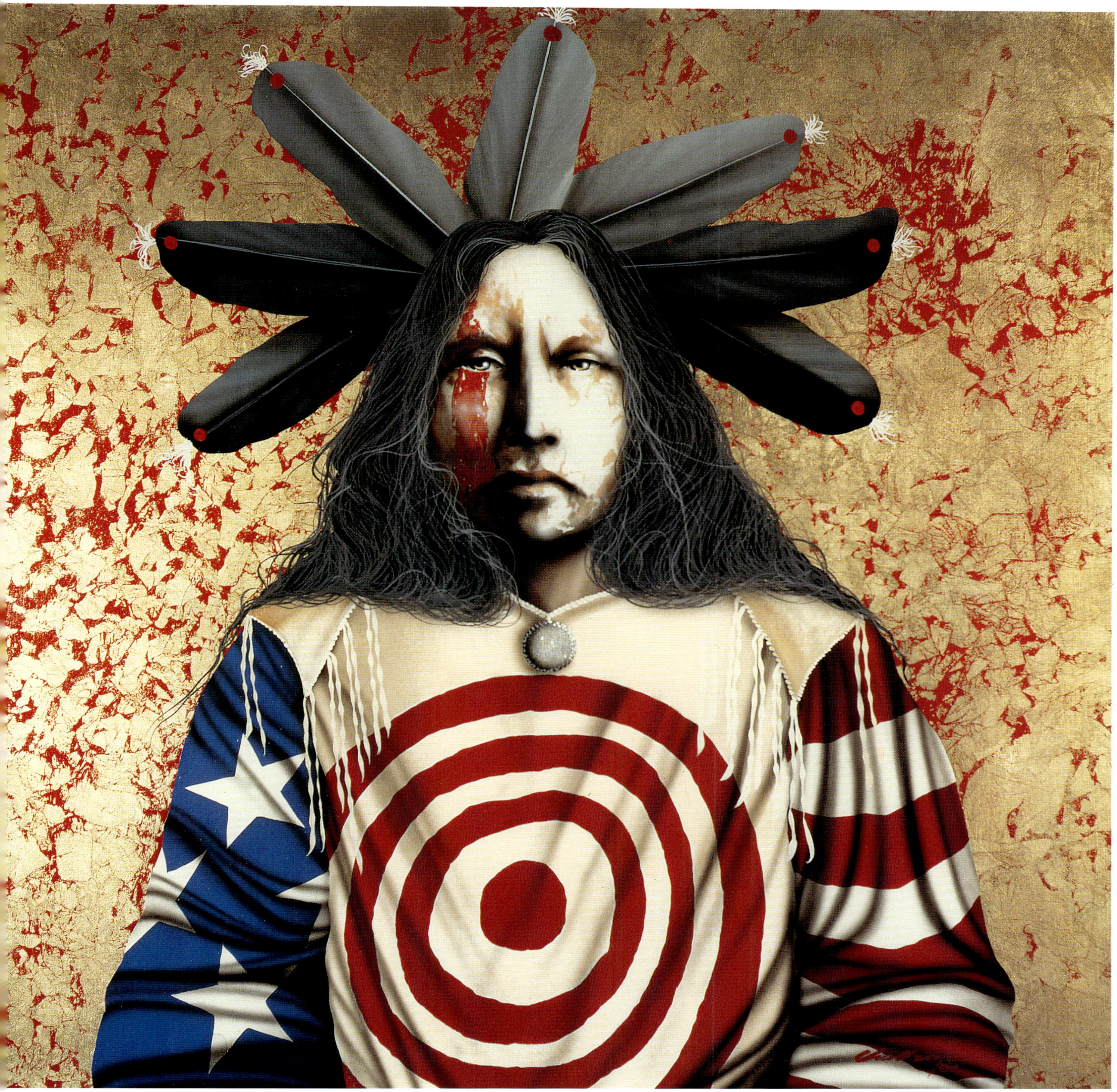

MOVING TARGET

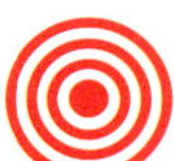

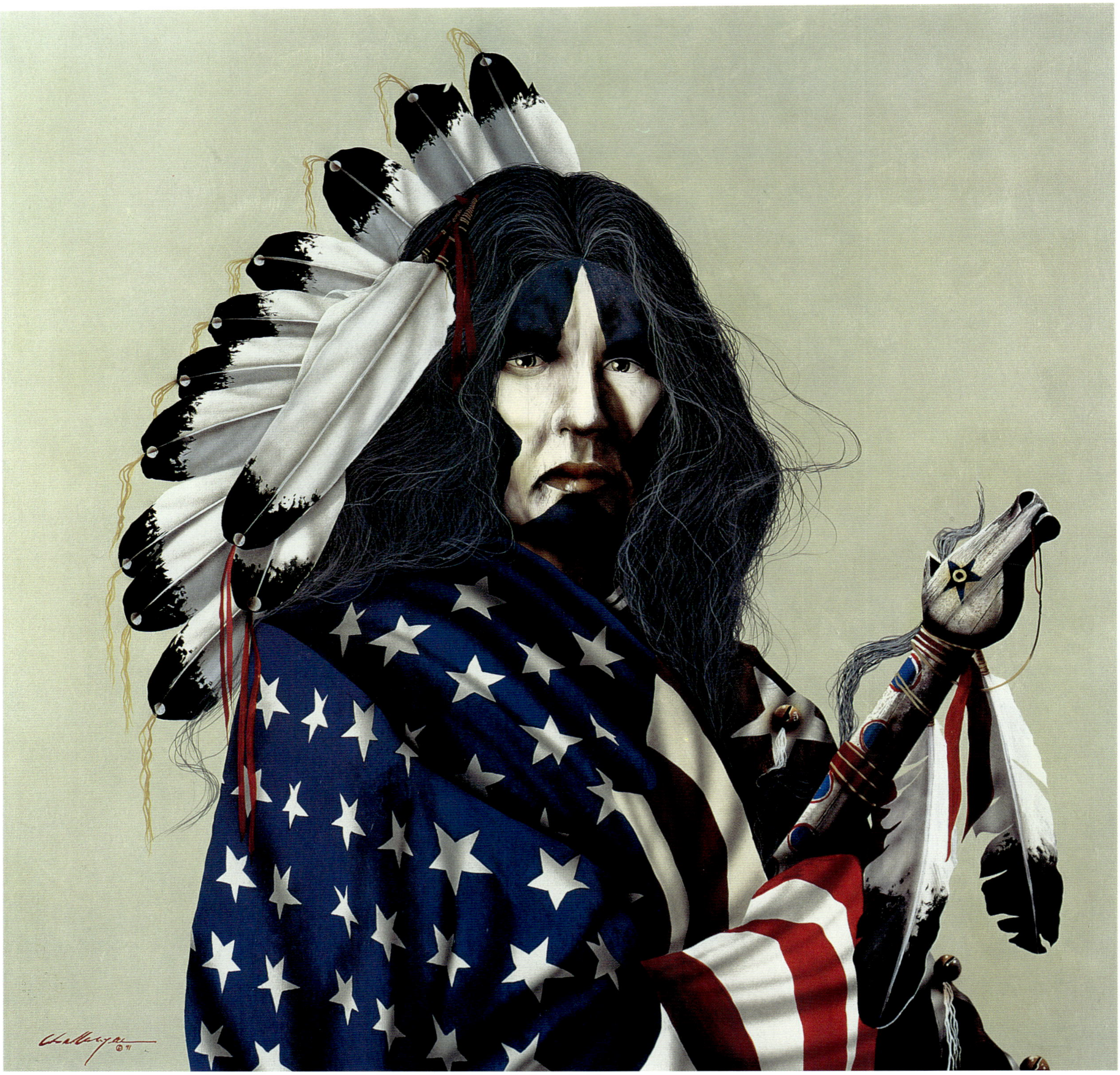

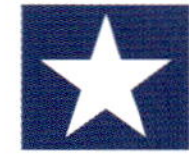

SPIRIT OF BLUE STAR

fighting. But rather than standing by them, they strapped themselves
to the lances along the battle front. They fought major battles only,
and in doing so, they inspired great courage. Once tied to their
lances, they would remain in place until one of their own members
pulled the lance from the ground and drove them away with a special
quirt.

The mysterious seventh degree, being the sacred number seven, performed secret
ceremonies known only to the order's members. Even the meaning of
the Arapaho word for this order is unknown.

The final and highest degree, the Water pouring men, included
seven of the oldest warriors of the tribe. They instructed all the
other degrees and performed their special duties in a designated sweat
lodge. Their name referred to water poured over hot stones, which
created steam in the sweat lodge ceremonies. The Water pouring men
were not required to enter battle, but one of the seven would often
travel with the warriors. In many ways, these venerated elders represented the essence of the tribe, passing the entire library of tribal
knowledge down to each succeeding generation.

Spreading knowledge and religious faith became a dangerous
responsibility for many Native American Ghost dance practitioners.
Kicking Bear, one of the primary Sioux Ghost dance leaders, braved
the consequences of restricted reservation policy and instigated the
ceremony across the Sioux reservation system. After successfully
engaging the camps of Sioux leaders Hump and Big Foot
along the Cheyenne River, he was asked by Sitting Bull to inau-
gurate the dance at Sitting Bull's camp on the Standing Rock
reservation. The reservation agent, hearing of Kicking Bear's arrival, sent a group of armed
officers and agency police to arrest him. But the group
returned to the agent, unable to overpower Kicking Bear,
expressing their fear of the Ghost dance leader's powerful medicine.

Religious leaders of the dance continued to travel from camp
to camp and reservation to reservation, delivering the doctrine
despite the danger of arrest and detention. Short Bull, one of the
principal leaders of the dance, expressed his beliefs to the people of Red
Leaf camp on Pine Ridge reservation just two short months before the
Wounded Knee tragedy: "Now there will be a tree sprout up, and there all the
members of our religion and the tribe must gather together. That will be the place where
we will see our dead relations. But before this time we must dance the balance of this
moon, at the end of which time the earth will shiver very hard. Whenever this thing
occurs, I will start the wind to blow. We are the ones who will then see our fathers, mothers, and everybody. We, the tribe of Indians, are the ones who are living a sacred life. God,
our father himself, has told and commanded and shown me to do these things."

Many Ghost dancers exhibited a remarkable personal commitment to their religious
beliefs in the face of adversity. Black Coyote, one of the primary southern Arapaho lead

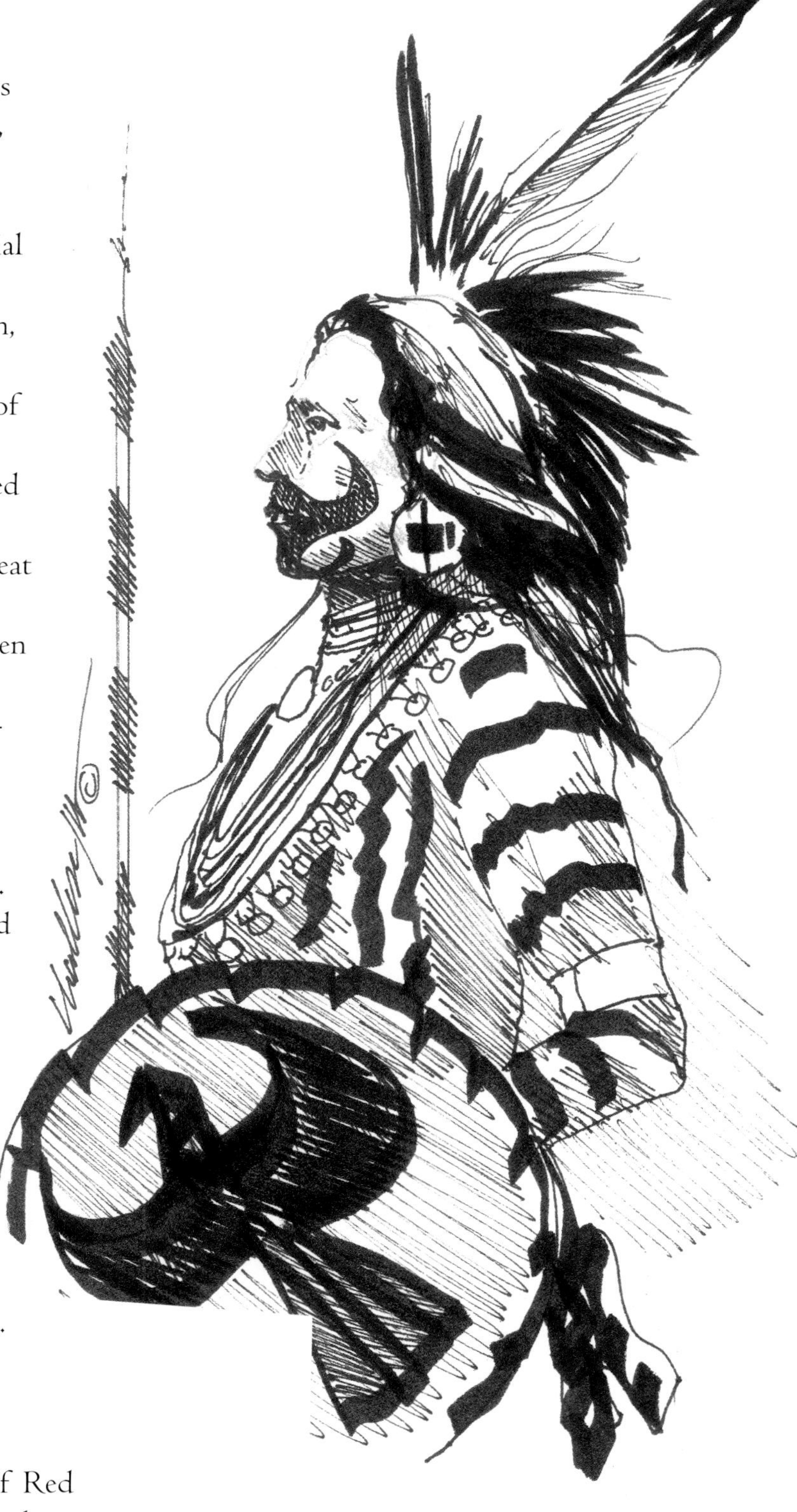

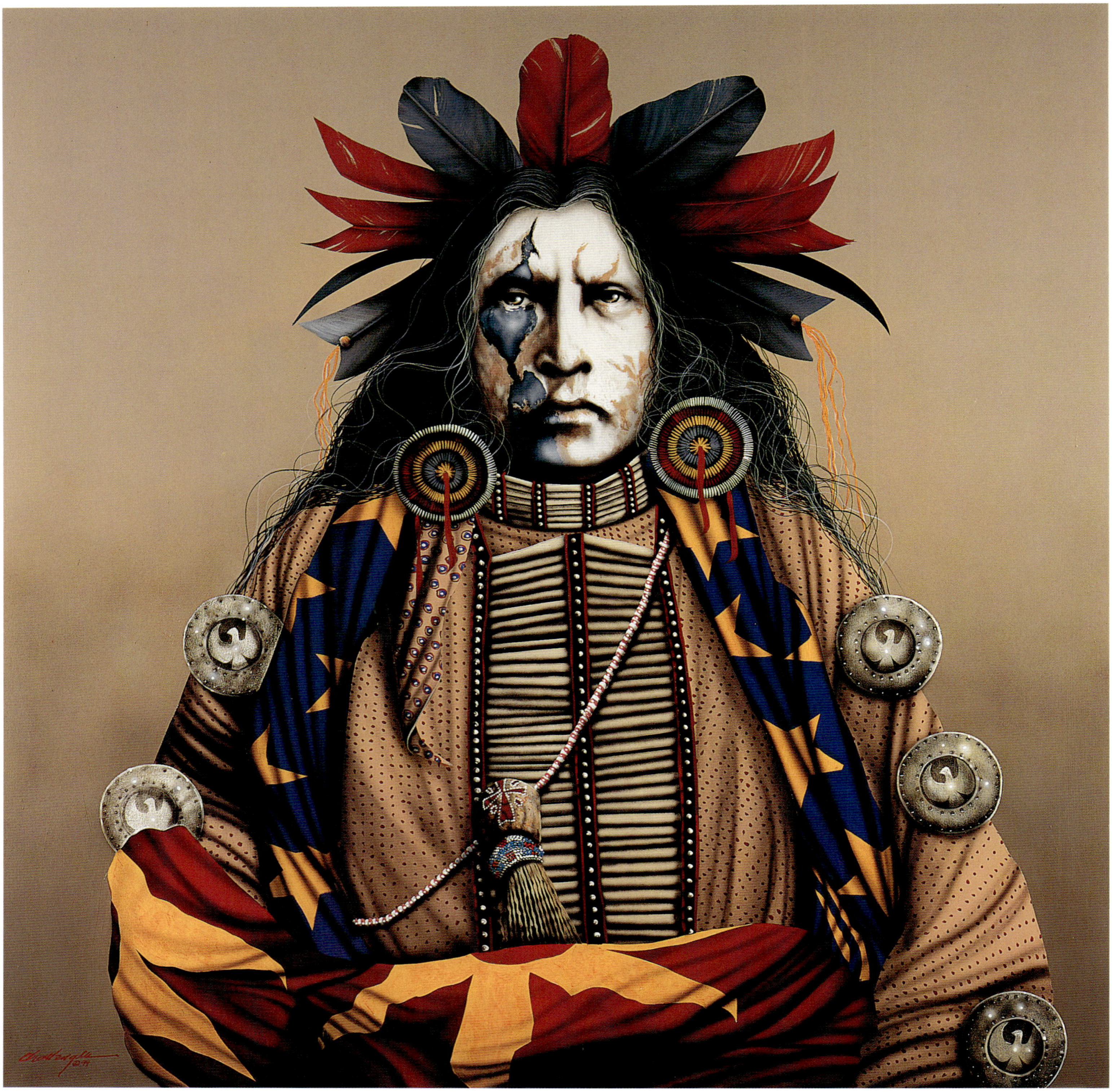

ABOVE:

PROUD STAR

OPPOSITE:

WHITE STAR

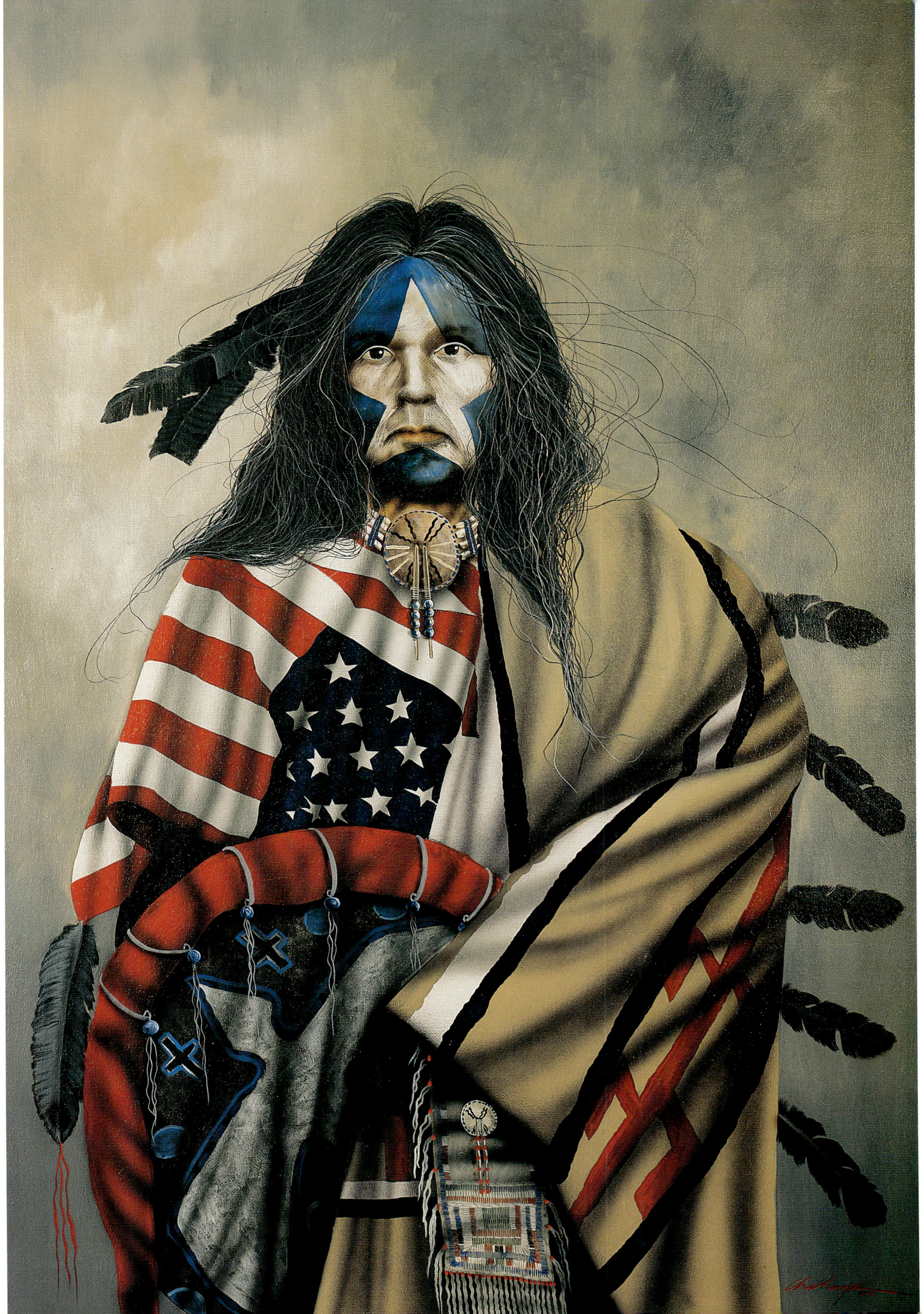

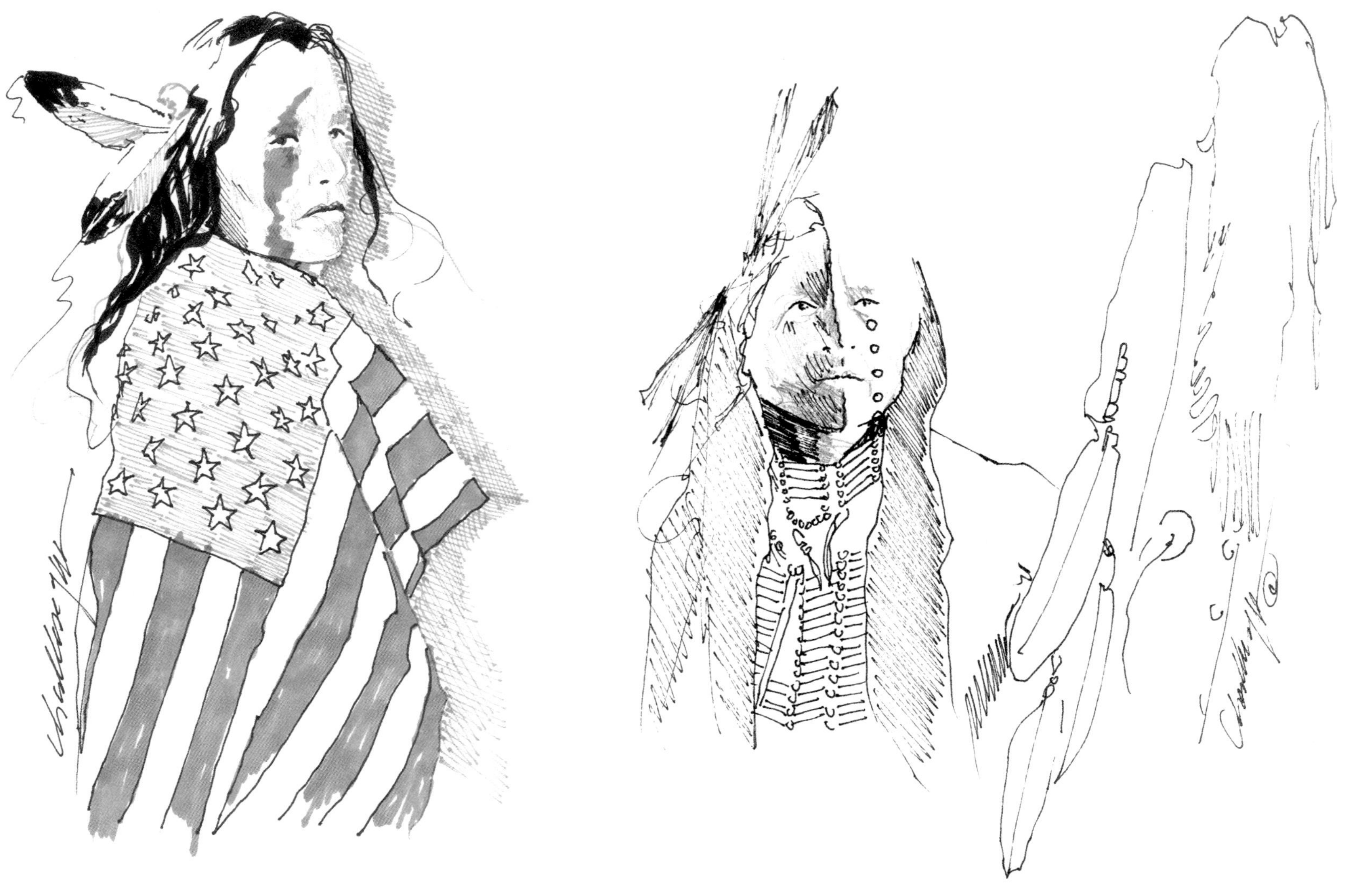

ers of the Ghost dance, embraced an unwavering strength of faith in his religious visions and his desire to preserve his family's well-being. "…A number of scars will be noticed on his chest and arms," Mooney recalls.

The full number of these scars is seventy, arranged in various patterns of lines, circles, crosses, etc., with a long figure of the sacred pipe on one arm. According to his own statement they were made in obedience to a dream as a sacrifice to save the lives of his children. Several of his children had died in rapid succession, and in accordance with Indian custom he undertook a fast of four days as an expiation to the overruling spirit. During this time, while lying on his bed, he heard a voice, somewhat resembling the cry of an owl or the subdued bark of a dog. The voice told him that if he wished to save his other children he must cut out seventy pieces of skin and offer them to the sun. He at once cut out seven pieces, held them out to the sun and prayed, and then buried them. But the sun was not satisfied, and soon after he was warned in a vision that the full number of seventy must be sacrificed if he would save his children. He then did as directed, cutting out the pieces of skin in the various patterns indicated, offering each in turn to the sun with a prayer for the health of his family, and then burying them. Since then there has been no death in his family. In cutting out the larger pieces, some of which were several inches long

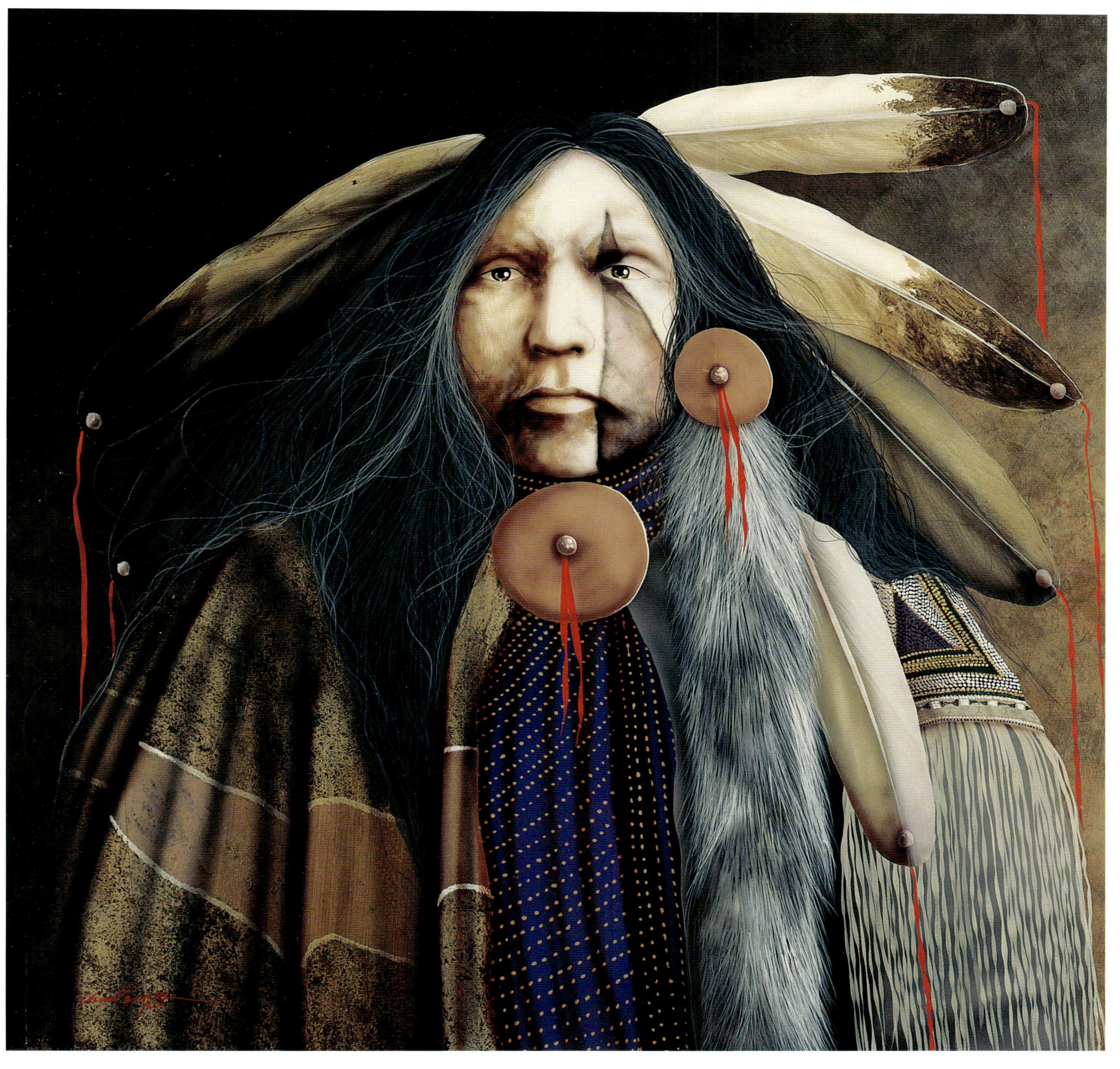

WARRIOR CIRCLE

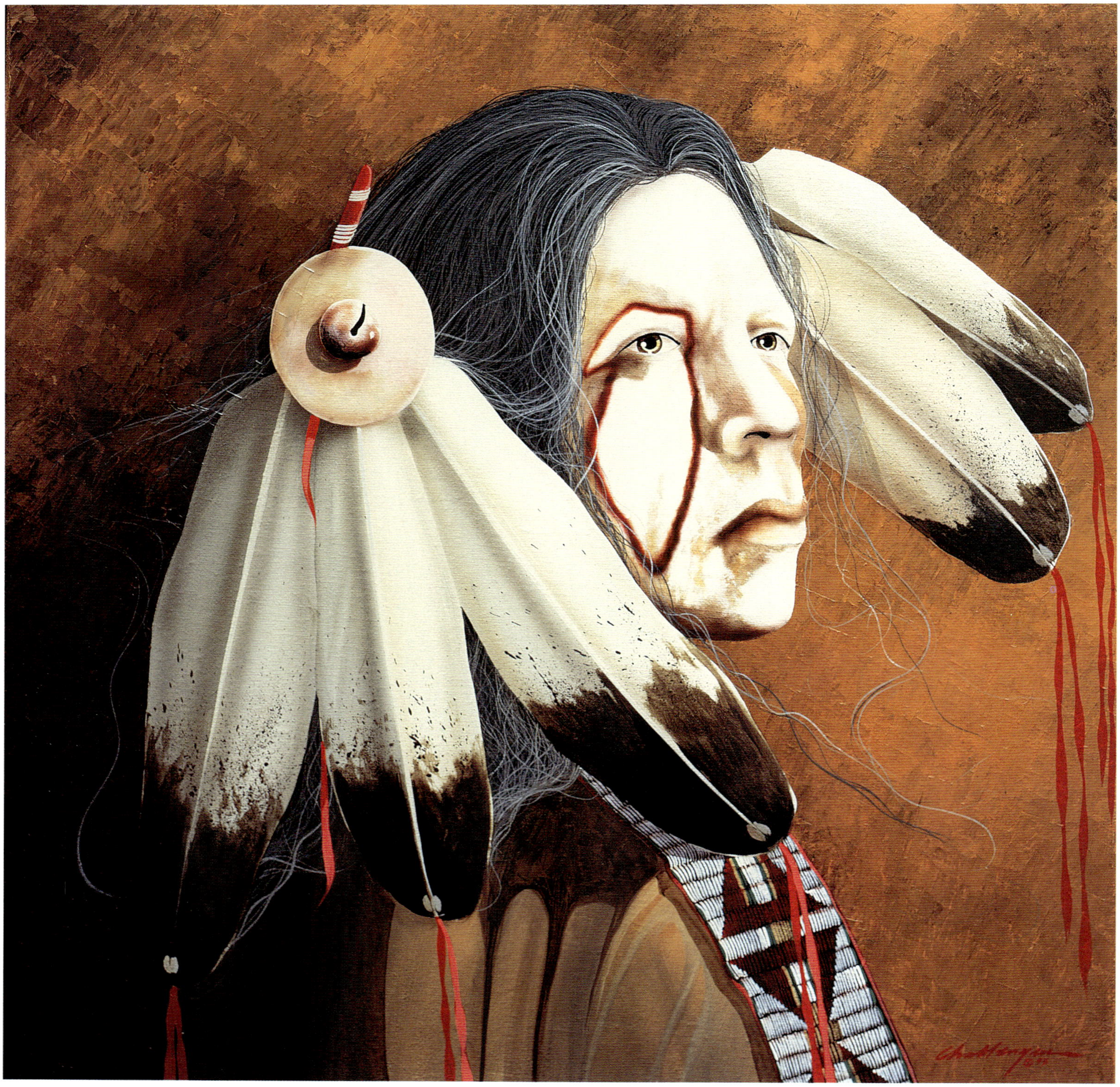

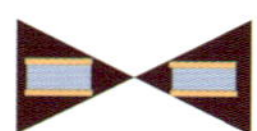

WE WILL ENDURE

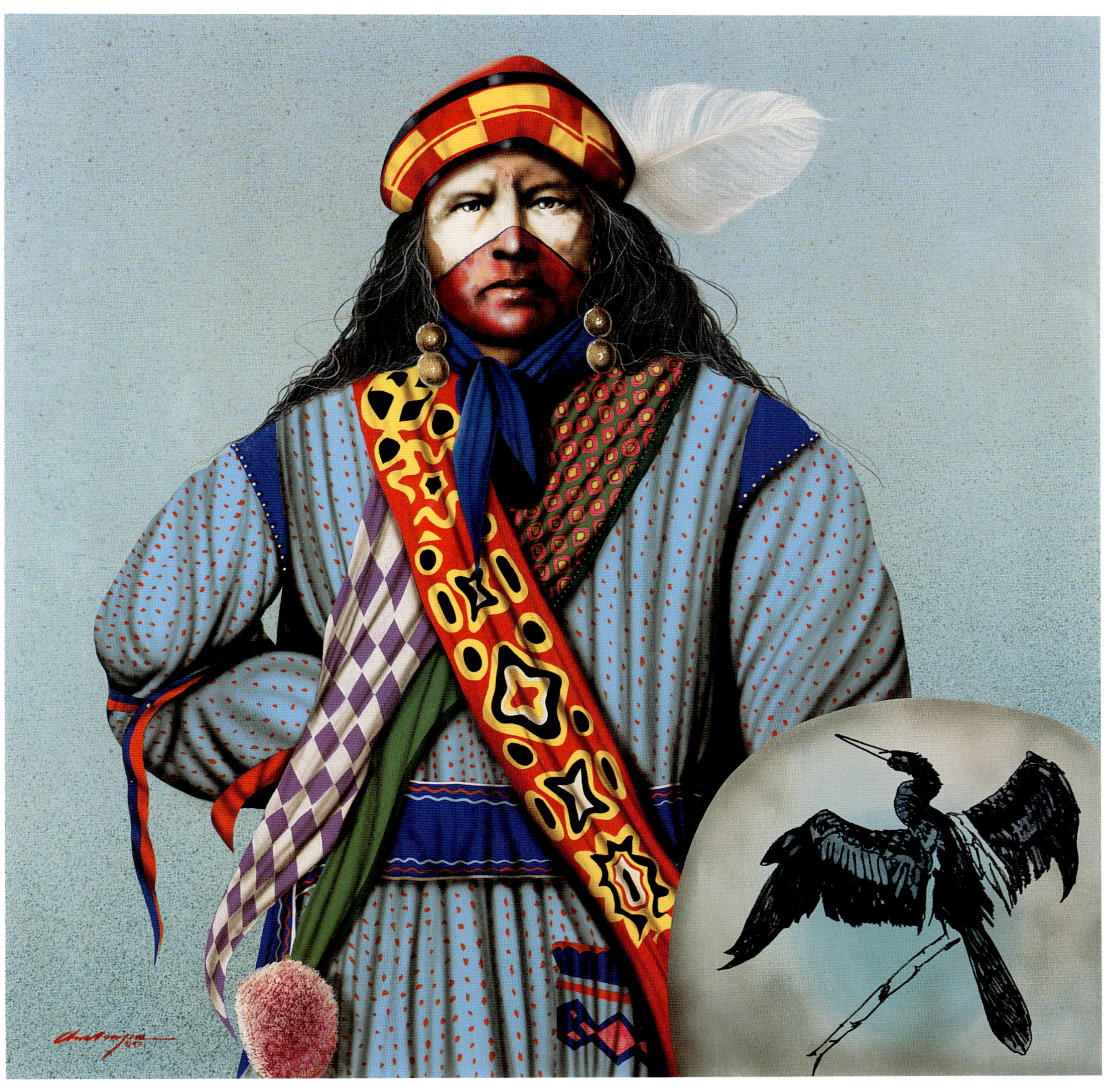

THE UNCONQUERED

and nearly half an inch wide, the skin was first lifted up with an awl and then sliced away with a knife. This had to be done by an assistant, and Black Coyote was particular to show me by signs, sitting very erect and bracing himself firmly, that he had not flinched during the process.

The Ghost dance legacy produced many brave women as well, including Little Woman, who composed many of the Ghost dance songs and became a leader in the Cheyenne Ghost dance. Reflecting the original teachings of Wovoka, Little Woman offered her people a way to remember and embrace loved family members lost. As a result of her devotion to the doctrine, she became known as the woman messenger from the spirit world and received the appropriate title "Crow Woman."

The Ghost dance doctrine generated many gentle heroes. But its oppressors created the fiercest, producing a flame of anger that perhaps burned brightest in the heart of the Teton Sioux Sitting Bull. One of the strongest proponents of the Ghost dance, Sitting Bull remained opposed to the cessation of Sioux land and all it stood for his entire life. What began as an attempt to arrest him for his Ghost dance practices resulted in his murder less than a month before the tragedy of Wounded Knee. Revered for his warrior victories, including the demise of General Custer at Little Bighorn, Sitting Bull had already spent two years in prison and, once released, set up camp along the Grand River at Standing Rock reservation. His camp became a center of rebellion, much to the concern of the reservation agency and the military. "Since the days of Pontiac, Tecumseh, and Red Jacket," General Miles exclaimed, "no Indian has had the power of drawing to him so large a following of his race and molding and wielding it against the authority of the United States, or of inspiring it with greater animosity against the white race and civilization."

Sitting Bull's sentence—and the punishment for thousands of his fellow Native Americans for fighting against the collapse of their culture, the loss of family and livelihood, and the demise of the world as they had known it for hundreds of years—would be death.

The loss of so many heroes marked the end of the dance and brought about the end of a remarkable era in the country's violent history. Over one hundred years have passed since the Ghost dance watermark, but the cultural sabotage caused by America's propensity for religious autocracy is a bitter lesson yet to be learned. The courage of the Native American people against this overwhelming adversity stands as a remarkable testament to the greatness of the human spirit. It is this indomitable spirit that will perhaps in the end prevail.

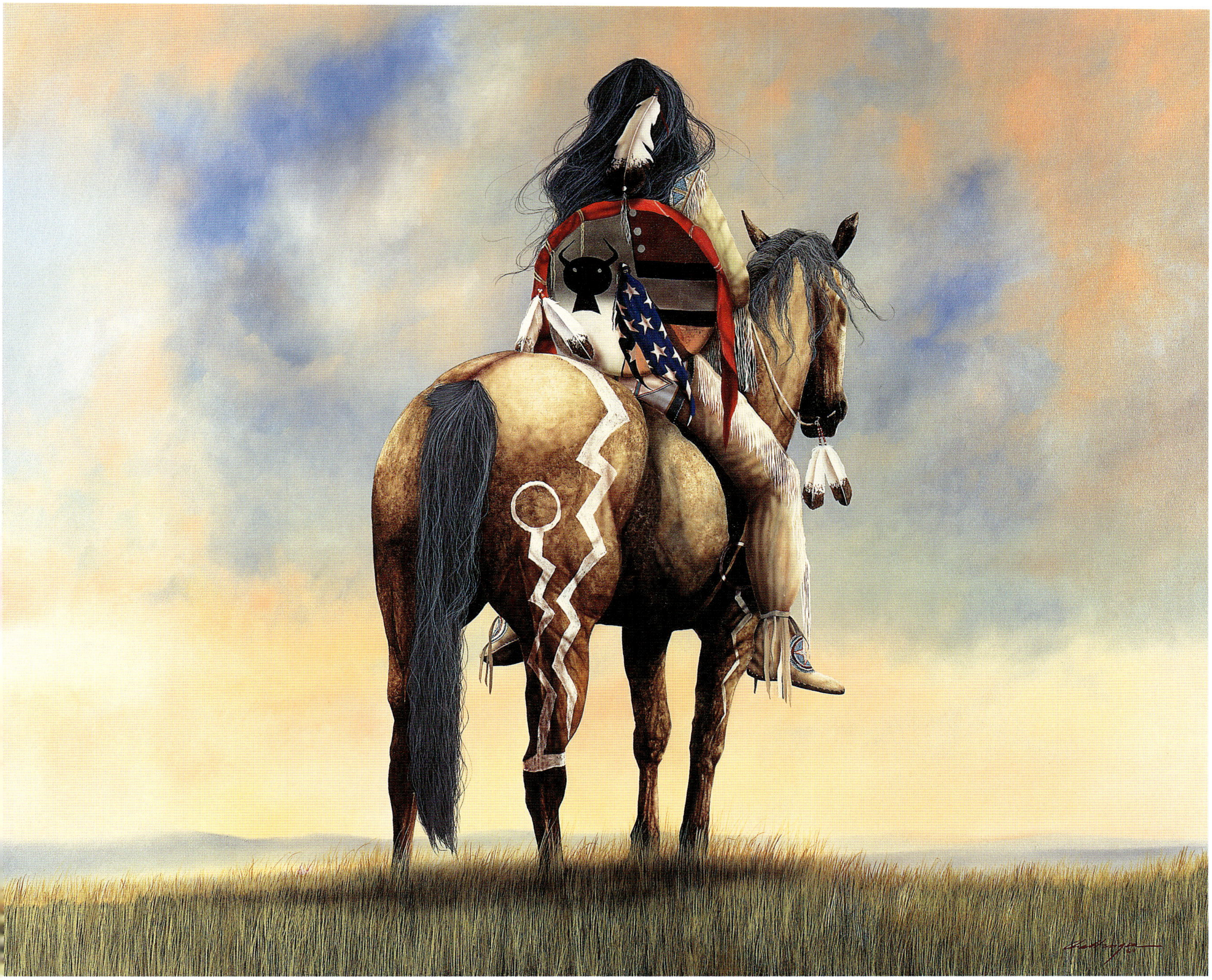

THE SPIRIT NEVER DIES

HEART OF A WARRIOR
THE SPIRIT LIVES

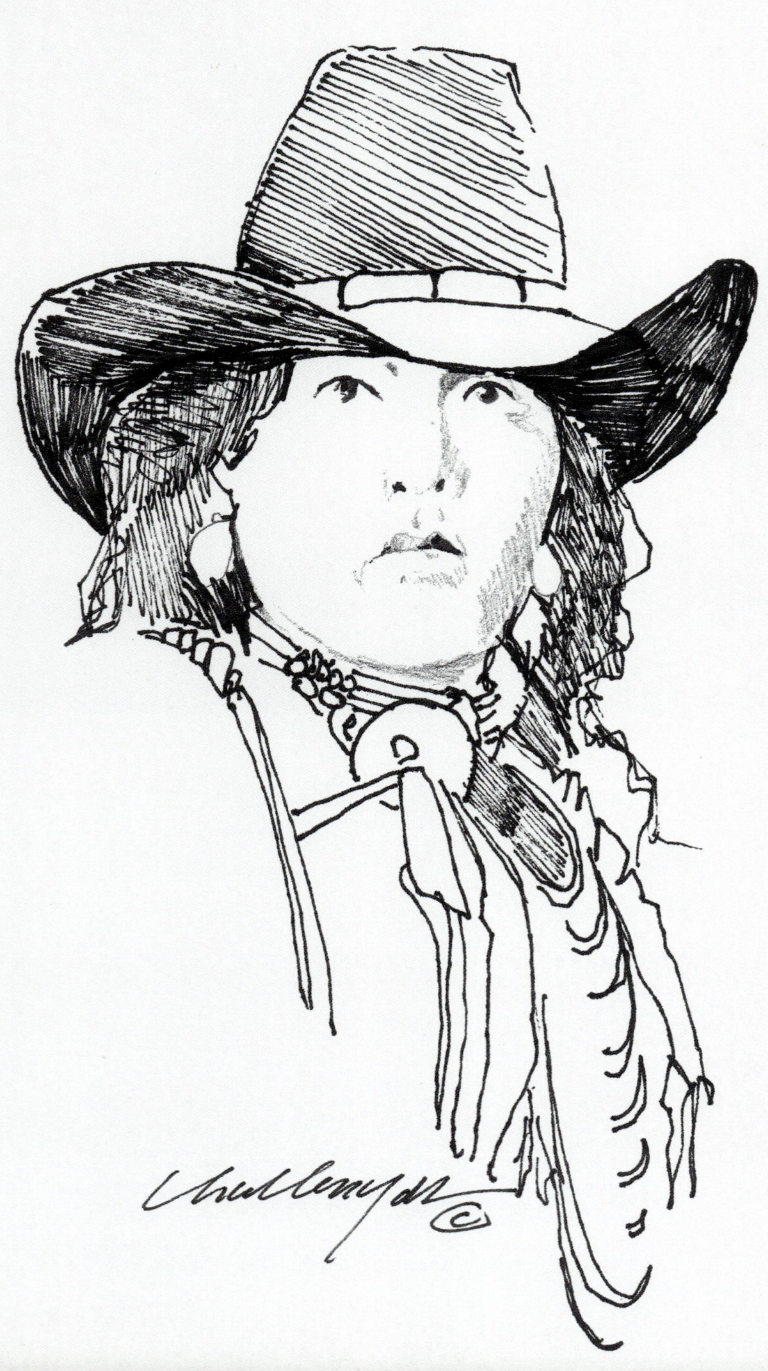

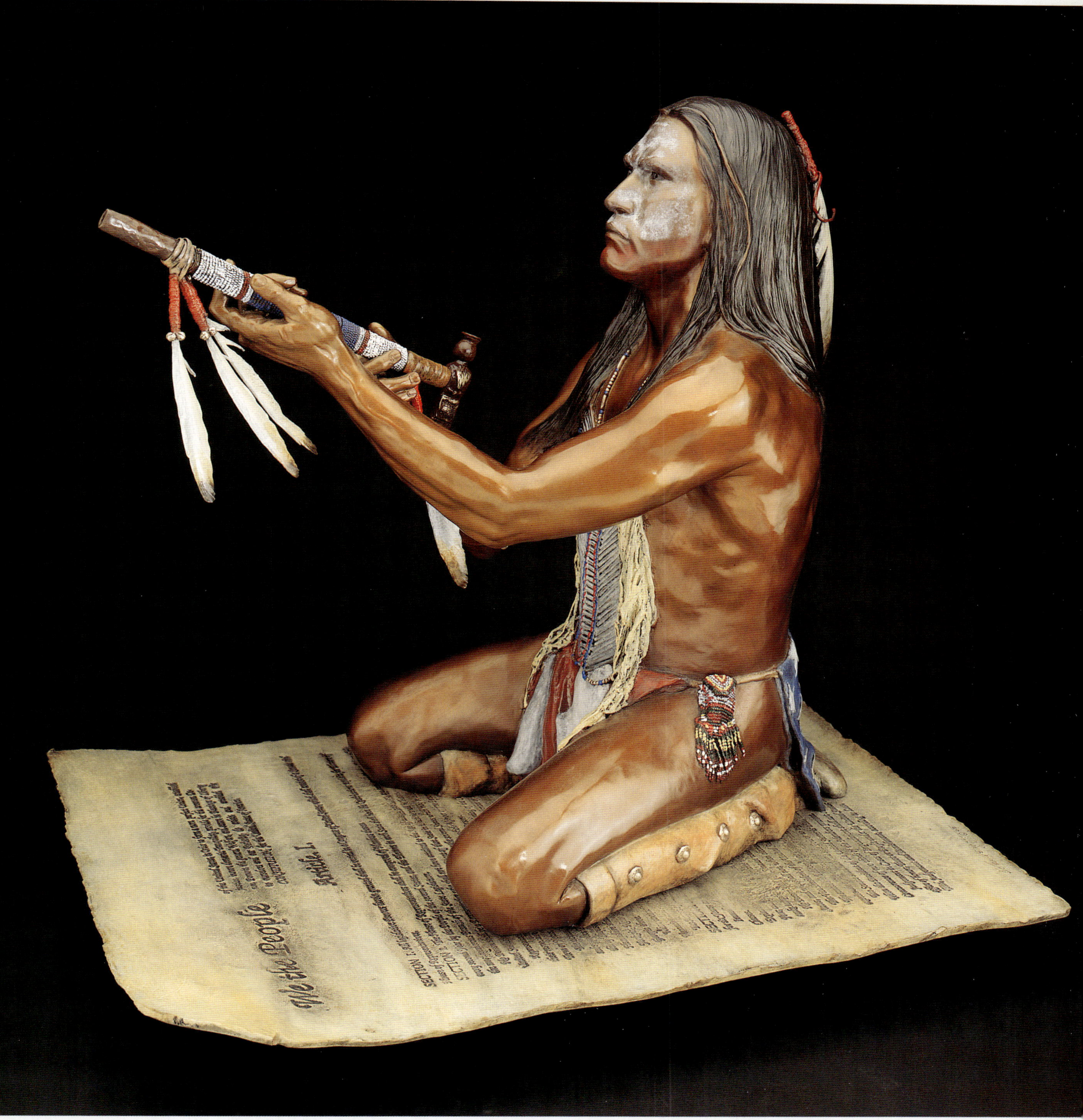
We the People
Article. I.
SECTION 1.
SECTION 2.

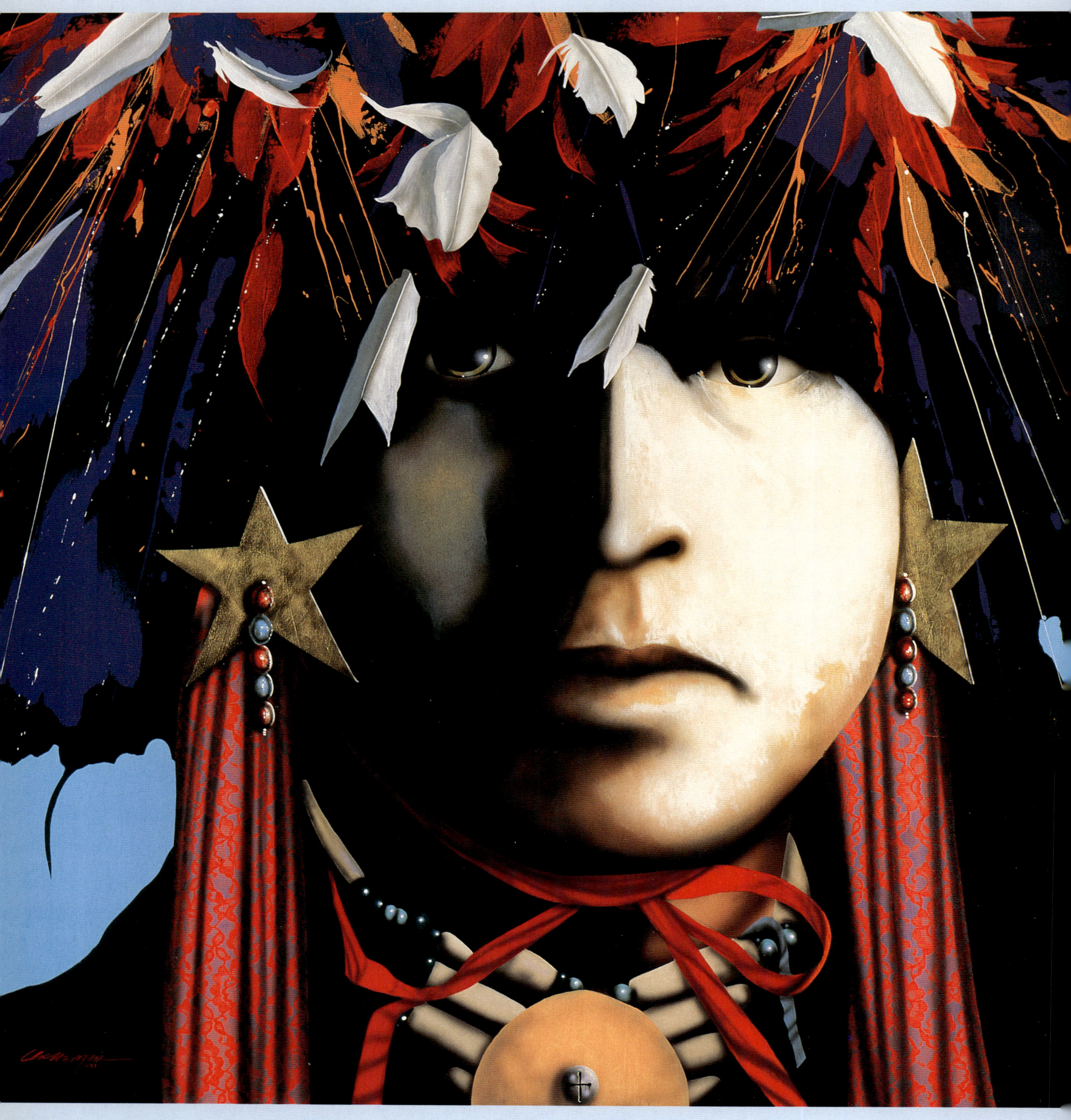

Many historians define the Ghost dance religion as a messianic movement, tarnishing Wovoka's vision with a savior's patina. But the real power of the religion relied on communal contributions rather than the works of a single entity. It created a multitude of messengers who brought hope to a people in need and to a culture denied its spiritual traditions. Its ceremonies empowered all practitioners—leaders as well as dancers—with the opportunity to contribute their personal offerings to the dance. Ghost dance visionaries created bridges to access the world of spirits; artisans constructed rattles, head dresses, ghost shirts, staffs, painted hides, and banners, while musicians composed the sacred songs and dancers bent and arched in the sacred movements.

The religion allowed the individual to prevail in spirituality, charging obedience not to an established hierarchy but a personal relationship with God. As a result, it is not an isolated messenger of the Ghost dance that has remained paramount over one hundred years later. It is, instead, the message.

"It was a moment I'll never forget," recalls JD Challenger.

I stood in the packed gallery surrounded by my paintings and shaking hands with collectors. I happened to look across the room and see this mountain cut through the crowd and come straight for me. This Native American was over six feet tall, huge shoulders, long braided hair and a face chiseled from rock. I didn't recognize him and he wasn't smiling. I thought to myself, "This isn't good. I've created all these paintings of his people and he's not happy about it at all." He came right up to me as I stuck my hand out to introduce myself. He grabbed it in both of his and it felt like my fingers were being squeezed in a vise. But then his eyes locked on mine and he said, "I have a message for you." Suddenly, I forgot about his grip and about my apprehension. Everything around me seemed to disappear—the gallery, the people—like some kind of magic, and it was just me and him standing there. Then he said, "You have the heart of a warrior. And through your art our warriors live."

As I listened to his message, all the feelings I had about what I wanted my art to accomplish kind of swelled up inside me. He made it clear that this message was not just his own. It came from all of his people. "A-ho," I remember saying to him. "A-ho," he replied and smiled. Then he was gone.

It's where I get the greatest rewards from being an artist, when I can connect like that. It's an unbeatable feeling.

OPPOSITE:
PRAYER FOR THE
ANCIENT ONES

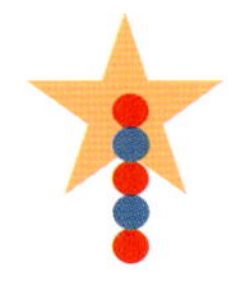

PAGE 127:
WE THE PEOPLE

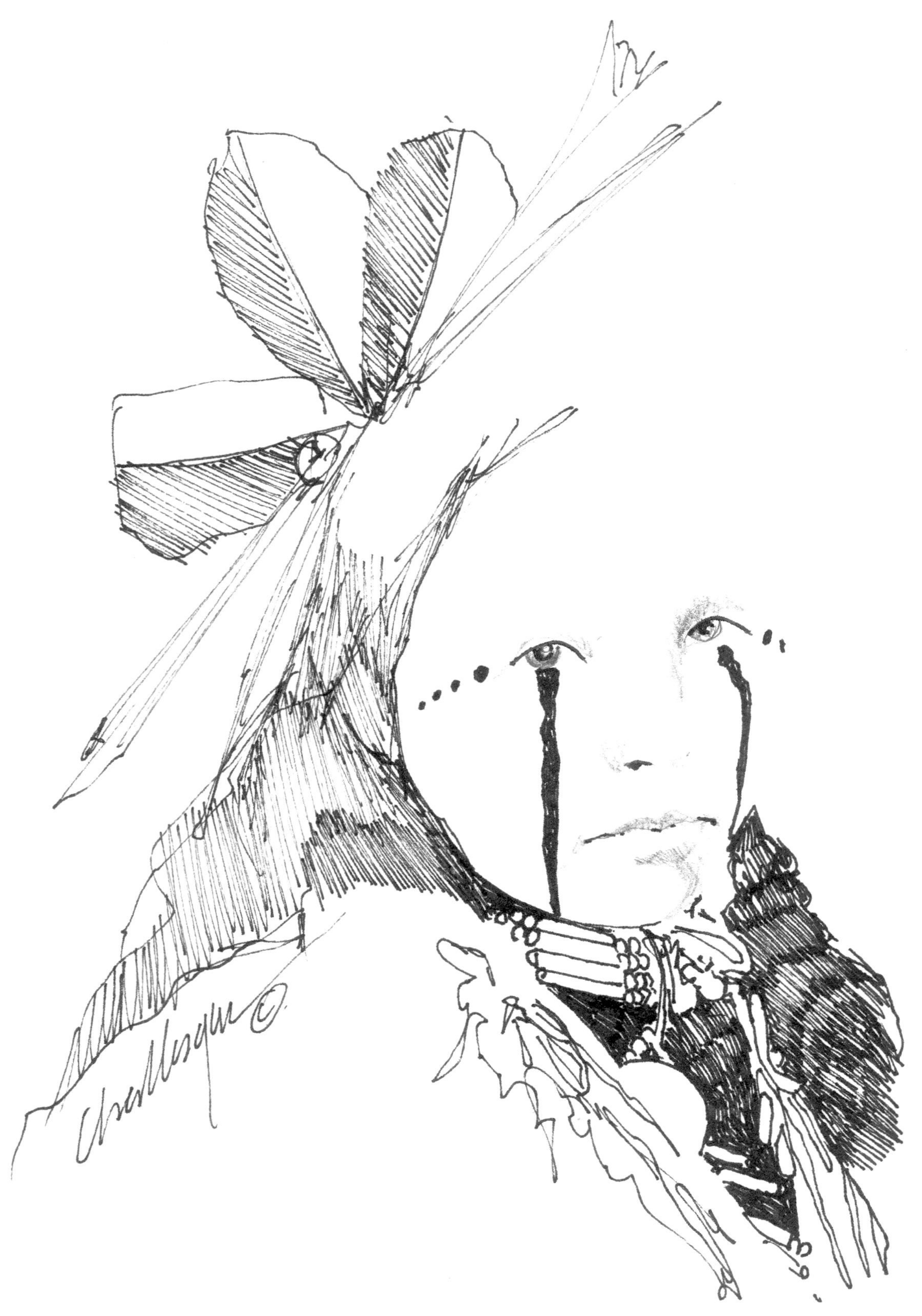

Challenger was drawn to Native American subject matter through a number of unusual circumstances, some of which are difficult for him to explain. "Something led me to the Native American culture and the Ghost dance era. I'm still not sure what it was. But it has been guiding me ever since."

After I created my first Ghost dance paintings, I called all my friends into my studio. I said, "Look, guys, this is what my heart tells me to do. Tell me where you want me to take this. Use me as an instrument, let me tell your story if

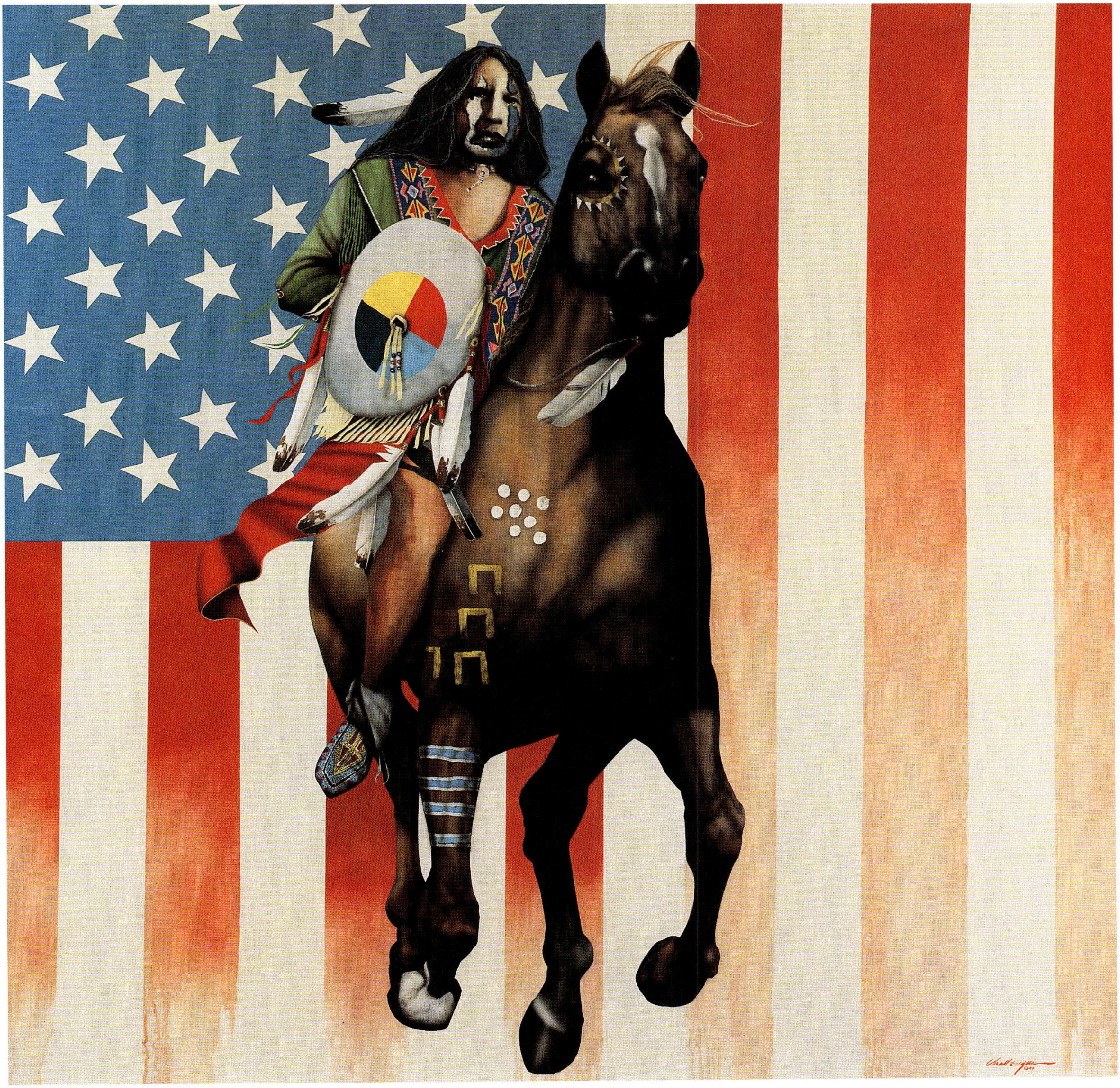

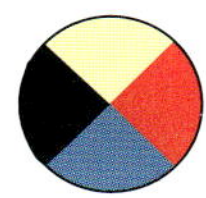

FADED GLORY

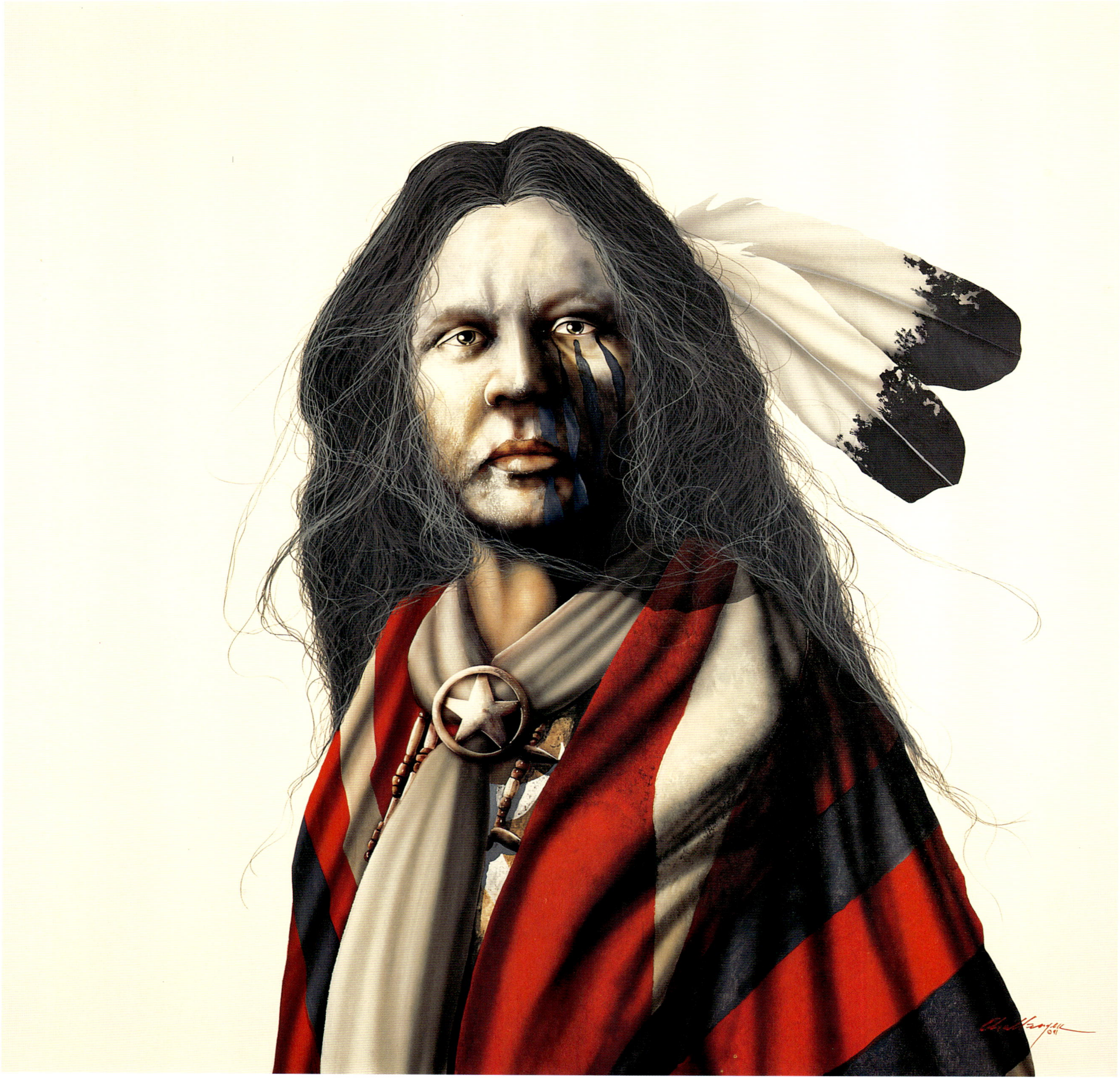

KNOWS HIS HEART

you want it told." I remember sitting there in my studio full of Native Americans, waiting for them to respond. I mean, these were my friends but they were also my most important critics. They spent a lot of time just looking at the paintings and then they started talking about them, calling the paintings "remembering," talking about the works' power. In the end, they gave me their blessing.

That was just the beginning. That was when I really began to learn. My friends started introducing me to some of their friends who they felt I should know. These men would come into my studio, unpack all their regalia, and put it on, then open up to me, sharing their culture. It was fascinating.

I had a small studio in the back of a store in Taos, New Mexico, many years ago. One afternoon this big guy comes through the door. I was sitting down at my easel, painting. I watched him as he moved through the studio, studying all the paintings. After a while, he introduced himself, knelt down next to me, said his name was Sky Hawk, and that he had something for me. Then he handed me a little red bundle tied with horse hair, his personal medicine bundle, and thanked me for portraying his people. I was overwhelmed. When he left, I called a buddy of mine, Three Hawks, and asked him to explain what had happened. He told me that Sky Hawk had paid me a great honor in giving up his personal medicine to me. He was now walking around unprotected, and it was my responsibility to keep the bundle safe. It has remained attached to my easel since that day.

Sky Hawk and I met by chance a year or so later. I was very happy to see him again and asked him to come and sit for me. He ended up sitting for many of my paintings. We would spend hours and hours talking together. He was guiding me. He showed me how hair was wrapped and how feathers were worn on the head and body, what certain symbols meant, and how to use them. It was an incredible experience.

"The color and expression in JD's paintings bring out the true Native American feeling and pride of the Ghost dance era," explains Augie Grayfox, a member of the Warm Springs tribe of the Eastern Chiricahua and frequent model for Challenger. "He is like a messenger for the Indian people."

"When you get down to it, it really is a responsibility," says Challenger. "So I have to do it right. To do it right, I need guidance. I am constantly learning. I feel very blessed to have the trust and friendship of so many Native Americans. Most of the history concerning them has been written by white men, but I am lucky enough to hear, directly from the ancestors, many of the Indian stories and ideas that have been passed down from generation to generation."

Approval of Challenger's work came as much from its authenticity as the artist's talent in combining objects, colors, and emotions to capture the warrior essence. The artist notes:

Once I began to exhibit the Ghost dance paintings regularly, Native American families would come in to the gallery during a show and the elders would use the paintings to explain the meaning of things to their children.

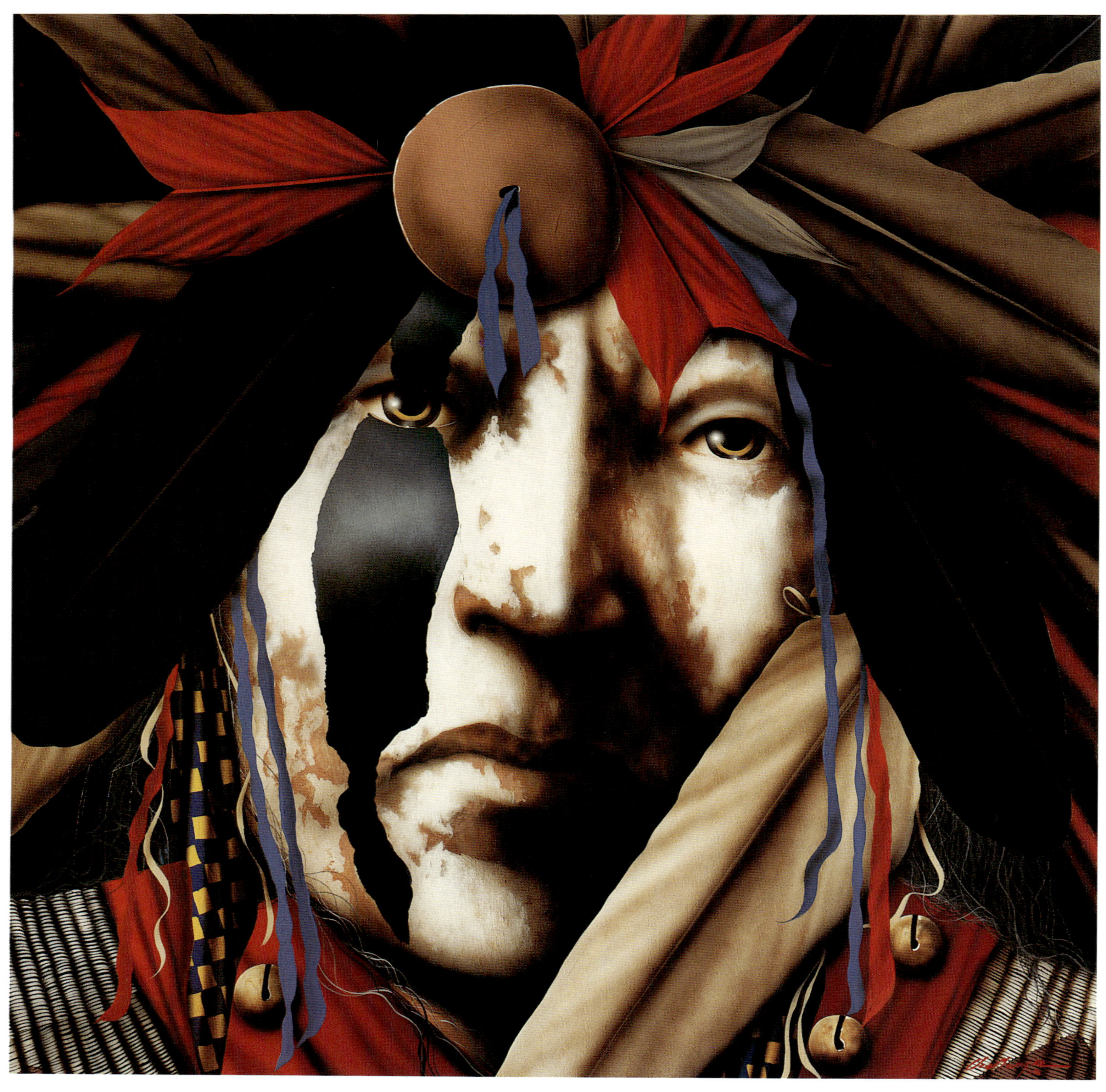

SONG FOR MOTHER EARTH

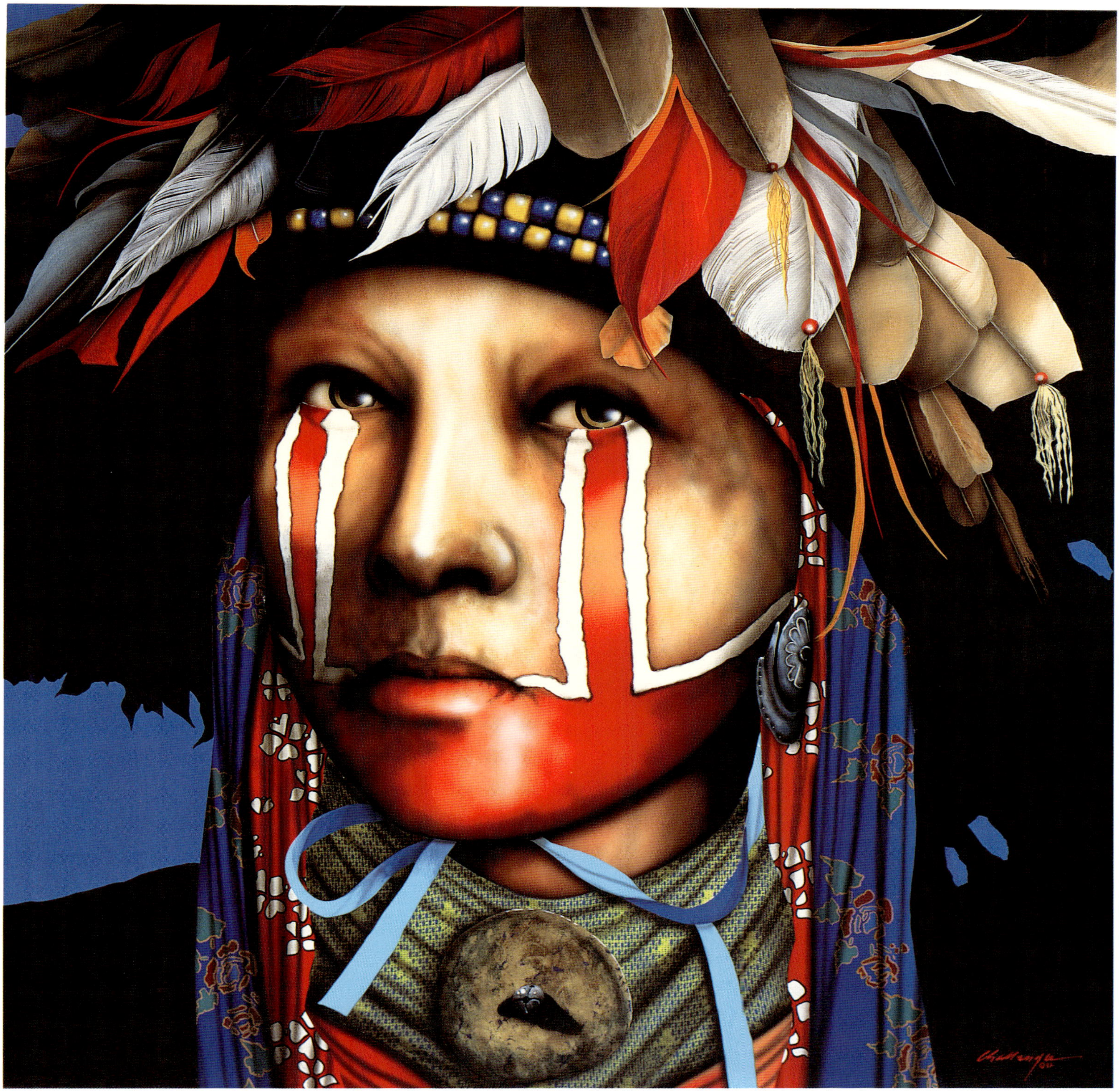

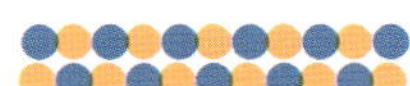

REMEMBERING THE SACRED WAYS

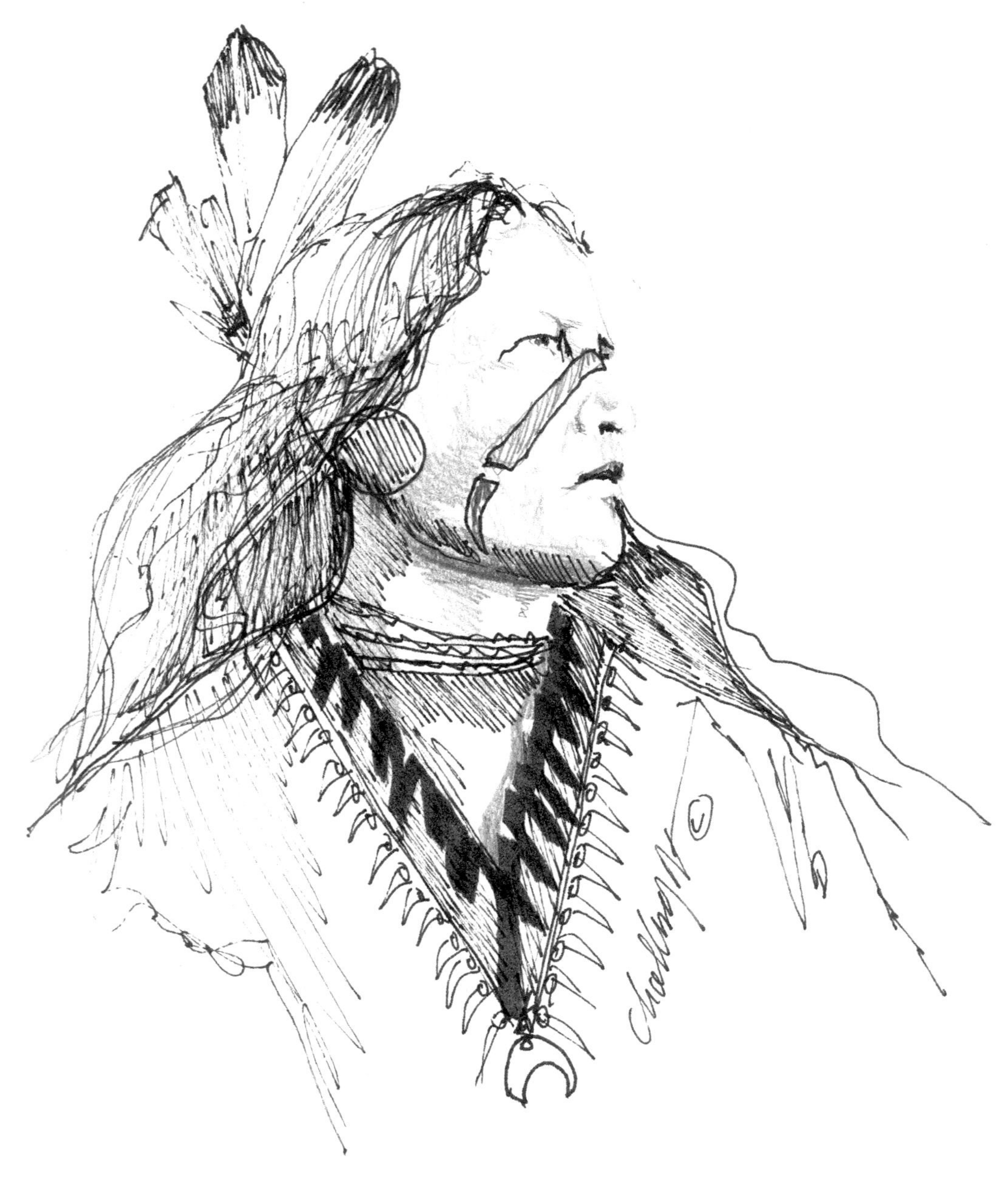

Success would be an elusive victory for Challenger through much of his youth. But he always knew he wanted to achieve recognition as a fine artist despite the odds he would face.

I was born in Oklahoma City. It was a tough beginning. But I ended up being able to take on anything that life threw at me.

Once I turned eighteen, I was ready to be on my own and try to make it as an artist. After rambling around for a while, taking whatever jobs I could get just to eat and paint, I ended up in Dallas, painting billboards.

I don't remember how many I painted. I lost count. I painted ten-foot waterfalls on Kool cigarette billboards until I was sick of them. They were pictorial boards, painted directly on the surface. I hated it, but it was great training. The experience gave me the ability to paint on any scale. But a time came when I realized that, if I painted one more billboard, I would be painting them the rest of my life. So I quit.

I still needed to eat, so I tried to get some work at a commercial art firm. I remember interviewing with this older gentlemen. He told me that after looking at my portfolio, he knew I was capable of doing anything he

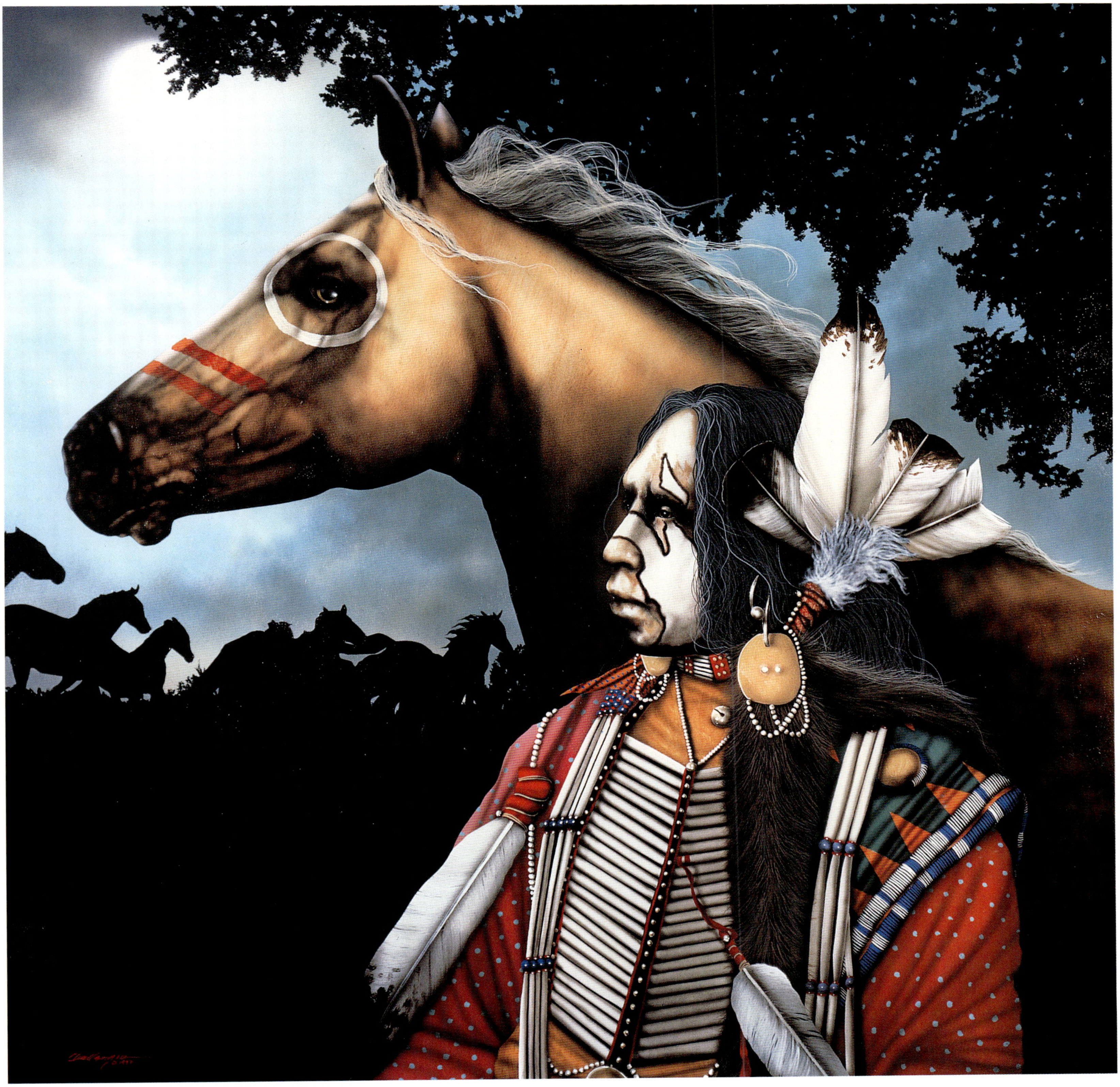

HORSE SPIRIT NIGHT

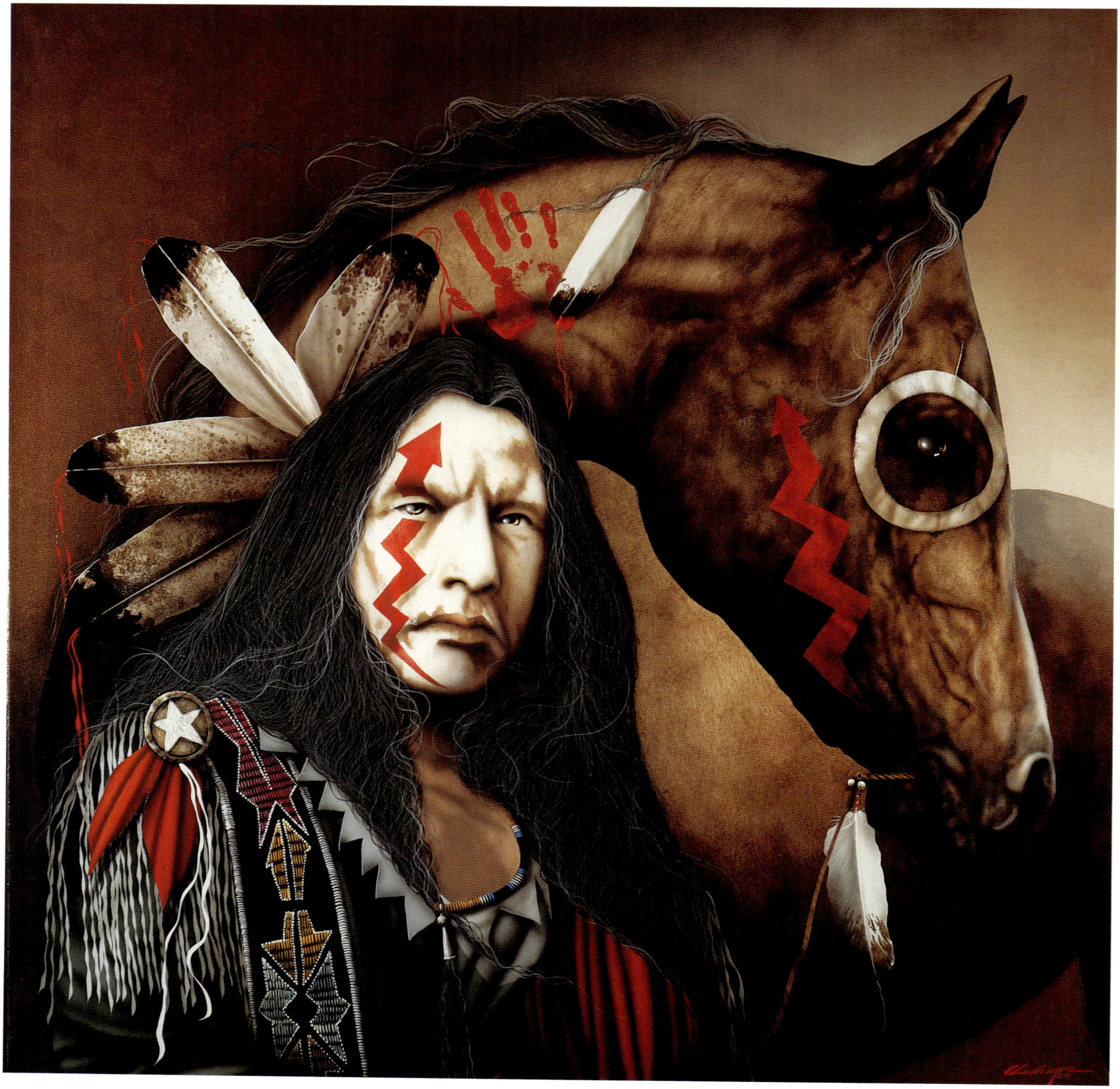

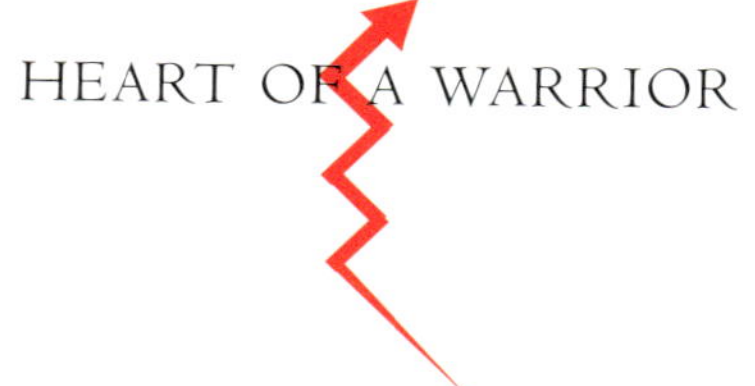

HEART OF A WARRIOR

asked me to paint, draw, or create. But he said he wasn't going to hire me.
He told me that he knew I needed a job and he needed somebody for a job.
But if he brought me in to the commercial art business, he said I would
never get out. He told me he didn't want to be responsible for preventing me
from pursuing a career as a fine artist. He loaned me twenty dollars and sent
me on my way.

   After losing pretty much everything I couldn't afford to keep, I hit the
road again. I was on my way to Los Angeles when my truck broke down
in New Mexico. So I stayed. That's how I ended up selling oranges to
the Pueblos.

At ease in the culture of the southwest and financially stabilized
by his frequent deliveries to the Pueblos, Challenger continued to
make the rounds to the galleries whenever he had a new body of
work. But he met with constant rejection.

I guess I was just too stubborn to give up.
   I always had this overwhelming feeling whenever I
walked into a gallery. I could smell the fresh paint on all the
canvases, the colors were so bright and beautiful and the paintings
were always perfectly lit. It was magic. It's what I wanted for my
own work—to be taken seriously, to be collected, to be hanging
there on the gallery wall. I just didn't know how to achieve it.
I would look at all these paintings by all these artists and
know for certain that I could paint their socks off. Why
wasn't I getting a chance to show it? I couldn't figure it out.
   When I look back at those days, I understand now that
it just wasn't my time. I was still paying my dues. I think a
person really has to or they don't appreciate what they have
when they finally get it. I've seen people who I thought were
the luckiest people in the world just burn it all down.

Challenger refused to give up despite constant rejection from galleries. "It seemed
like every time I tried to go forward one step, I would take ten steps back. I finally ended
up back in Oklahoma City, miserable and feeling like a failure. But then Denise showed up
and my whole world started to turn around.

   I hadn't seen her in several years. Denise and I were childhood sweet-
hearts. I'd been crazy about her since the first time I met her. In fact, I knew
then that she was it. But we were just kids. We dated all through high school. I
was traveling around and trying to be an artist by the time she turned eighteen.
I wanted to marry her. But she went away to college as soon as she graduated.
After she left, I was heartbroken.
   So here I was, back in Oklahoma after being away for a couple of years. I
was having some dinner and I saw her walk in to the café. My heart just
jumped up and ran off. She came up to me and stuck out her little hand and I

took it in mine. It felt like I had stuck my fingers in a light socket. All the feelings were still there. So I looked in her eyes and told her that we had better fix
it up permanently or end it for good. So we got married.

I was wilder than hell. I was frustrated, angry, and tired of being hungry,
tired of failure. I was my own worst enemy. She calmed me. She was all the
things that I was missing in my life and when she married me, she made me
complete.

Denise, Challenger's wife of twenty-two years, became his closest companion and
greatest strength. But it would be a long time before anyone else would realize what Denise
had always known—that Challenger was a unique talent with tremendous potential.

Even when times were bad, she always believed in me. And times did get
worse. When we were first married, I remember we came up against a real
financial problem—how to pay the rent. I had no idea what I was doing.
Running around the country as a single guy was one thing, but now I was
married and had responsibilities. Denise kept encouraging me to paint, but we
had bills to pay and I couldn't pay them with paintings of landscape.

We were overdue on rent by two months already and it was the beginning
of the third month. We had enough cash for one month's rent. I remember
driving down the street in Oklahoma City and seeing this little used car for
sale. It was a tiny car, a little Fiat. It gave me an idea. I stopped the truck and
got out, told Denise to wait for me, and walked over to the used car lot. I
asked the dealer if the Fiat ran. He told me that it ran great but nobody wanted it because it was so small. It really was a small car. When I sat in the driver's
seat, I could reach out the passenger window and adjust the side mirror. I gave
him three hundred and fifty dollars for it, the rent money, and told Denise to
follow me home in our truck. I didn't tell her what I was doing, I just asked
her to trust me. And she did.

I put the little Fiat in the garage while Denise started working on keeping the bill collectors at bay. I spent several days in the garage, spray painting
the car lime green, yellow, and pink. I installed a little tape player inside. Then
I painted Peanuts characters all over the side of the car and lettered "Charlie
Brown's Hot Roasted Peanuts" across the side. Then I took all the cash we had
left, about forty-seven dollars, and bought some little bags and a bushel of
peanuts at a produce wholesaler. I loaded up the trunk with bagged peanuts
and drove it out of the garage. Denise stood there smiling, and said, "That's
the cutest car I've ever seen! Now what?" I told her she'd married the peanut
vendor and that he was leaving for work and wouldn't return home until he
made some money.

It took just three hours to sell all the peanuts. I started making two and
three hundred dollars a day. I paid the rent and the utilities and bought some
art supplies. I could paint all day and then take the nutmobile out to softball
fields, used car lots, and other outdoor places that drew crowds in the
evenings. Sometimes Denise would go with me. We did it for so long that I
developed a route.

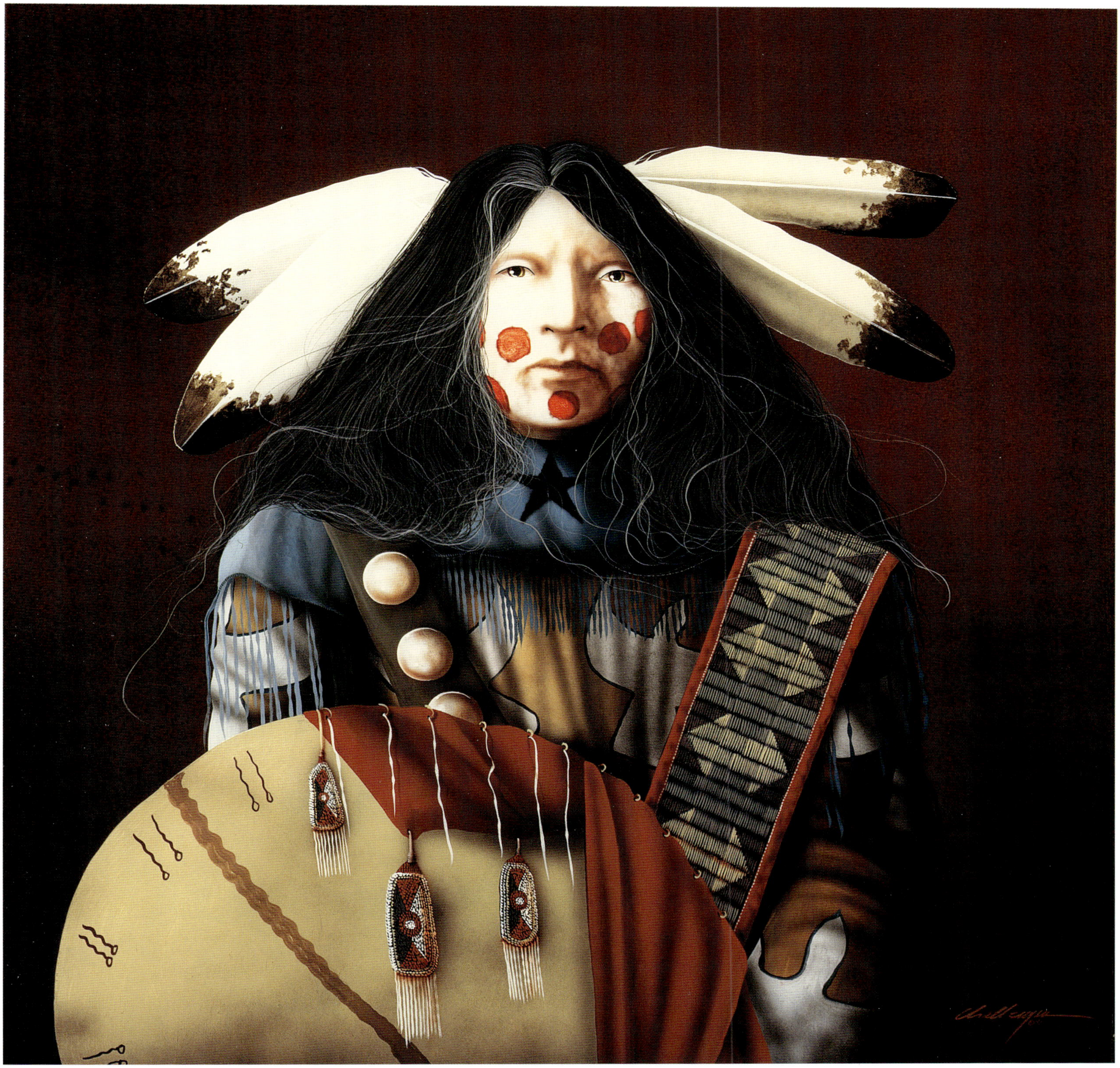

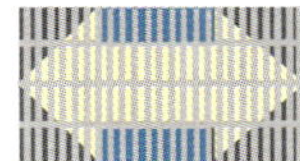

MESSENGER OF HOPE

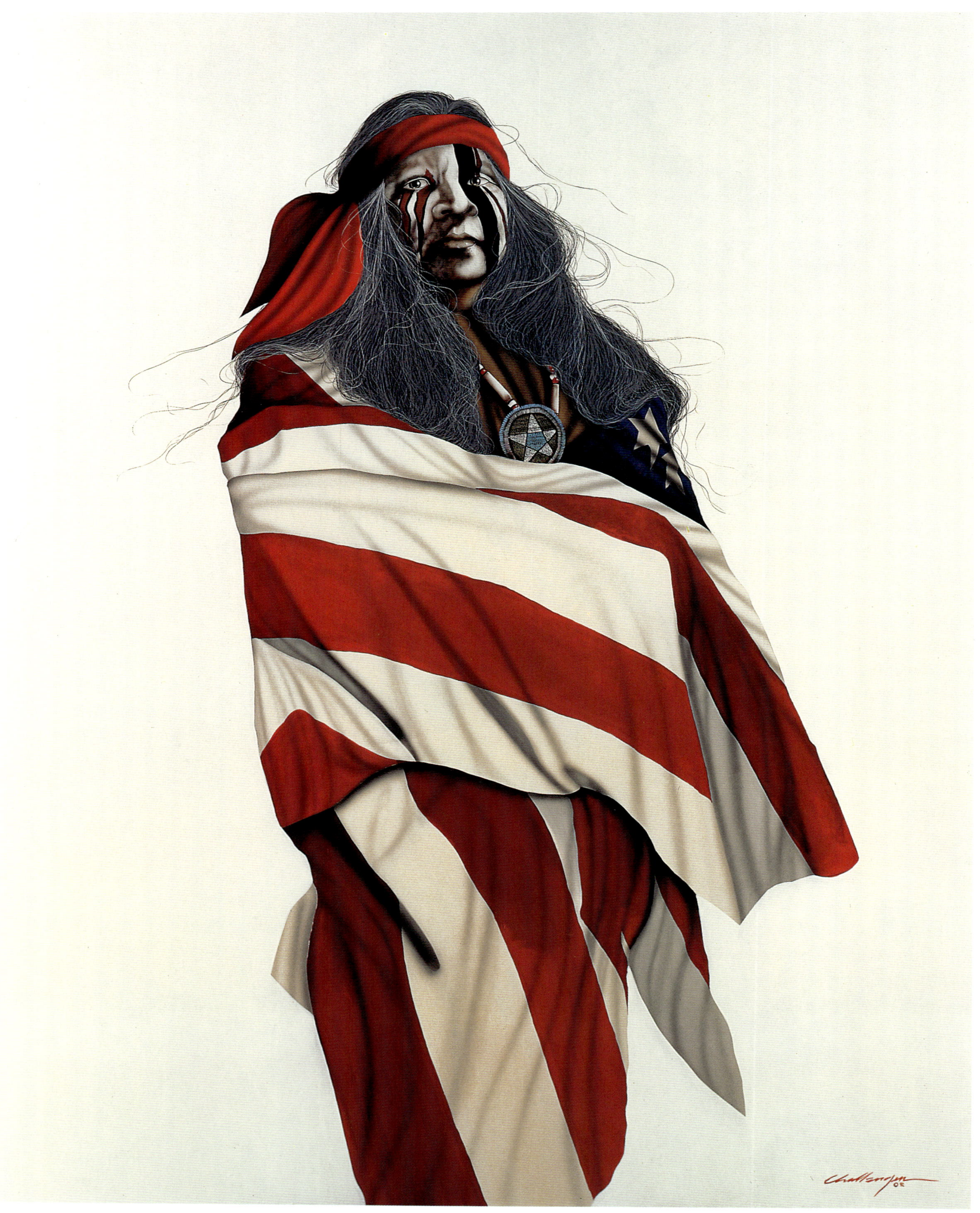

Finally, the bottom fell out of the peanut market. There was a blight or drought or something, and we couldn't afford the peanuts when we could get any peanuts at all.

I kept painting, but nothing was happening. I finally started my own sign-painting company, contracting for billboards. I was stuck, back where I started. I felt miserable, trapped. Denise knew it. One day she turned to me and said, "Let's move to Taos." I asked her what she thought we were going to do in Taos. "The same thing we're doing here—starve—but at least in Taos we'll be starving someplace pretty. You need to be around other artists, JD, because you aren't going to make it here in Oklahoma." I told her that I wasn't going to make it in Taos either. She said, "Yeah, you will. We'll both go for it this time."

Denise was right, thank goodness, but she was right about the whole situation. We ended up starving in Taos. It got bad. Finally, I was driving to the plaza in Taos and ran out of gas. I walked into one of the galleries on the plaza and told them that I was not there to show my work, I was there for a job. Denise and I started working for twenty dollars per day, ten for each of us and a little percentage of anything we sold. By the end of the year, that gallery was making some money. We sold paintings, sculptures, turquoise jewelry, and Navajo rugs.

We couldn't afford both an apartment and a studio, so I talked our boss into letting me set up my easel at the gallery. Denise would wait on customers and I would sit in the doorway, painting Taos and Santa Fe watercolors—landscapes, missions, adobe houses—and I started selling them. I was pretty good at it. I mean, if I'm painting rain, you're going to get wet. But I think people would buy them because they liked them and because they could watch me paint and talk to me about what I was painting. Collectors like to know where the work is coming from in a lot of different ways. But whatever the reason, I was actually starting to make a living painting. We went to the grocery store more often and put some much needed shocks on the Bronco.

The owner of the gallery store next door saw how well we were doing, not just selling my own paintings but selling the rest of the stuff in the gallery. He made us an offer and we moved next door. Eventually, we became partners.

It was in the old La Fonda Hotel, right on the Taos plaza. I tore out part of an old kitchen connected to the store and turned it into my studio. People continued to come in while I was painting and talk with me and sometimes buy the paintings right off the easel. Everything started going better than it ever had. Then, one day, I stopped coming into the store.

I started staying home at this little house we were renting and working on a new series of paintings in the garage. It was a tiny building with no heat. It was very cold. But I wouldn't show the work to anyone, including Denise. I just kept telling her that I needed to be painting what I felt compelled to paint, not what I think I should be painting. She understood. She would come home from running the store and ask me what I had done all day and there would be nothing but a bunch of crumpled-up paper lying on the floor.

I had spent all this time on the reservation, I had forged these great friendships, and I was surrounded by this remarkable Native American culture.

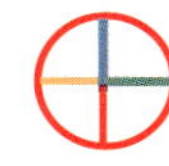

It inspired and affected me more dramatically than anything else in my life. It was truly what I wanted to paint. But I didn't know how. I had to teach myself how to paint all over again.

When I started painting as a boy, I would pick a leaf from a tree and lay it down on some white paper. Then I would paint it and paint it until you couldn't tell the difference between the leaf and the painting of the leaf. Well, now I had feathers to figure out how to paint, and beads, porcupine quills, and brain-tanned leather, not to mention hair, eyes, lips, and painted skin. It was a real struggle, but I eventually completed the first Ghost dance painting.

I had finally found a gallery in Santa Fe willing to carry my landscapes by this time, so I took the first Ghost dance painting there and hung it on the wall. About three days later, the gallery owner called me and said, "Come get this painting, JD!" I asked her why. "Because people come in here and they get real emotional about it. They either love it or hate it. And because something's happening with it and I don't understand it. And because it scares me. Now come and get it out of here!" I took it down and brought it back to our little store and hung it in the office.

Every time I would leave the store to pick up lunch or deliver something, Denise would get it and hang it out front. I would come in and take it down and put it in the back. This went on until one day I walked in and there it was, hanging in the front of the store for the umpteenth time. I called Denise back to the office and told her I wanted it down and did not under any circumstances want it hanging back up. Anywhere! She said, "Fine, you tell that to the guy who just bought it."

After she sold the next two or three Ghost dance paintings, for more money than I ever thought I would get for any of my paintings, I created an entire body of work. That is when I called all my friends in to my studio and asked for their guidance.

Challenger considers himself a very lucky man. His studio, easel, brushes, and paints have been blessed in special Native American smudge ceremonies, despite the fact that he has never requested such an honor. "It would have been inappropriate. For me, it's like saying thanks for helping. It's part of what guides me."

"In many ways, I have a limited control over my work. I finish a painting and I say to it, 'Now go tell your story.' It knows where it's going. I don't have any control over that. I am just a tool. I am just two hands and a body that can make this happen. If I'm going in the wrong direction, the canvas tells me. The color is wrong, everything drips, the brushes fall from my hands. Once I begin, the canvas gets a hold of me and it won't let go until it's complete no matter how much I struggle. But sometimes the work falls into place, time disappears and it flows. I tune everything out and sit for hours just painting. It's like magic."

Challenger has finally achieved success as his wife Denise predicted. A celebrated artist with a national reputation, Challenger is fulfilling his greatest desire. But in many ways, Challenger's art has exceeded even its creator's success.

Collectors purchase Challenger's art for its beauty and authenticity. They embrace the work for its aesthetic pleasures, enjoying the benefits of owning exquisite fine art. In addition, the paintings, prints, and bronzes surpass the collector's investment, generating real financial gain for the owner as the work increases in value, anchoring it in the solid realities of art and finance.

But there is a separate reality at work in these paintings. It is the reality of the Thunderbird, of the turtle and the crow, of heroes and great warriors, of visions in a sky of uncompromised purity, of dances across a land unabused by greed and dreams of a world restored. Like the whirlwind, JD Challenger draws this reality to earth, unraveling its mysteries across the canvas and creating a province in which the Spirit is very much alive.

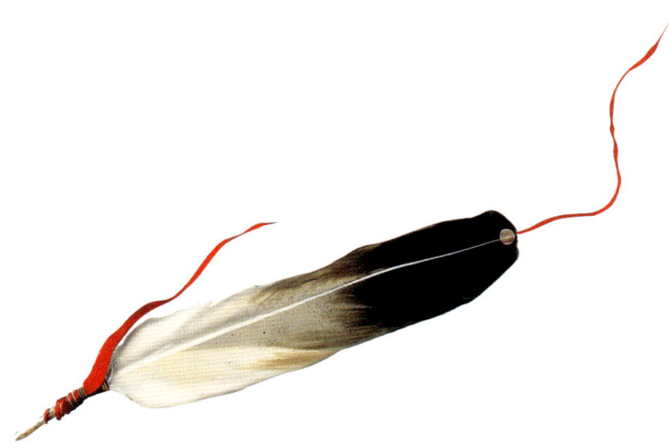

ARTIST'S ACKNOWLEDGMENTS

A-ho. Special thanks for sharing. All my relations. A-ho.

Augie Grayfox, Rodney A. Grant, Sammy "Tonekei" White, Bill Miller, Flint "Duivitsie" Carney, Robert Mirabal, Richard Skyhawk, Caesar Gomez, Marion D. Threehawks, Nelson Fernandez, Andersen Kee, Michael Horse, James A. Jennings, Phillip Yogie Bread, Bearheart Williams, Harvey Beartrack, Mitchell Cypress, Sonny Billie, Ronnie Jimmie, Sally Tommie, Pete and Arnie Oceola, the Seminole Tribe of Florida, Inc., E. M. Hinton, and "George."

Special acknowledgment and thanks to: A. Dwain Wilkinson, Jr.; Chris Bowman; T. L. Bowman; Edwin O. Minx; Taos, NM; M.M.M.; Michael McCormick; Joan Marcus Fine Art; Houshang and Associates; Marian Levy - PAC; The Lady in #109; Larry Smith; Mark Eaker; Stephanie Allen; Shirley Jackson; and the exceptional staff at Somerset House Publishing and Gregory Editions

AUTHOR'S ACKNOWLEDGMENTS

This text would not have been possible without the valuable contributions of James Mooney and his The Ghost Dance Religion and the Sioux Outbreak of 1890, Fourteenth Annual Report of the Bureau of Ethnology, 1892–93, Part Two, published by the Government Printing Office, Washington, DC, in 1896. I have included excerpts from Mr. Mooney's eyewitness accounts, interviews, and observations throughout this book. Special thanks to the National Museum of Natural History and the Smithsonian Institution.

The quotes by Black Elk are reprinted from Black Elk Speaks, by John G. Neihardt, by permission of the University of Nebraska Press. Copyright 1932, 1959, 1972, by John G. Neihardt. Copyright © 1961 by the John G. Neihardt Trust.

The quote by Dick Fool Bull is reprinted, with permission, from American Myths and Legends by Richard Erdoes and Alfonso Ortiz, Copyright © 1984 by Richard Erdoes and Alfonso Ortiz. Published by Pantheon Books, a division of Random House, Inc.

Excerpts from the Indian–Pioneer Histories occur throughout the text and appear courtesy of the Oklahoma Historical Society's Archives and Manuscripts Division.

Special thanks to Ruthie Emehahtubbee Imes, Phyllis Adams, and William D. Welge of the Oklahoma Historical Society Archives.

My highest respect and deepest regard for Mr. Ronnie Jimmie.

BIBLIOGRAPHY

Andrist, Ralph K. The Long Death: *The Last Days of the Plains Indian.* New York: The Macmillan Company, 1 964.

Asanap, Herman. Interview. *Indian–Pioneer Histories.* Vol. 99. Oklahoma City: Oklahoma Historical Society, 1937–38.

Barney, Garold D. *Mormons, Indians, and the Ghost Dance Religion of 1890.* Lanham: University Press of America, 1986.

Berkhofer, Jr., Robert F. *The White Man's Indian: Images of the American Indian from Columbus to the Present.* New York: Alfred A. Knopf, Inc., 1978.

Blake, E. E. Interview. *Indian–Pioneer Histories.* Vol. 75. Oklahoma City: Oklahoma Historical Society, 1937-38.

Brine, Lindsey. *The Ancient Earthworks and Temples of the American Indians.* First published by Farmer and Sons, London, 1894. Royston: Oracle Publishing, Ltd., 1996.

Bourke, Captain J. G. *The Medicine-Men of the Apache,* Ninth Annual Report of the Bureau of Ethnology. Washington, DC: Government Printing Office, 1892 .

Brown, Dee. *Bury My Heart at Wounded Knee.* New York: Holt, Rinehart & Winston, Inc., 1971.

Carmody, Denise Lardner, and John Tully. *Native American Religion.* New York: Paulist Press, 1993.

Challenger, Denise. Personal communication. 1997.

Chapman, Abraham, ed. *Literature of the American Indians: Views and Interpretations.* New York: The New American Library, Inc., 1975.

Chippewa Music. Bureau of American Ethnology, Bulletin 45. Washington, DC: Government Printing Office, 1910.

Chippewa Music II. Bureau of American Ethnology, Bulletin 53. Washington, DC: Government Printing Office, 1913.

Converse, Harriet M. *Myths and Legends of the New York State Iroquois.* New York State Museum Bulletin, Number 125, 1908.

Corey, Melinda, and George Ochoa. *The Encyclopedia of the Victorian World.* New York: Henry Holt and Company, 1996.

Cox, Guy. Interview. *Indian–Pioneer Histories.* Vol. 2 . Oklahoma City: Oklahoma Historical Society, 1937–38.

Creeping Bear, Joe. Interview. *Indian–Pioneer Histories.* Vol. 100. Oklahoma City: Oklahoma Historical Society, 1937–38.

Day, A. Grove. *The Sky Clears.* New York: The Macmillian Company, 1951.

Deer, Ada E. *The Contract with America: A Return to Termination.* Online report. Bureau of Indian Affairs, 1997.

Deloria, Vine, Jr. *Custer Died for Your Sins: An Indian Manifesto.* New York: Avon Books, 1970.

Densmore, Frances. *The American Indians and Their Music.* New York: n.p. 192 6.

Dorsey, J. O. *The Social Organization of the Siouan Tribes.* Journal of American Folklore, Vol. 4, No. 14. Boston, 1891.

Erdoes, Richard, and Alfonso Ortiz. *American Indian Myths and Legends.* New York: Pantheon Books, 1984.

Foreman, Grant. *Indian Removal: The Emigration of the Five Civilized Tribes of Indians.* Norman: University of Oklahoma Press, 1932 .

Grayfox, Augie. Personal communication. 1997.

Hauptman, Laurence M. *Between Two Fires: American Indians in the Civil War.* New York: Simon and Schuster Inc., 1995.

Heckewelder, J. *History, manners, and customs of the Indian nations who once inhabited Pennsylvania and the neighboring states.* Vol. 1. Transactions of the American Philosophical Society. Philadelphia: 1876.

Hultkrantz, Ake. *The Religions of the American Indians.* Berkeley: University of California Press, 1979.

Indian Religious Freedom Issues. Hearing Before the Subcommittee on Civil and Constitutional Rights of the Committee on the Judiciary, House of Representatives, Ninety-seventh Congress, Second Session on Indian Religious Freedom Issues. Serial No. 58. Washington, DC: U. S. Government Printing Office, 1982 .

Jimmie, Ronnie. Personal communication. 1997.

Kehoe, Alice Beck. *The Ghost Dance: Ethnohistory and Revitalization.* New York: Holt, Rinehart and Wintson, 1989.

Kroeber, Alfred L. *The Arapaho.* Bulletin of the American Museum of Natural History, Vol. 18, 1902 , 1904, and 1907. Lincoln: University of Nebraska Press, 1983.

La Farge, Oliver. *A Pictorial History of the American Indian.* New York: Crown Publishers, Inc., 1956.

Lorrin, Nora, and John L. Rice. Interview. Indian–Pioneer Histories. Vol. 52 . Oklahoma City: Oklahoma Historical Society, 1937–38.

Louthan, M. B. Interview. *Indian–Pioneer Histories.* Vol. 78. Oklahoma City: Oklahoma Historical Society, 1937–38.

Lyman, Stanley David. *Wounded Knee 1973: A Personal Account.* Lincoln: University of Nebraska Press, 1991.

MacMurray, J. W. *The Dreamers of the Columbia River Valley in Washington*

Territory. Transactions of the Albany Institute, Vol. 11. Albany: 1887.

Mail, Thomas E. *The Mystic Warriors of the Plains.* New York: Doubleday, 1972.

Ma-na-ka, Mary. Interview. *Indian–Pioneer Histories.* Vol. 106. Oklahoma City: Oklahoma Historical Society, 1937–38.

Marriott, Alice, and Carol K. Rachlin. *American Epic: The Story of the American Indian.* New York: G. P. Putnam's Sons, 1970.

Martineau, LaVan. *The Southern Paiutes: Legends, Lore, Language, and Lineage.* Las Vegas: KC Publications, 1992 .

Matlock, Stacey. Interview. *Indian–Pioneer Histories.* Vol. 34. Oklahoma City: Oklahoma Historical Society, 1937–38.

Methvin, J. J. Interview. *Indian–Pioneer Histories.* Vol. 36. Oklahoma City: Oklahoma Historical Society, 1937–38.

Miller, David Humphreys. *Ghost Dance.* New York: Duell, Sloan and Pearce, 1959.

Mooney, James. *The Ghost Dance Religion and the Sioux Outbreak of 1890.* Fourteenth Annual Report of the Bureau of Ethnology, 1892 –93, Part 2 . Washington, DC: Government Printing Office, 1896.

Mosier, Lotta Harris. Interview. *Indian–Pioneer Histories.* Vol. 37. Oklahoma City: Oklahoma Historical Society, 1937–38.

Murie, Jim. Interview. *Indian-Pioneer Histories.* Vol. 107. Oklahoma City: Oklahoma Historical Society, 1937–38.

Neihardt, John G. *Black Elk Speaks: Being the Life Story of a Holy Man of the Ogalala Sioux.* Lincoln: University of Nebraska Press, 1932 .

One Year Later: A Clinton Administration Progress Report to the Federally Recognized Tribal Nations One Year After the Historic April 29, 1994 Meeting with President Clinton and the Tribal Leaders. The White House Domestic Policy Council. Washington, DC: 1995.

Parker, Z. A. *The Ghost Dance at Pine Ridge.* Vol. 4. Journal of American Folklore, No. 13. Boston: 1891.

Perdue, Theda. *Nations Remembered: An Oral History of the Five Civilized Tribes, 1865–1907.* Westport: Greenwood Press, 1980.

Peterson, Scott. *Native American Prophecies.* New York: Paragon House, 1990.

Petter, Rodolphe. Interview. *Indian–Pioneer Histories.* Vol. 70. Oklahoma City: Oklahoma Historical Society, 1937–38.

Pevar, Stephen L. *The Rights of Indians and Tribes: The Basic ACLU Guide to Indian and Tribal Rights.* Carbondale: Southern Illinois University Press, 1992 .

Revard, Franklin N. Interview. *Indian–Pioneer Histories.* Vol. 41. Oklahoma City: Oklahoma Historical Society, 1937–38.

Sandos, James A. and Larry E. Burgess. *The Hunt for Willie Boy: Indian-Hating and Popular Culture.* Norman: University of Oklahoma Press, 1994.

Simmons, Marc. *Witchcraft in the Southwest: Spanish and Indian Supernaturalism on the Rio Grande.* Lincoln: University of Nebraska Press, 1974.

Starkloff, Carl F. *The People of the Center: American Indian Religion and Christianity.* New York: The Seabury Press, 1974.

Terrell, John Upton. American *Indian Almanac.* New York: Barnes and Noble Books, 1994.

Thomas, R. B. Interview. Indian–Pioneer Histories. Vol. 46. Oklahoma City: Oklahoma Historical Society, 1937–38.

Turpin, Solveig A. *Shamanism and Rock Art in North America.* San Antonio: Rock Art Foundation, Inc., 1994.

Valleire, Frank. Interview. *Indian–Pioneer Histories.* Vol. 48. Oklahoma City: Oklahoma Historical Society, 1937–38.

Vecsey, Christopher, ed. *Handbook of American Indian Religious Freedom.* New York: The Crossroads Publishing Company, 1991.

Ward, Geoffery C. *The West: An Illustrated History.* New York: Little, Brown and Company, 1996.